The Priest:
His Dignity and Obligations

By
Saint John Eudes

Translated from the French by
Reverend W. Leo Murphy

With an Introduction by
The Late Reverend Charles Lebrun, C.J.M., S.T.D.

Foreword by
Most Reverend John T. McNally D.D.
Archbishop of Halifax, N.S.

Loreto Publications
Fitzwilliam, NH 03447
AD 2008

Imprimi Potest:
A. D'Amours, C.J.M.
Praepositus Provincialis

Laval-des-Rapides, P.Q.,
die 6ª Maii 1946

Nihil Obstat:
† John M. A. Fearns, S.T.D.
Censor Librorum

Imprimatur:
Francis Cardinal Spellman
Archbishop, New York

December 20, 1946

Published by:

Loreto Publications
P. O. Box 603
Fitzwilliam, NH 03447
603-239-6671
www.LoretoPubs.org

ISBN: 1-930278-69-1

Printed and bound in the United States of America

Part I

A MEMORIAL
OF
THE ECCLESIASTICAL LIFE

GENERAL PREFACE

St. John Eudes has been called "the wonder of his age." Missionary, founder, reformer of the clergy, he crowded into a life of seventy-nine years so many and such varied accomplishments that one marvels how a single man could achieve so much. In addition to the activities of an incessant and many-sided apostolate, he wrote a number of valuable books, which rank him among the most prolific ascetic writers of the seventeenth century.

For many years the devotional works of St. John Eudes were practically unknown.[1] Occasionally a volume was discovered in the library of some seminary or religious house. Many others preserved in manuscript form were lost in the chaos of the French Revolution.[2] At the beginning of the present century the sons of St. John Eudes united in a tribute of filial piety to bring out a complete edition of the works of their spiritual father, seeking them in public and private libraries throughout the world.[3] About twenty volumes were found and edited in 1905 by the late Fathers Charles Lebrun, C.J.M., and Joseph Dau-

---

[1] Before the French Revolution the works of St. John Eudes were popular in France. In 1792 the houses of the Congregation of Jesus and Mary were confiscated by the Government and its members were massacred or dispersed throughout Europe. With the suppression of the Eudists, their rich literary heritage was widely scattered and partially destroyed. It was not until the re-establishment of the Congregation of Jesus and Mary in 1826 that effort was made to recover the printed and manuscript works of St. John Eudes. The research was carried on until the latter part of the nineteenth century. In the "Préface Générale" to the *Oeuvres Complètes* (Vannes, 1905), Father Charles Lebrun points out that one of the purposes of the edition was "to unearth these works buried too long in oblivion," *exhumer ces ouvrages ensevelis depuis trop longtemps dans l'oubli* . . .

[2] The following manuscripts were not found: *The Christian Man, All Jesus, The Divine Office, The Admirable Sacrifice of the Mass, Meditations* (2 vols.), *Sermons of St. John Eudes* (3 vols.), *Favors Obtained by the Diocese of Coutances through the Blessed Virgin, The Divine Childhood of Jesus, The Devotion to the Sacred Heart of Jesus, The Admirable Life of Mary des Vallées* (incomplete copy found at Laval University Library, Quebec) and *Correspondence of St. John Eudes.*

[3] Cf. *Oeuvres Complètes*, p. xiv.

phin, C.J.M. The first edition in French, *Oeuvres Complètes du Vénérable Jean Eudes,* ran into twelve octavo volumes with introductions, explanatory notes, analytic and alphabetic indexes of great value. These writings constitute a complete summa of ascetic and pastoral theology. The list is as follows:

Volume I. The Life and Kingdom of Jesus in Christian Souls. In this work the Saint develops his spiritual teaching on the Christian life, namely, that the Christian life is simply the life of Jesus extended and continued in each one of us.

Volume II. This volume contains six short treatises on subjects relating to the Christian life:

1. *A Treatise on the Respect Due to Holy Places,* which is an echo of the fiery denunciations he pronounced during his missions against profaners of the temple of God.

2. *Meditations on Humility,* a series of meditations on the profession of humility as used daily in his order of priests, the Congregation of Jesus and Mary.

3. *Interior Colloquies of the Soul with God,* meditations on creation, the end of man and the grace of Baptism.

4. *Man's Contract with God in Holy Baptism,* a summary of the teachings of Sacred Scripture and Tradition on the Sacrament of Baptism.

5. *The Practice of Piety,* a brief explanation of what is necessary in order to live a Christian life.

6. *Catechism of the Mission,* an outline of the catechetical instructions given during a mission.

Volume III. Contains two important works on sacerdotal perfection:

1. *The Memorial of the Ecclesiastical Life,* an explanation of the dignity and duties of the priesthood.

2. *A Manual of Piety for Use in an Ecclesiastical Community,* in which the author explains how the means of sanctification he recommended to his priests should be practically applied in their daily lives.

Volume IV. Comprises significant works on the priestly ministry.

1. *The Apostolic Preacher* is one of the first treatises written on the ministry of the Word of God and is even yet one of the most practical.

2. *The Good Confessor* explains the qualities and obligations of the minister of the Sacrament of Penance.

3. *Counsels for Mission Confessors* suggests practical means of assisting penitents to make their examination of conscience and excite themselves to contrition.

4. *The Manner of Serving Mass* explains the dignity and holiness of this act and what one must do to perform it devoutly and worthily.

Volume V. The Admirable Childhood of the Most Holy Mother of God. This book treats of the holy childhood of Mary and the practical means of honoring the mysteries and virtues of her early life.

Volumes VI, VII, VIII contain the entire writings of the Saint on the Sacred Hearts of Jesus and Mary. The work is entitled: *The Admirable Heart of the Most Holy Mother of God.* It comprises twelve books covering the complete theology of the devotion to the Sacred Hearts. Eleven books discuss the theory, history, and practice of the devotion to the Immaculate Heart of Mary. The last book deals with the devotion to the Sacred Heart of Jesus. It is this work, together with the Offices of the Sacred Hearts, that merit for him the title of Father, Doctor and Apostle of the Devotion to the Sacred Hearts.

Volume IX. The Rules and Constitutions of the Congregation of Jesus and Mary.

Volume X. Contains *The Rules and Constitutions of the Order of Our Lady of Charity,* the *Directory* of the Order, and a collection of two hundred and forty letters.

Volumes XI and *XII* embrace the Saint's *Liturgical Works,* comprising twenty-five Offices and Masses for feasts to which he urged special devotion, the *Memorial of God's Blessings* and several other minor works.

The second French edition appeared in 1935, *Oeuvres Choisies de Saint Jean Eudes,* prepared under the direction of Father Lebrun, the leading authority on Eudistic research. It comprises nine volumes: *The Life and Kingdom of Jesus in Christian Souls, Meditations of Various Subjects, Regulae Vitae Christianae et Sacerdotalis, Man's Contract with God in Holy Baptism, Letters and Minor Works, Writings on the Priesthood, The Sacred Heart of Jesus, The Admirable Heart of Mary,* and *The Admirable Childhood of the Mother of God.* The format of these volumes is compact and more convenient than the 1905 edition, which is now out of print.

The publication of the works of St. John Eudes revealed the extent and depth of their spiritual doctrine. Cardinal Pitra, who was associated with the cause of Beatification, discovered in the writings of St. John Eudes a remarkable depth of thought and purity of doctrine. Cardinal Vivès has more recently expressed his admiration:

I was acquainted with the Doctors of the Order of Saint Francis; I was acquainted with Saint Teresa and Saint John of the Cross, the mystical writers of my own country, Spain; but I was completely ignorant of the writings of Father Eudes. As a member of the Sacred Congregation of Rites it was my duty to study his life and his works, and I am in admiration. Blessed John Eudes must be ranked with the great lights of the Church. His spiritual doctrine is profound and of wonderful exactitude. He is one of the writers who has best propounded the doctrine of the Gospel.[4]

The late Father Ange Le Doré, for fifty years Superior General of the Congregation of Jesus and Mary, wrote:

The works of Blessed John Eudes, although they do not bear the scientific touch of the professional theologian, are nevertheless proof of his remarkable theological, ascetic and scriptural knowledge. . . . He is not a Doctor after the fashion of the scholastics of the thirteenth century or of the great theologians of the sixteenth and seventeenth centuries. As they, he might have built up theses and composed books didactic in form; but he was before all a saver of souls. For him the science of theology found its chief field of usefulness in the practice of virtue and in the acquisition of sanctity of which it is the principle. . . . He was a Doctor after the manner of the Apostles, the Fathers of the Church, St. Francis de Sales and St. Alphonsus de Liguori. The science which shines in his works not only emits light; it engenders piety and sanctity.[5]

The spiritual doctrine expounded by St. John Eudes follows the teaching of Cardinal Pierre de Bérulle and Father Charles de Condren, two prominent members of the seventeenth-century French School of Spirituality. St. John Eudes applies this doctrine to the devotion to the

---

[4] Quoted by P. A. Bray, C.J.M., *Saint John Eudes* (Halifax, 1925), p. 116.
[5] Quoted by Bray, *op. cit.*, p. 117.

Sacred Hearts of Jesus and Mary, developing and rendering it more precise and practical. He has the rare gift of expressing the most sublime truths in simple, familiar language. He also excels in condensing into a few pages a complete scheme of Christian life and perfection.

The wish was repeatedly expressed that these inspirational writings could be made available to English-speaking readers. Excellent abridged editions of certain books were published in England and in Canada, but they did not do justice to the literary value of the Saint. Consequently, the Eudist Fathers commemorating their tercentenary in 1943 resolved to publish a complete translation of the principal works of their founder. Competent translators were secured and much time and effort were expended to produce readable volumes in modern English, faithful to the spirit and style of the original.

The first English edition, *Selected Works of Saint John Eudes,* is the result. In presenting it to the public the Eudist Fathers and the Religious of Our Lady of Charity of the Refuge, and of the Good Shepherd, wish to thank all those who contributed to the success of this comprehensive undertaking. They are especially grateful to the distinguished churchmen who have so graciously accepted to introduce these volumes to Catholic readers, because they consider that the works of St. John Eudes should be more widely known. The Saint in his apostolic work and in his writings ranks with the eminent figures who belong not to one country and to one religious order but to the universal Church. Three centuries have passed since he wrote the works now being printed in the new world, a striking illustration that he wrote for all time. He still speaks in accents that penetrate the mind and heart of the reader to enlighten, purify and sanctify so that Jesus Christ may live and reign in the Christian soul.

WILFRID E. MYATT, C.J.M.
PATRICK J. SKINNER, C.J.M.
Editors

Holy Heart Seminary
Halifax, N. S.
Feast of St. John Eudes, 1945

CONTENTS

PART I

A MEMORIAL OF THE ECCLESIASTICAL LIFE

PART II

THE APOSTOLIC PREACHER

PART III

THE GOOD CONFESSOR

PART IV

MEDITATIONS

on

THE PRIESTLY OBLIGATIONS

PART V

MEDITATIONS

on

TONSURE AND HOLY ORDERS

PART VI

MEDITATIONS

for

THE ANNUAL RETREAT

PART VII

OFFICE AND MASS

for

THE FEAST OF THE HOLY PRIESTHOOD

FOREWORD

THIS LATEST WORK of St. John Eudes to be presented to the public in the English language, *The Priest, His Dignity and Obligations,* will prove a valuable addition to ascetic theology, in the vernacular of most of this continent.

It is a treatise whose wording springs from a heart filled with zeal for God's house. To me, quite a number of its expressions and assertions seem extravagant and exaggerated, more so, doubtless, in their English dress than they do in the French version in which they were first set down, but we are dealing with the spiritual outpourings of a sainted soul and must take his presentation as it stands.

Surely, the glory of the priestly state can hardly seem overdrawn, until we think of the weakness and fickleness of ourselves who have dared to accept that exalted dignity. *Habemus autem thesaurum istum in vasis fictilibus.* Its very sublimity fills our souls with awe and trepidation. It is *magna dignitas, mira potestas, sed excelsum et pavendum officium,* and as such we dare embrace its lofty character and its tremendous obligations only because we feel not only privileged, but almost obliged to do so, by the beneficent call of God. "Neither doth any man take the honour to himself, but he that is called by God, as Aaron was" (Heb. 5, 4).

To follow the counsels outlined by our saint is by no means easy to our capricious souls. Their numberless repetitions in the volume under consideration may sometimes grate upon our patience, but salutary precepts and wholesome advice must be ceaselessly urged

xvii

upon us priests, as we in turn do it in the guiding of others, in season and out of season, so as to imprint their effect upon our too mutable minds.

If we seek a proof of the value of this treatise on priestly obligations, we need only to look at the results so cogently portrayed to us in the congregation founded by this glorious saint, and in the work they accomplish in the formation of the clergy of God's holy Church. What we have experienced in dealing with the priests of the Congregation of Jesus and Mary, in their institutions in this diocese, has given ample proof of their loyal obedience to, and respect for, their superiors, both within and without their ranks; and of the eminently careful and intensive training, by word and example, of the young clerics entrusted to their system of sacerdotal formation.

For this we devoutly thank God and the unfailing protection of His sainted director of priestly perfection. Never did the world need more keenly than now the exalted example and the devoted zeal of holy and apostolic priests.

May this volume prove to countless numbers of them a precious guide and a sacred inspiration!

✠ JOHN T. McNALLY
Archbishop of Halifax

Halifax, Nova Scotia
May 15, 1946

INTRODUCTION

ONE of the main ambitions of St. John Eudes was the sanctification of the clergy. In the early years of his career as an Oratorian missionary he began to deliver special lectures once or twice a week to the priests of the district in which the mission was being preached. With all the warmth and earnestness of his deep convictions he strove to impress upon his hearers the sublime dignity of the priestly state and the gravity of the obligations it entails. Later, in 1643, he left the French Oratory and founded the Congregation of Jesus and Mary for the establishment of seminaries and for the training of young aspirants for the priesthood.

But St. John Eudes did even more. He wrote a number of excellent works on the life and functions of the priest. The best-known are *A Memorial of the Ecclesiastical Life, The Apostolic Preacher* and *The Good Confessor*. These writings cover all the duties of the priestly life. They are not pretentiously learned works but simple practical handbooks, filled with beautiful thoughts on the dignity of the priesthood and with helpful suggestions for the carrying out of its weighty obligations. These three works have been brought together in this volume of the *Selected Works of St. John Eudes*. A brief outline of each book with its salient characteristics will be of great benefit to the reader.

I. *A Memorial of the Ecclesiastical Life*

St. John Eudes began his *Memorial of the Ecclesiastical Life* in 1668, but did not complete it until a few days before his death in 1680. Father Blouet de Camilly, second superior general of the Congregation of Jesus and Mary, had it published at Lisieux the following year.

The *Memorial* is not a lengthy treatise on the priestly life nor is it a detailed exposition of the duties of a priest. The seventeenth cntury has left us several books of that nature, of which the best known is Father Olier's *Treatise on Holy Orders,* which was published in 1675. St. John Eudes certainly read and appreciated the *Treatise* because his ideas on the priesthood as well as on the Christian life fully corresponded with those of the venerable founder of Saint Sulpice.

While the *Treatise* and other seventeenth-century works on the priesthood were considered excellent, they were not, in the judgment of the Saint, sufficient for the clergy of the day. Priests needed shorter and more practical books which they could always have at hand and which would sum up their duties and how best to fulfil them. St. John Eudes's *Memorial* was intended to fill this need. It was to serve as a reminder of all the qualities and obligations of the priestly life as also of the manner of performing the sacerdotal functions. In other words, it was to be a manual to help priests to correspond to their exalted vocation and to carry out its duties in a saintly manner.

It is a well-established fact that so long as a priest has only commonplace ideas of his state and duties, he does not feel the necessity of aspiring to perfection and experiences none of the holy ardors of true zeal. St. John Eudes realized this better than anyone, and so he began his *Memorial* by reminding priests of the sublimity of their calling. This is the theme of the first two chapters of his work. In both, the Saint's style is highly colored and distinctly oratorical. Very possibly they are merely extracts from conferences given by him to the clergy. At all events, they are certainly faithful echoes of his lectures and enable us to have an idea of that ardent and devotional eloquence that so strongly impressed his hearers and communicated to them something of the apostolic zeal that filled his heart. One cannot read them without being struck by the admiration and the enthusiasm with which he writes on the sublimity of the priesthood. It would be impossible to find more striking and more accurate ideas on the subject.

The third chapter of the *Memorial* is a summary of the duties that devolve on the priest. This part is called the "memorial" or reminder by St. John Eudes, but that word is now given to the whole book. It would seem that this chapter is the oldest part of the volume, the nucleus of the complete work. In any case, it is superb and supplies fresh evidence of the Saint's ability to condense a whole programme of life into a few pages. The thirty-four articles to be found in it contain everything essential for the practice of priestly perfection. St. John Eudes deals with the fundamental rules of the priest's life, the principal dangers to be guarded against, the care that must be exercised over souls and the devotional exercises suited to the clergy. In these few pages one finds no exaggeration or even hyperbole, so commonly used by orators. The exactness and moderation of his teaching is matched by the precision of his style so that together they make this memorial or reminder a model of its kind.

The fourth and fifth chapters contain a series of pious exercises for the spiritual and the apostolic life of the priest. The Saint dwells on the interior dispositions necessary for achieving personal sanctity and for sanctifying souls through the ministry.

The last chapter is called the Directory of Retreats. It is very short and contains the usual method followed by retreatants in the seminaries conducted by the Congregation of Jesus and Mary. It also has brief notes on the various exercises of the retreat. The chief interest is found in the "extraordinary examens" inserted by the author, which have valuable instructions on the priestly virtues and which find a fitting place in a reminder of the priestly dignity and duties.[1]

II. *The Apostolic Preacher*

One of the principal functions of the sacred ministry is the preaching of the Word of God. Jesus Christ, the model of the priest, spent His public life in prayer and in preaching. The first mission that the Saviour of the World gave His Apostles was to announce the Gospel to all creatures. Moreover, the supernatural life of the soul is grounded on faith, and faith is engendered and developed by preaching. *Fides ex auditu* (Rom. 10, 17).

St. John Eudes belonged to the century of great French preachers. He himself was a born missionary. God had endowed him with extraordinary talents and special aptitudes for the holy ministry of preach-

---

[1] These examens are usually separated from the chapter and printed as "Meditations for the Annual Retreat." In the present English edition they are the last series of meditations.

ing. Noble and majestic of bearing, with a strong, flexible and pleasing voice, a rich and vivid imagination, and an ardent and impetuous character, he was destined in the course of his fifty-five years as a missionary to sway multitudes and to move and convert souls. To these qualities were added a burning zeal for the glory of God and the salvation of souls, boundless compassion and sympathy for sinners and great personal sanctity which was universally recognized.

During his missions St. John Eudes invariably gave conferences to his young and inexperienced missionaries on the manner of preaching usefully. In order to conserve these rules in the Congregation of Jesus and Mary and to ensure their practice after his death he decided to bring them together into a volume with the significant title, *The Apostolic Preacher*. Though he labored at the work for a long time, he did not complete it until the end of his life and it was his successor, Father Blouet de Camilly, who published it in 1685.

In *The Apostolic Preacher* the Saint dwells upon the excellence and importance of preaching and elaborates some beautiful thoughts that are not usually found in books on the subject. He insists on the supernatural character of preaching and urges the preacher to raise himself above all thoughts of vanity and self-interest and to aim solely at instructing and touching his hearers. He goes into numerous details on the preparation and the composition of the sermon, gives many simple plans, adds some practical advice concerning delivery and points out the ordinary faults of preachers with countless other details that he drew from his own experience. What he desires, above all, is that the preacher be a man of prayer and that he be the first to practise what he preaches to the people.

III. *The Good Confessor*

In 1644 St. John Eudes published a small book called *Advice to Missionary Confessors,* which he wrote for his auxiliary priests on the missions that it might guide and help them to maintain uniformity of method in the tribunal of penance. In its contents as in its title, this book recalls *Advice for Confessors* by St. Francis de Sales. St. John

Eudes took care, however, to add to the meekness of the Bishop of Geneva the firmness of St. Charles Borromeo, whose regulations he followed on the delaying and refusing of absolution. The Saint's booklet had a rapid success and appeared in a second edition. But this volume was merely an essay, and the day came when St. John Eudes wished to complete it by adding the fruits of his long experience in the confessional. He quickly realized that the only way of doing this successfully was to revise the work completely. Thus he produced an entirely new book, *The Good Confessor,* which appeared in 1666. It was given a most cordial welcome by the clergy and became very popular. This explains why it was re-edited so often in the seventeenth and eighteenth centuries.[2]

The Good Confessor is an excellent handbook of pastoral theology, whose purpose is to teach priests how to administer the Sacrament of Penance. Gifted with a practical spirit, the Saint knew that the best means to inspire his fellow priests with a love of this office, so fruitful but often so fatiguing, was to point out first its greatness and sublimity. This he does in the opening chapters. Then he develops the necessary qualifications of the good confessor and offers some helpful advice on dealing with sinners in the confessional.

"Of all the books," says Martine, "given by Father Eudes to the public, *The Good Confessor,* brought him the most honor. He received from all sides the thanks and praises that he merited for publishing a work of such great utility."[3]

A little later Pierre Cousin wrote, "We might say that this little book, the first that has appeared in France since the reform of the confessional, has two advantages over most works on the same subject. The first is that the method it teaches is so easy that no one can fail to understand and to practise it faithfully. And the second is that the duties of confessors are there exposed not drily, but with a devotion that arouses that of the reader even as it instructs him."[4]

[2] Sixteen editions appeared from 1666 to 1733.
[3] Martine, *Vie du P. Eudes,* Vol. II, p. 121.
[4] Father Pierre Cousin was appointed superior general of the Eudist Fathers in 1727. The quotation is taken from the introduction to the 1732 edition of *The Good Confessor.*

IV. *Meditations*

The present volume includes three series of meditations for the use of the clergy. The first group have as their object the chief obligations of a priest: obligation to seek perfection, hatred of sin, self-denial, love of Christ, of the Blessed Virgin Mary, and of the Church. These meditations are remarkable for the conciseness of their style as well as for the loftiness and solidity of their doctrine. With a little development they would make an excellent clergy retreat.

The other meditations fall into two distinct groups. The first deals with tonsure and holy orders, the material being extracted for the most part from the *Pontifical.* It was obviously the Saint's intention that they should be used by those to be ordained and possibly they were written for them. The second group, *Meditations for the Annual Retreat,* were formerly found in the Directory of Retreats at the end of the *Memorial.* They are the extraordinary examinations of which we have previously spoken.[5]

The Priest: His Dignity and Obligations, like all the other works of St. John Eudes, was bound up with his apostolic labors, and its only object was to ensure the success of the latter. It is not a learned work but a practical book written to meet the needs of his own Congregation and to help all priests to lead a life conformable to their sublime vocation. Written simply and clearly, without any literary object, it is permeated with the Saint's penetrating unction and delicate piety. No priest can read it seriously without deriving great benefits from it for his personal sanctification and for his priestly work for the salvation of souls.

Charles Lebrun, C.J.M.

[5] See p. xxi.

DEDICATION

TO

THE HOLY PRIESTS OF THE
CHURCH TRIUMPHANT

O great saints, chosen from all eternity by Jesus Christ, the Saint of saints, to be clothed in an especial manner with His admirable sanctity; glorious priests selected from thousands of men by Jesus, the Supreme High Priest, to be His associates in the Divine Priesthood, prostrate at your feet with all respect and humility I salute you!

I honor you by every means in my power as my masters and spiritual fathers, as shining lights in the firmament of the Church, as true shepherds of the flock of Christ, as oracles of the Eternal Word, as prophets of His holy teaching, as chiefs in the celestial militia, as captains of the army of the Great King, as princes of His realm, as kings of His empire.

I revere you as members of the greatest and most dignified order in heaven and on earth, the Eternal Priesthood, founded and established by Jesus Christ, the Son of God.

I hail you as the solid pillars supporting Mother Church, as the unshakable foundation of the house of God. I respect you as custodians of the keys of heaven, as cherubim stationed with flaming swords at the gates of paradise to prevent the unworthy and profane from entering its portals. I see in you living and perfect images of the Sovereign Priest, Jesus Christ, the Only Son of God, with whom you are one, being clothed with the very Priesthood conferred upon Him by His Eternal Father, and one with Him as all members are one with their head.

With all my heart I thank God for having elevated you to the highest dignity in his heavenly kingdom and in the family of His

Divine Son. I rejoice that you are now crowned with glory and happiness, commensurate with the loftiness of your priestly dignity.

From my innermost soul I thank you for the heroic service you have rendered here on earth to our Divine Master and to His Holy Church, by the faithful discharge of your sacerdotal duties, and for the glory you have rendered God in time and eternity.

Who can tell the ardor of the love for Holy Mother Church which consumed you? Who can ever express in words the vigilance and zeal with which you labored in her interests? You realize now more than ever her great need in our materialistic age for priests who will follow in your footsteps, imitating your virtue and holiness. You understand how true is the saying of the Eternal Truth Himself that the harvest is great but the laborers few.

Permit me to address to you the prayer that Our Lord and Saviour recommended to all His children: "Pray ye therefore the Lord of the harvest, that he send forth labourers into his harvest" (Matt. 9, 38). But pray that He send workers "approved unto God" (2 Tim. 2, 15), workers seeking not their own interests, but having as their only goal the glory of the Master and the salvation of the souls which He purchased with the shedding of His Precious Blood. Pray that He may send to His Church priests after His own heart, who will walk the same road you trod while you were on earth.

O saintly priests, you know full well the importance and necessity of having holy priests in the Church of Christ. It is the most ardent longing of all true Christians who are animated with the love of God and the zeal for His Church. It is the sole desire that inflames my heart, and though I am the lowliest and most unworthy of all His priests, there is nothing that I would not undergo or suffer to further such a worthy consummation. This conviction constrained me to publish this work on the dignity and obligations of the priesthood. Those who take the trouble to use this book will find in its pages a compendium of their duties, and through its guidance they will exercise more worthily their priestly functions and be holy in all their actions.

Yet, because we labor in vain on earth unless our work be approved and blessed in heaven, deign, O holy priests of God, to accept this work and bless it, offering it in turn to the Sovereign Priest and to His

Blessed Mother that they may smile in benediction upon it. Plead
with Jesus and Mary that they may employ this book as a means of renewing the spirit of holiness and piety in priests on earth. Ask them to
make all priests worthy to share your happiness in heaven, that your
brothers in the Sacred Ministry may one day be associated with you in
paradise to chant forever the praises of the Most Blessed Trinity, whose
glory and majesty fill heaven and earth.

SAINT JOHN EUDES
1601-1680

Part I

A MEMORIAL OF THE ECCLESIASTICAL LIFE [1]

CHAPTER I [2]

THE DIGNITY OF THE PRIESTHOOD [3]

In the dedication of this work I prostrated myself before the holy priests of the Church Triumphant to invoke their blessing. I now address myself to you, brother priests of the Church Militant, in the words that St. Peter, the Prince of the Apostles, addressed to all Christians: *Vos autem genus electum, regale sacerdotium, gens sancta, populus acquisitionis ut virtutes annuntietis ejus qui de tenebris vos vocavit in admirabile lumen suum.* "You are a chosen generation, a kingly priesthood, a holy nation, a purchased people; that you may declare his virtues, who hath called you out of darkness into his marvellous light" (1 Pet. 2, 9).

You are a *chosen generation,* for the Saint of saints has elected you to the holy office of the priesthood. To you particularly He addresses these words: "But according to him that hath called you, who is holy,

---

[1] *Memorial:* There is no exact equivalent in English for the French word "Mémorial." We have decided to retain the word with the sense of *reminder,* which it sometimes has in English. St. John Eudes says himself: "I wish to put this book in your hands as a reminder (memorial) of all the qualities and the merits, the obligations and the duties of your profession, as also of the method of exercising in a holy manner all the priestly functions." Cf. *Oeuvres Complètes du Vénérable Jean Eudes,* Vol. III, p. 21.

[2] The French work is divided into parts, not chapters. Chapter divisions are used in this edition.

[3] In the original edition this chapter is the second dedication.

be you also in all manner of conversation holy; because it is written: 'You shall be holy, for I am holy' " (1 Pet. 1, 15-16).

You are clothed and adorned with *a kingly priesthood*. You are priests and kings as Jesus Christ Himself is the Supreme Priest and King.

You are *a purchased people* in a very special significance. It is true that Our Blessed Redeemer purchased all mankind at the price of His Blood and that Almighty God gave Him to all nations. Nevertheless Jesus acquired you in a particular manner and so His Heavenly Father manifests a unique love for you.

After the Blessed Virgin Mary you represent our Divine Saviour's most glorious conquest. You are the most precious of all gifts that the Eternal Father has bestowed upon His Only Son. You are the first and most excellent fruit of His work, the worthiest price of His blood, His principal portion. You embody His most noble heritage from which are derived fruits for the glory of God more acceptable than from all His other possessions.

The Son of God chose you, not only that you yourselves might serve and love Him, but also that you might make Him loved and served by others. He selected you that you might *announce* to the world *the virtues,* that is, the perfections and excellence, the mysteries and marvels of Him who "hath called you out of darkness," from the darkness of sin and hell, "into His marvellous light."

Jesus Christ, speaking of Himself, says, "I am the light of the world" (John 8, 12). He says also of priests, "You are the light of the world" (Matt. 5, 14), and "to you it is given to know the mystery of the kingdom of God" (Mark 4, 11) and to make it known to other men. To you has been opened the treasury of wisdom and grace that you may be dispensers of these gifts.

You are persons elevated by the infinite goodness of God to the highest dignity of heaven and earth, second only to the divine motherhood of the Blessed Virgin Mary.

You are the noblest personnages in God's house. You are clothed with genuine nobility for, as Christians and certainly much more as priests, you may be called in the words of St. Paul "the offspring of

God" (Act. 17, 29). You are children of God, His first-born sons. You are of the royal blood of Jesus, a part of His genealogy; you are His brethren and members in a degree much higher than any other Christians. You are clothed with the royal priesthood, and your priesthood is one with His. Since there is but one priesthood, *unum est sacerdotium*,[4] centered in Christ and extended to all other priests, so there is but one Priest, Jesus Christ. All other priests are one with Him, united to Him according to His own prayer: "The glory which thou has given me, I have given to them: that they may be one as we also are one: I in them, and thou in me; that they may be made perfect in one . . ." (John 17, 22-23).

You are governors, judges, princes and kings of the empire of the supreme Monarch of the World. You are governors, not *tenebrarum harum* (Eph. 6, 12), that is, of this world, which is darkness and nothingness, but of faithful souls purchased with the Precious Blood of Christ, one drop of which is worth more than a thousand worlds.

You are judges, not of bodies but of souls, not of earthly but of heavenly things. Your judgments are not transitory; they endure forever. They are written, not on paper nor on parchment with ink, but in eternity with the adorable Blood of the Son of God. Thus the most eminent persons in the land recognize you as judges of their souls, divinely appointed by Providence. Humbly they kneel before you and accept your judgment as the very judgment of God Himself.

You are princes of God. Your principality is not terrestrial; it is immortal and imperishable. You are kings of His empire, the Church. It is to you that He says: *Ego dispono vobis sicut disposuit mihi Pater meus regnum.* "And I dispose to you, as My Father hath disposed to me, a kingdom" (Luke 22, 29). Your royalty is not temporal but eternal, a participation in the royalty of Jesus Christ.

Since Christ is Priest and King, so, too, you are priests and kings. Since you share one priesthood, so, too, you participate in one kingship with Him. Since the Eternal Father has given His Divine Son a name and a power above every name and every power (Phil. 2, 9), so He has given you, His priests, a name and a power incomparably

---

[4] Summach. Papa, *Ep.* 10 *ad Eonium, Arelat. Episc.*

greater than all names and all powers in this world and in the world to come.

Did God say to any of the angels: "Thou art a priest for ever according to the order of Melchisedech?" (Ps. 109, 4). Did He ever pronounce to the Archangels, the Principalities or the Powers what His Son said to you: "Whatsoever thou shalt bind upon earth, it shall be bound also in heaven: and whatsoever thou shalt loose on earth, it shall be loosed also in heaven?" (Matt. 16, 19). To which of the Cherubim or Seraphim did He ever give the power to forgive sin, to bestow grace, to close hell and open the gates of heaven, to bring God into the hearts of men in the Blessed Sacrament? To whom in the universe did He grant the power of offering the Holy Sacrifice of the Altar, to immolate Him and give His Body and Soul to the faithful?

To which of the heavenly spirits did God ever speak the words He says to every priest, "As the Father hath sent me, I also send you?" (John 20, 21). In other words, I send you for the same purpose for which My Heavenly Father sent Me, to preach the gospel, to dispense grace, to administer the sacraments, to destroy the tyranny of Satan, to dispel the darkness of sin and to spread the divine light of grace throughout the world. I send you to establish the reign of God and to exercise on earth the very functions which I exercised, to continue My work of redemption, to lead the same life that I led and to practise the same virtues that I practised.

Thus, it is clear that you are not only the visible angels of the God of Armies; you are far greater than angels in power and authority. Hence, you must live a life more perfect in purity and sanctity than that of the angels.

It is not surprising that your power surpasses that of the angels, for, as the King of the Angels has made you participants in His kingship, so He has vested you with His own power. Consequently, you may say with Him, although in a different sense, "All power is given to me in heaven and on earth and in hell;" *in heaven* for you have the keys to open and close the gates of the kingdom; *on earth* for daily you exercise among men an infinite power which is God's alone by the remission of sins, the bestowal of grace, the formation of Christ in men's hearts and in the Blessed Eucharist; *in hell* for the Master has given you the power to crush and destroy the dragons of hell and to drive demons from the bodies and souls of the faithful.

Furthermore, you have power over the Sovereign Lord Himself in heaven and on earth. Do you not envision Our Lord Jesus Christ, King of angels and men, Who was subject to His Mother and to St. Joseph on earth, *erat subditus illis* (Luke 2, 51), actually subjected to the power of His priests? Does He not obey their commands and their words? Does He not hear their voice when they summon Him to come into their hands at the consecration of the bread and wine in the Holy Sacrifice of the Mass? Have they not power over His Mystical Body, which is the Church, over His Holy Spirit, over His grace and His mysteries? Is it not through priests and their ministry that the Holy Spirit is imparted to the faithful, that the treasures of grace are distributed and that the secrets of the eternal mysteries are made manifest? For that very reason Sacred Scripture attributed to them the function of "dispensers of the mysteries of God" (1 Cor. 4, 1).

Above all else, how wonderful is the power of priests over the very Body and Blood of the Saviour! That power not only gives them the right to bring Our Lord down upon the altar whenever they wish or to transport Him from one place to another; it also extends to the point of sacrificing Him every day, and of annihilating Him so far as it is possible to annihilate Him, because sacrifice means the destruction of the object sacrificed. Whoever possesses sacrificial power likewise must have power to destroy what he sacrifices. This is indeed the greatest and most absolute power God Himself can exercise over His creatures, to destroy and annihilate them for His glory.

Thus, God has honored the sovereign Priest, His Divine Son, and all those whom He has called to this holy state of the priesthood. He who can make creatures more perfect, angels more beautiful and worlds far greater and lovelier, cannot institute a priesthood more worthy and more admirable than the Christian priesthood. The sacerdotal dignity and power are so exalted that even Our Lord Himself cannot make priests capable of exercising functions more marvelous than yours when you form Christ in the Holy Eucharist, when you offer Him in sacrifice, or give Him to the faithful in Holy Communion or when you forgive sins in the Sacrament of Penance.

What more shall I say? You are the first officers in the court of the great Monarch of the universe. You are the chief ministers of His state, the treasurers of His mercy, His faithful stewards. Into your hands He has committed His riches, His entire glory, the treasures of His grace, the keys of His kingdom, the sacraments of His religion, the sanctity of His divine mysteries, the virtue of His word, His Mystical Body, His very flesh and His Precious Blood.

You are the most noble part of the Mystical Body of Christ. You are the eyes, the mouth, the tongue, the heart of the Church, in other words, of Jesus Christ Himself.

You are His eyes for through you the Good Shepherd watches over His flock. Through you He enlightens and guides His sheep. Through you He weeps over the transgressions of those who fall by the wayside, or become prey of the wolves. Through you He weeps over the death of His dear Lazarus, that is, of the souls of those who are dead through sin.

You are His mouth and His tongue. Through you He speaks to His people, continuing to preach the gospel that He Himself preached during His public life.

You are His heart. Through you He imparts true life, the life of grace on earth and the life of glory in heaven to all the members of His Mystical Body. What marvels, what favors, what greatness in the sacerdotal dignity! Yet there is still more!

You are the associates of the Father, the Son and the Holy Ghost, in most sublime and mysterious intimacy. I hear the great Apostle Paul announce to all Christians that they have been called by God to be members of the society of His Divine Son. *Vocati estis in societatem Filii ejus Jesu Christi.* "You are called unto the fellowship of his Son Jesus Christ our Lord" (1 Cor. 1, 9). With truth I say that priests are called unto the fellowship of the Father, and the Son and the Holy Ghost. *Vocati estis in societatem Patris, et Filii, et Spiritus Sancti.*

God the Father associates you with Himself in the highest of all functions, the generation of His Divine Son. He embraces you in His divine paternity, making you fathers of that very Son since yours is the power to form and generate Him in the souls of the faithful. He has chosen you to be fathers of His people, real fathers in word and action. You bear within you the living image of the divine paternity. "O Priest," cries St. Augustine, "thou are the vicar and father of Christ!"

God the Son associates you with Himself in His noble perfections and His divine operations. He makes you participants in His role as mediator between God and man, in the dignity of Judge of the universe, in His name and office as Saviour of the world. He gives you power to offer with Him to His Eternal Father the sacrifice of Redemption which He renews daily on the altars of the world, the most sublime action that He ever performed and ever will perform.

God the Holy Ghost associates you with Him in His divine actions. Why did the Holy Spirit come into the world? Was it not to dispel the darkness of ignorance and sin? Was it not to enlighten men's minds with a celestial light, to fire their hearts with divine love, to reconcile sinners to God, to destroy sin, to communicate grace, to sanctify souls, and to establish the Church? Was it not to apply to mankind the fruits of the passion and death of the Redeemer, to destroy the old man and bring to life within us Jesus Christ Our Lord?

Is not your daily duty to concern yourselves with all these miraculous functions? Are you not sent by God to bring Christ into all hearts? Is it not true that all the offices of the priesthood are designed for the sole purpose of forming and causing God to live in the souls of His people?

Truly then, you have an intimate alliance with the Three Eternal Persons of the Blessed Trinity. You are their associates and their coadjutors. You are cooperators with the Most High in all His works. *Dei adjutores, cooperatores veritatis* (1 Cor. 3, 9). You are co-laborers with the Almighty, sanctifiers of souls, mediators between God and man, judges of nations, saviours of the world. The Divine Redeemer has appointed you here on earth to serve in His place, to continue and complete His own work, the redemption of the universe.

In Sacred Scripture, Almighty God has given you the name of

saviour, for of priests He says, by the mouth of the Prophet **Abdias** (Abdias 13, 21), *Ascendent salvatores in montem Sion.* Clement of Alexandria attributes to priests the role of redeemers.[5]

It may even be said of you that you are other Christs, living and walking among men for you bear the exalted name of the Son of God, the name of Jesus and Saviour. You represent His authority and His divine perfections. You act in His name, are employed in His service, continuing to live on earth the very life He led here below.

You are visible gods in this world, children of God, fathers of **God.** In his work, *The Celestial Hierarchy,* St. Dionysius invests you **with** these three attributes: You are gods because you take the place of **God** in this world and are clothed with His qualities, His prerogatives **and** powers. You are children of gods because you are the children of your bishops who in turn are gods in yet a higher degree than you. You are fathers of gods, because you are fathers of Christians who likewise **are** gods, though in a lower degree than you. *Ego dixi dii estis* (Ps. 81, 6). "A priest," says St. Gregory Nazianzen, "is a god who produces gods." *Deus deos efficiens.*[6]

O incomparable excellence! O incomprehensible dignity of **the** Priesthood of Jesus Christ, shared with all His priests! How indebted we should be to Him who has raised us to so elevated a state, and has showered upon us such extraordinary gifts! O noble vocation! What a grace, what a privilege, what an inestimable blessing to have been called to an order so divine and so exalted!

[5] Clem. Al. *in Oseam.*
[6] *Orat. Apolog.*

CHAPTER II

QUALITIES OF A HOLY PRIEST

THE MOST EVIDENT MARK of God's anger and the most terrible castigation He can inflict upon the world are manifested when He permits His people to fall into the hands of clergy who are priests more in name than in deed, priests who practice the cruelty of ravening wolves rather than the charity and affection of devoted shepherds. Instead of nourishing those committed to their care, they rend and devour them brutally. Instead of leading their people to God, they drag Christian souls into hell in their train. Instead of being the salt of the earth and the light of the world, they are its innocuous poison and its murky darkness.

St. Gregory the Great says that priests and pastors will stand condemned before God as the murderers of any souls lost through neglect or silence. *Tot occidimus, quot ad mortem ire tepidi et tacentes videmus.*[1] Elsewhere St. Gregory asserts that nothing more angers God than to see those whom He set aside for the correction of others, give bad example by a wicked and depraved life.[2] Instead of preventing offenses against His Majesty, such priests become themselves the first to persecute Him, they lose their zeal for the salvation of souls and think only of following their own inclinations. Their affections go no farther than earthly things, they eagerly bask in the empty praises of men, using their sacred ministry to serve their ambitions, they abandon the things of God to devote themselves to the things of the world, and in their saintly calling of holiness, they spend their time in profane and worldly pursuits.

When God permits such things, it is a very positive proof that He is thoroughly angry with His people, and is visiting His most dreadful

[1] *Homil. 12 super Ezech.*
[2] *Homil. 27 in Evang.*

9

anger upon them. That is why He cries unceasingly to Christians, "Return, O ye revolting children . . . and I will give you pastors according to my own heart" (Jer. 3, 14-15). Thus, irregularities in the lives of priests constitute a scourge visited upon the people in consequence of sin.

On the other hand, the greatest effect of God's mercy, the most precious grace He bestows upon mankind, is to send worthy priests, men after His own heart, seeking only His glory and the salvation of souls. The greatest blessing that God bestows upon a church, the most signal manifestation of divine grace, is to have a saintly shepherd, be he bishop or priest. This is indeed the grace of graces and the most priceless of all gifts for it includes within itself every other blessing and grace. What is a priest after God's heart? He is an inestimable treasure containing an immensity of good things.

The holy priest is one of the treasures of the Great King, having in his keeping the infinite abundance of God's mercy to enrich worthy souls. He is an inexhaustible fountain of living water, open and accessible to all those who long to come to drink the waters of salvation.

He is a tree of life planted by God in the paradise of the Church, bearing on its branches at all times fruits of everlasting life, freeing from sin and hell, giving grace and eternal bliss to those who will but eat. Those fruits are the words, instructions, exhortations, prayers, intercession and example of the life and work of the holy priest.

He is an ever burning and shining light set in the candelabra of Mother Church, burning before God and shining before men: burning in his own love for God, shining by his charity for his fellow man; burning with the perfection of his inner life, shining by the perfection of his exterior deportment; burning in fervent prayer for his people, shining by his preaching of the word of God.

The priest is a sun cheering the world by his presence and bearing. He brings heavenly blessings into every heart. He dispels the ignorance and darkness of error and radiates on every side bright beams of celestial light. He extinguishes sin and gives life and grace to the multitudes. He imparts new life to the weak, inflames the lukewarm, fires more ardently those who are aglow with the sacred flame of divine love.

He is an angel purifying, illuminating and perfecting the souls that God has entrusted to him. He is a seraph sent by God to teach men the science of salvation which is concerned only with knowing and loving Almighty God and His Divine Son, Jesus Christ.

The priest is an archangel and a prince of the heavenly militia, waging constant war against the devil who strives to drag countless souls into the depths of hell.

He is the real father of the children of God, with a heart filled with love which is truly paternal. That love urges him to work unceasingly to nourish his flock with the bread of the sacred word and of the sacraments, to clothe the faithful with Christ and the Holy Ghost, to enrich them with celestial blessings and to secure for them every possible assistance in the salvation of their souls.

Above all else, the priest is the father, the advocate, the protector and defender of the poor, widows, orphans and strangers. He is the refuge of the afflicted, of the desolate and the discouraged. He is happy to visit and console the sorrowful, to bring them what assistance he can, taking upon himself their burdens and defending them against their oppressors.

He is a captain in the mighty army of God, always ready to battle for the glory of God and the defense of Holy Mother Church. He is ever prepared to lay siege to the world, the flesh and the devil. For him the conquest of kingdoms means only the salvation of souls for each soul is a kingdom more precious than all the empires of the world.

The priest is a prince of the realm of God, one of the kings of Christ's empire, the Church. He is appointed to rule by the maxims and laws of the gospel as many kings and queens as there are Christians committed to his care. His duty is to make them worthy to possess in eternity the very kingdom of the Sovereign Monarch of the world.

The priest is an evangelist and an apostle whose chief work is to preach publicly and privately, by word and example, the Gospel of Jesus Christ; to continue and perpetuate the functions that the apostles were commissioned to perform, and to practise the virtues that they practised.

He is the sacred bridegroom of the divine spouse, the Church of Christ. He is so consumed with love that his thoughts are concerned only with seeking means to adorn and embellish the Church in the eyes of men, and to render her yet more worthy of the eternal love of the heavenly and immortal Bridegroom.

The priest is a mediator between God and man, causing the Eternal Father to be known, loved, adored and served, as well as feared, by men. His office is to make known the will of God to men, urging them to be faithful to their every duty. His concern is to be devoted unceasingly to "the things that appertain to God" (Heb. 5, 1).

The priest is one of the chief parts of the Mystical Body of Christ because he occupies the principal parts of that Body, namely, the head, the eyes, the mouth, the tongue and the heart. He is the head with the Chief Shepherd, sharing the right to rule and govern in His place. He is the eyes watching over the other members to enlighten and guide them, and to weep over them when they sin. The priest is the mouth and the tongue to speak the language of heaven, to utter on all occasions the words of eternity. He is the heart circulating the blood stream of Christ's Precious Blood to quicken and vivify the other members, that their works and functions may be ennobled and perfected.

A holy priest is a saviour and another Christ, taking the Master's place on earth, representing Him, clothed with His authority, acting in His name, adorned with His qualifications, exercising His judgment on earth in the tribunal of penance. He is consecrated to exercise the highest functions Christ ever performed on earth, to continue the work of salvation. In imitation of His Redeemer he gives himself, mind, heart, affections, strength, time, all for God. He is ever ready to sacrifice his very blood and even life itself to procure the salvation of souls, particularly those of his own flock.

He is a god, living and walking on earth; a god by grace and by participation, clothed with the perfections and attributes of God, namely, His divine authority, power, justice, mercy, charity, benignity, purity and holiness. He is a god delegated to carry on God's noblest works, the sacerdotal and pastoral duties, as great St. Dionysius says: *Omnium divinorum divinissimum est cooperari Deo in salutem animarum.* "The most divine of all divine things is to cooperate with God in the salvation of souls." [3]

[3] *De Coelesti Hierarchia,* cap. 5.

St. Gregory Nazianzen asserts that the priest is a "God who makes gods," *Deus deos efficiens,*[4] that is, Christians who are given the name of gods in Sacred Scripture.

He is a shepherd bearing within himself the living image of the goodness and the vigilance of the Good Shepherd, a guardian who never deserts his flock lest the wolves devour it. He is a shepherd who knows his sheep, their needs, their maladies, their infirmities, that he may cure them. He is a shepherd who nourishes them by word and example.

What more shall I say? "Who speaks of the priesthood," says St. Dionysius, "speaks of an order which contains within itself all that is most sacred and most holy."[5] "Who speaks of the priesthood," avers St. Ignatius Martyr, "speaks of the fullness of the blessings of God."[6] "Who speaks of a priest," adds St. Dionysius, "speaks of a man who is divine."[7]

Whoever refers to a priest adorned with virtue and holiness becoming the dignity of his calling, bespeaks the greatest degree of sanctity found in Holy Church, a sanctity which is the source and wellspring of grace and love, for the priesthood is the fountain of all holiness.

Such a priest is a man called to the sacerdotal dignity not by men, not by the will of flesh and blood, not by his parents or by the spirit of ambition, not by avarice or human motives, but by vocation from God.

Such a priest is a man endowed with the marks and perfections outlined in the first Chapter of St. Paul's Epistle to Titus, and in the third Chapter of his First Epistle to Timothy: "a man without crime, as the steward of God; not proud, not subject to anger, not given to wine, no striker, not greedy of filthy lucre; but given to hospitality, gentle, sober, just, holy, continent: of good behaviour, chaste, given to hospitality, a teacher; one that ruleth well his own house having his children in subjection. . . . But if a man know not how to rule his own house, how shall he take care of the church of God?" (Tit. 1, 7-8); (1 Tim. 3, 2-5).

Such a priest employs his revenue and income not in vanities nor sinful excesses nor to enrich his relatives or his own estate, but to en-

[4] *Orat. Apolog.*
[5] *De Eccl. Hierarch.* cap. 1, 3.
[6] *Epist.* 10 *ad Smyrna.*
[7] *Loc. cit.*

hance the glory of God. He adorns altars, clothes the naked, feeds the hungry, refreshes the thirsty, frees prisoners, assists religious institutions, builds churches and hospitals, and carries out good works of every description.

Such a priest is seen frequently in the hospitals, prisons and the homes of the poor. He consoles, instructs and assists the people in their spiritual and corporal necessities. He applies himself diligently to the consideration of his duties; he studies the needs of his flock in order to exercise the utmost efficiency in supplying their wants. He ferrets out any disorders which may exist among his charges in order to eradicate them; he gives himself unselfishly to the advancement of the glory of God and the salvation of those souls under his direction.

The saintly priest employs his mind and heart, thoughts, affections, words and actions, his time, his life, all that he has, to destroy the tyranny of Satan and sin, and to establish the reign of Christ in the hearts of those whom God has entrusted to him.

The worthy priest is an angel of purity in mind and body, a cherub of light and knowledge, a seraph of love and charity, an apostle of zeal in work and sanctity, a little god on earth in power and authority, in patience and benignity. He is the living image of Christ in this world, of Christ watching, praying, preaching, catechizing, working, weeping, going from town to town, from village to village, suffering, agonizing, sacrificing Himself and dying for the souls created to His image and likeness.

He is the light of those who sit in darkness and in the shadow of death. He is the destroyer of error, schisms and heresies, the converter of sinners, the sanctifier of the just, the strength of the weak, the consolation of the afflicted, the treasure of the poor. He is the confusion of hell, the glory of heaven, the terror of demons, the joy of angels, the ruin of Satan's kingdom, the establishment of Christ's empire, the ornament of the Church, the crown of the Supreme Shepherd.

In a word, the holy priest embodies a world of grace and benediction for the entire Church, but especially for that portion which God has called him to govern and guide.

CHAPTER III

DUTIES OF THE PRIESTLY STATE

FROM ALL that has been written in the foregoing chapters, it is obvious that the priest is favored with far more graces than any other human being except the Blessed Virgin Mary. It follows, then, that no one on earth is held to a greater perfection and sanctity of life than the priest, especially if he is charged with the care of souls.

Thus, it is most important and necessary for you to consider often and seriously before God the dignity and excellence of your vocation, the obligation and duties which it involves and the manner in which you discharge them.

Consequently, it is profitable for you to have a summary of these duties, to read and reread, that thus you may engrave your responsibilities on your heart, and give expression to them in your life and conduct.

The compendium that I have drawn up with this intention in mind, formulates the principal sacerdotal duties under thirty-four headings, in honor and commemoration of the thirty-four years[1] of the life on earth of Jesus Christ, the great High Priest, who is the model of all priests. If you seek to follow a rule filled with love, sweetness and perfection you must do as follows:

[1] The exact duration of Christ's public life is uncertain. St. John Eudes follows the opinion of St. Jerome that the ministry of Jesus lasted three years and a half. Assuming as do many authoritative writers that Our Lord began His public life at the age of thirty, St. John Eudes concludes that the entire life of the Savior extended over a period of thirty-three years and six months. Our Lord therefore died in His thirty-fourth year. This accounts for the fact that St. John Eudes asks us to honor the thirty-four years of our Lord's life on earth.—For the chronology and duration of Christ's life, see Filion, *Vie de N.S. Jesus Christ* (Paris, 1925), vol. II, p. 11 and *The Catholic Encyclopedia*, vol. VIII, "Jesus," p. 379.

1

Establish in your heart a firm resolution to live inwardly and outwardly in such a way that your life may be above reproach, following the words of St. Paul to Timothy which apply to priests as well as bishops, "It behoveth therefore a bishop to be blameless" (1 Tim. 3, 2). Make of your life a living gospel, a continual sermon, a perfect rule of life and morals for those whom you govern.

2

Make a lofty and generous profession to conduct your life always according to the maxims of faith and of the gospel, being assiduous in reading and studying them. Christ brought His divine maxims down from heaven and taught them to His apostles for this very purpose. Why else did He inspire the writings of Sacred Scripture except that they be followed? Who will follow them if not the priests who should learn these truths and preach them to the people? How shall they learn and preach these truths if they do not take the trouble to read the exhortations of Our Lord Jesus Christ, where they are to be found, especially in chapters five, six and seven of St. Matthew?

3

Be not concerned with the world. Rather renounce its maxims, its spirit and everything associated with it. True Christians are not of this world, even as the Master Himself is not, according to His own words: "Because they are not of the world, as I also am not of the world" (John 17, 14). If the Holy Ghost forbids the faithful to be concerned with the things of this world, even commanding them to hate them, how much more so do His words apply to priests? "Love not the world, nor the things which are in the world. If any man love the world, the charity of the Father is not in him" (1 John 2, 15).

4

Engrave on your heart the words of St. Paul and follow them faithfully: "Be not conformed to this world" (Rom. 12, 2). Renounce as much as lies in your power everything worldly in dress or habits. It surely demeans the priesthood when you who are supposed to be the salt of the earth, that is, the wise men of the world, follow the fashions of the day and the inane spirit of the times, manifested in thoughtlessness and perpetual changes. *Stultus ut luna mutatur* (Ecclus. 27, 12).

5

Avoid all familiarity with the laity, especially worldlings and women, except in charity and necessity. Even then, your aim should be to avoid being alone with them. At all times, whether your conversation be with women or other people of the world, speak the language of the Heavenly Father, conversing chiefly of the things of God and eternal salvation: "If any man speak, let him speak, as the words of God" (1 Pet. 4, 11). "For we are the good odour of Christ unto God; providing good things, not only in the sight of God but also in the sight of all men, that he, who is on the contrary part may be afraid, having no evil to say of us" (2 Cor. 2, 15; Rom. 12, 17; Tit. 2, 8).

6

Always dress in your clerical attire which is the ornament and glory of the priest. Be mindful that you should avoid anything which suggests foppishness or vanity. Likewise, you should be careful to be neat and tidy so that your appearance suggests order and cleanliness. Your bearing at all times should denote humility, simplicity and modesty.

7

Deny to avarice any part in your life, and shut the door of your heart firmly against any inroad. Engrave upon it these words of the Holy Ghost, "Let your manners be without covetousness, contented with such things as you have. For He hath said, *I will not leave thee: neither will I forsake thee*" (Heb. 13, 5). "For they that will become rich fall into temptation and into the snare of the devil and into many unprofitable and hurtful desires, which drown men into destruction and perdition. For the desire of money is the root of all evils: which some coveting have erred from the faith and have entangled themselves in many sorrows. But thou, O man of God, fly these things: and pursue justice, godliness, faith, charity, patience, mildness" (1 Tim. 6, 9-11).

You should always remember that, when you embraced the clerical state, you made your profession in these words, *Dominus pars haereditatis meae,* meaning that you would seek no other portion, no other heritage than Jesus Christ Himself. Consequently, He is the only treasure to fill your heart, and you should seek no other treasures on earth. The Fathers of the Church tell us that the priest who enriches himself or his relatives at the expense of the Church will be condemned by God as guilty of theft and sacrilege. As St. Bernard puts it: *Furtum est, rapina, sacrilegium.*[2]

8

Hold in horror the spirit of the Pharisees, that is, the spirit of ambition and vanity which loves the point of honor, which preaches but does not practise, which seeks only the praise and tribute of man, and which is concerned only with appearances and the plaudits of humans. That spirit dares to ignore the frightful anathemas hurled by the Saviour Himself against the haughty Pharisees: "Woe to you when men shall bless you: for according to these things did their fathers to the false prophets" (Luke 6, 26). To avoid such a tendency, consider well and practise the words of Sacred Scripture: "The greater thou art, the more humble thyself in all things: and thou shalt find grace before God" (Ecclus. 3, 20). And Christ Himself counsels us thus, "Go sit down in the lowest place" (Luke 14, 10). "Learn of me, because I am meek and humble of heart" (Matt. 11, 29).

9

Fear the sentence pronounced against the unworthy servant: "And the unprofitable servant cast ye out into the exterior darkness" (Matt. 25, 30). Have a wholesome dread lest this verdict be hurled against you. To safeguard particularly against this, avoid idleness, the mother of all vices. Regulate and occupy your time with prayer and study, and in the exercise of devotion, charity or other useful works. Remember that no group of men on earth is more obliged to make profitable use of time than priests for they are charged with the most important duties on earth—the glory of God and the salvation of souls.

[2] *Epist. ad Falconem.*

10

Learn to hate intemperance in eating and drinking. Avoid every occasion in which sinful excesses may be committed. This vice is low and bestial and most definitely contrary to the sanctity and dignity of the priest, who should be an angel among men.

11

Abhor impurity. Avoid with the most scrupulous exactitude the places, persons or things which might constitute the slightest peril or suggest even the smallest shadow of that abominable vice. What could be more necessary and becoming to the life of the priest consecrated to God, the priest whose life is spent in the church near the altar, whose time is spent performing angelic functions amidst divine mysteries, what is more necessary and becoming than purity of mind and body? What can be more terrible than an impure priest? He is a monster, a Judas, an antichrist.

12

Consider the words of St. Paul: "If any man have not care of his own, and especially of those of his house, he hath denied the faith, and is worse than an infidel" (1 Tim. 5, 8). Lest, therefore, you be condemned by God as apostates, learn to rule and govern your household that it may be a shining example of virtue, modesty, charity and piety for all Christian families to behold and imitate.

13

Keep a constant eye on the needs of your flock, anticipating their every want. Be mindful that the slightest negligence on your part renders you culpable in the eyes of God for He will demand a rigorous account of all the souls committed to your care. "I will require his blood at thy hand," says Sacred Scripture in Ezechiel (3, 18). Likewise, the Master will brand you as the murderers of those who perish because of your sloth, as witness the terrible words of St. Gregory: *"Tot occidimus quot ad mortem ire tepidi et tacentes videmus."* [3]

[3] Homil. 17.

14

Eradicate those evils for which you can find a remedy. Seek to destroy as far as is possible, scandal, disorders and sin by prayer, example and preaching. Thus, you shall fulfil the words of St. Paul: "Preach the word; be instant in season, out of season; reprove, entreat, rebuke in all patience and doctrine" (2 Tim. 4, 2). Banish blasphemies, swearing, injury and injustice, the oppression of the poor, the pomps of Satan. Crush the implements of the devil, immoral dancing, obscene plays, lascivious books and shows, immodest dress and lewd fashions. Abolish blasphemy, lying, fraud and every such type of sin. Above all else, preach and wage incessant war against drunkenness, the source of so much evil.

15

Be the protector and defender, the consoler, the father and the refuge of the poor, widows and orphans. Be the strength of those who are helpless and oppressed. Be assiduous in catechizing and preaching the gospel. Visit prisoners and the afflicted, encouraging them to turn their trials to their spiritual advancement.

16

Cultivate a very special charity for the sick and visit them frequently. Administer the sacraments and try to be with them at the hour of death. Be exact in your devotion to the poor as well as to the rich, to the humble as well as to the great.

17

Strive your utmost to instruct those under your care in their Christian obligations. In this respect be faithful in preaching and exhorting, not only in the pulpit and in public, but even in private, in the home, on the street, everywhere, in imitation of the first Christian priests. "And every day they ceased not in the temple, and from house to house, to teach and preach Christ Jesus" (Acts 5, 42). Let it be said of you as of St. Paul, "I am clear from the blood of all men. For I have not spared to declare unto you all the counsel of God. . . . For three years I ceased not, with tears to admonish every one of you night and day" (Acts 20, 26-31).

18

Watch over the school, being especially careful in the selection of teachers. Frequently visit the class rooms to teach catechism, and to hear the children say their morning and night prayers. Encourage them also in the practice of the utmost respect for the House of God.

19

Try to adjust differences which may arise between various members of your flock and strive to establish the reign of peacefulness and Christian charity among those committed to your charge by God.

20

Cultivate an ardent love for the Church which God has given to you as a spouse to whom you must surrender your whole heart. Carefully protect her interests; seek unflaggingly to advance her mission; labor unceasingly for her growth and sanctification; be unfailing in your zeal for the salvation of souls, burning into your very heart the words of St. Dionysius, *Omnium divinorum divinissimum est co-operari Deo in salutem animarum.*[4]

21

Let your chief glory and happiness consist in seeking to carry out holily and reverently the noble duties of the priestly life, especially the offering of the Holy Sacrifice of the Mass, the recitation of the Divine Office, the administration of the sacraments, preaching and instructing. Above all else, endeavor to form the saintly habit of doing everything not simply by routine, not in a slovenly, careless manner, but with devotion and exactitude worthy of God, as St. Paul counsels, *digne Deo* (Col. 1, 10), that is, worthy of His eternal majesty and infinite sanctity. To attain this goal, observe the dispositions and practices which will be suggested later on this point.

[4] *De Coelesti Hierarchia,* cap. 3.

22

Be most devoted to hearing confessions, regarding this function as one of the chief duties of the priest and as a most necessary, most powerful and most effective means of cooperating with God in the salvation of souls.

23

Take great care not to violate the command of our Divine Master, namely: "Give not that which is holy to dogs; neither cast ye your pearls before swine" (Matt. 7, 6). Let no unworthy person, no public sinner approach the holy table; withhold absolution from those unworthy of it, particularly those who persist in living in the proximate occasion of sin or constitute themselves such occasions for others; those, too, who live at enmity with their fellow men, refusing all attempts at reconciliation; those who remain constantly in the state of mortal sin without purpose or desire of amendment.

Be solicitous for the sanctity of the Sacrament of Matrimony, being particularly careful that none shall enter that holy state unless they are free from all canonical impediments and are thoroughly familiar with the obligations of marriage as well as its rights.

Regarding the Sacrament of Baptism, likewise be on guard against permitting unworthy godparents to assume the duties of sponsors, for these spiritual fathers and mothers cannot discharge the duties of their high office unless they are properly instructed and fitted for the task.

24

Be diligent in your care of the church, the cemetery and all places set aside for the service of God. Let all appointments reflect the sanctity that must characterize a consecrated environment. Everything should be neat and clean and in good order, especially the objects inside the Sanctuary. There the Great King should be served and honored with a dignity and excellence befitting His exalted position; there above all else the sacraments should be administered with the most exacting care; there the Divine Office should be recited with gravity and devotion, and every ceremony carried out with grace and dignity. The

House of God should be a place where the worshipper conducts himself with modesty, respect and appreciation of the Real Presence.

Be insistent in your zeal for the observance of Sunday and Holy Days. Discourage their profanation by unseemly conduct or unbecoming amusements. Above all else, fulminate against such sinful practices as drunkenness and debauchery.

25

Cherish an ardent devotion to the Blessed Virgin Mary and her holy spouse, St. Joseph, and endeavor to implant it also in the lives of those under your charge. Likewise impress upon your congregation the necessity of honoring the patron saints of the diocese and of the parish. Have a special devotion to all holy Pontiffs, Priests and Levites. Let it be felt that the observance of their feast days is actually the celebration of the feasts of our own brothers and fathers: *Filii sanctorum sumus* (Tob. 2, 18).

26

Have a most profound devotion to the Blessed Sacrament, for it is the unspeakable treasure of the priest, who should have in his own heart a burning zeal towards so holy a possession. It should be his one and constant desire to honor the Blessed Sacrament and to make it honored by others and to see that the abiding place of the Lord is clean, honorable and edifying. The priest should be unfailing in his efforts to teach the faithful to act reverently in the presence of Christ in the Tabernacle; he should spare no pains to encourage them to assist frequently and devoutly at Holy Mass.

27

Never spare yourself when it is a question of establishing the reign of the Master in the Holy Family of Christ, that is, in the intimate circle of priests and clerics consecrated to His service. Let the most important duty of your life be to implant virtue, piety and sanctity in the minds and souls of the chosen ones of God.

28

Read carefully the thirty-fourth Chapter of the Prophet Ezechiel, the tenth Chapter of St. John's Gospel, the sixth Chapter of the Second Epistle of St. Paul to the Corinthians and his Epistles to Timothy and Titus. In these texts you shall hear the voice of God speaking to priests, outlining their duties, which are summarized in the following words which you should engrave upon your hearts: "In all things show thyself an example of good words, in doctrine, in integrity, in gravity. The sound word that cannot be blamed: that he who is on the contrary part may be afraid, having no evil to say of us" (Titus, 2, 7-8). "Be thou an example of the faithful in word, in conversation, in charity, in faith, in chastity . . . Attend unto reading: to exhortation and to doctrine. Neglect not the grace that is in thee, which was given thee by prophecy, with imposition of the hands of the priesthood. Meditate upon these things: be wholly in these things: that thy profiting may be manifest to all. Take heed to thyself and to doctrine: be earnest in them. For in doing this thou shalt both save thyself and them that hear thee" (1 Tim. 4, 12-16).

29

Weigh deeply and ponder the following words:

1. "This is the will of God, your sanctification" (1 Thess. 4, 3). "But according to him that hath called you, who is holy, be you also in all manner of conversation holy: because it is written, *You shall be holy, for I am holy*" (1 Pet. 1, 15-16).

2. "Did you not know, that I must be about my Father's business?" (Luke 2, 49).

3. "For all seek the things that are their own: not the things that are Jesus Christ's" (Phil. 2, 21).

4. "He is . . . the shepherd of the sheep. To him the porter openeth: and the sheep hear his voice. And he calleth his own sheep by name and leadeth them out" (John 10, 2-3).

5. "Feed the flock of God which is among you, taking care of it, not by constraint, but willingly, according to God: not for filthy lucre's sake but voluntarily" (1 Pet. 5, 2).

6. "I lay down my life for my sheep" (John 10, 15).

30

Realizing your incompetence, cultivate a true love of prayer, having recourse to it at all hours and on every occasion. Never attempt anything till you have first prayed, being mindful that only thus may you hope to draw down upon yourself divine light and grace. You should constantly implore the aid of Our Lord, the Sovereign Priest, of His Blessed Mother, and of the angels and the saints.

31

Keep constantly before your eyes the life of the Great High Priest and Supreme Shepherd of souls, the life of the Blessed Virgin Mary, who is the mother of all Christians, but particularly of the priests and doctors of Holy Church. Study their actions and their virtues, and the excellence of all holy persons, making them the model of your life, the rule you should follow, according to which you shall be judged hereafter.

32

Be assiduous in spiritual reading, setting aside at least a quarter of an hour daily for this purpose. Let your reading be done attentively and let it be unhurried.

33

Take the time at least once a month to read these rules, or at least a portion of them, with great attention, in the presence of God. Examine yourself to see how you have transgressed. Ask God's pardon for your faults. Make a firm resolution to be more faithful in the future. As a means of finding strength, invoke the Divine mercy and the intercession of the Blessed Virgin Mary, the angels and the saints, particularly your heavenly patron.

34

Finally, make an eight-day or a ten-day retreat every year in imitation of Our Saviour, who spent forty days in the desert before beginning His public life, and even during His journeys through Galilee often retired into the mountains alone to pray. Imitate also the Apostles and disciples who spent ten days in prayer shut away from the world, preparing themselves for the coming of the Holy Ghost, Who was to animate their entire being for the great work of the salvation of souls.

Let your retreat be made in a seminary or in some secluded place where your soul may be alone in its communings with its Maker. Let every moment of that precious period be given to exercises of devotion and virtue, so that the words of the Holy Spirit may be fulfilled, as spoken by St. Paul in his Epistle to Timothy: "Take heed to thyself and to doctrine" (1 Tim. 4, 16). Take heed especially "to thyself," that is, apply yourself wholly to the considerations of the obligations of your state in life. Consider your lapses, humbling yourself before God, penitently resolving to amend your life, to fortify yourself against temptations, invoking for this purpose the light and help of heaven.

CHAPTER IV

THE SPIRITUAL LIFE OF THE PRIEST [1]

1. Morning Exercise

ON AWAKENING in the morning, pronounce fervently the holy names of Jesus and Mary. Make the sign of the cross with great devotion, saying the words with the intention of adoring the Most Blessed Trinity and of consecrating yourself to the Father, the Son and the Holy Ghost.

Renew the profession of faith made at baptism, saying with all your heart the words, *Abrenuntio tibi, Satana,* including therein sin, the world and the devil; and then add, *Adhaereo tibi, Christe.*

If you wish to make a longer renewal of your baptismal profession of faith, you may say the following prayer:

"O Jesus, for love of Thee I renounce sin, the evil spirit, the world, myself, all my inclinations and whatever is of the old man. I give myself entirely to Thee and consecrate to Thee my heart in honor of Thy Most Sacred Heart; my body with all its members in honor of Thy Sacred Body; my soul with all its faculties; my whole life in honor of Thy life; all my thoughts, actions, works and sufferings in honor of and in thanksgiving for all Thy thoughts, words, actions, works and sufferings.

"O Jesus, take complete possession of me so that I may be entirely consecrated to Thee and may be sacrificed with Thee for the honor and glory of the Eternal Father.

"O Mother of Jesus, to thee I give myself; give me in turn to thy Divine Son.

---

[1] In this translation we have separated into two chapters the part dealing with the dispositions to exercise the priestly functions in a holy manner.

27

"Angels of God, saints of God, I give myself to you. Give me, I beseech you, to God for ever."

On arising, recall the infinite love with which Our Lord came forth from the bosom of His Heavenly Father to enter into this valley of tears and darkness. At the moment of His Incarnation He left behind the infinite glory and happiness of heaven to embrace the cross and its humiliating sufferings. In union with that great love of Jesus, arise saying: "I will rise, . . . and seek Him whom my soul loveth" (Cant. 3, 2). As you say the words, "whom my soul loveth," have the desire to pronounce them as far as possible with all the love that is offered to Jesus Christ both in heaven and on earth.

While you are dressing, recite vocal prayers, such as the hymn, *Veni Creator,* or one of the psalms or recall some passages of Sacred Scripture. Fill your mind with holy thoughts, for example, the consideration of the fact that God has subjected you to the necessity of being decently clothed to protect your body; recall also that there are many who are more worthy than you in His sight and who dwell in poverty. Then raise your soul to God and say:

"O my Saviour, I acknowledge that I have deserved because of my sins the frightful punishment of being hurled unclothed into hell fire. I bless Thee with all my heart for having given me these garments. I give myself to Thee in this action of dressing which I now perform, with all the sentiments that animated Thee when Thou didst clothe Thyself with our humanity. O Dear Jesus, rid me of the old man, clothe me with the new, make me live the words of St. Paul: 'Put ye on therefore, as the elect of God, holy and beloved, the bowels of mercy, benignity, humility, modesty, patience, and charity'" (Col. 3, 12).

When you are fully dressed, kneel and adore the Blessed Trinity. Offer thanks for having been preserved during the hours of sleep; consecrate the day to God's glory, saying three times: "Glory be to the Father and to the Son and to the Holy Ghost."

Adore Jesus Christ, as the God-Man, thanking Him and consecrating yourself to His glory, saying at the same time, "We adore Thee, O Christ, and we bless Thee, because by Thy holy cross Thou hast redeemed the world. Thou didst suffer for us; O Lord Jesus, have mercy on us."

Invoke the assistance of the Blessed Virgin in the recitation of the *Hail Mary*.

Salute your guardian angel with this prayer: "O my holy Guardian Angel, I honor thee by every means at my disposal; I thank thee for all the favors which have come to me through thy special intercession; I offer myself to thee that thou mayst offer me to God and beseech Him to keep me from sin and grant me the grace of always doing His holy will."

Salute all the other angels and saints of heaven in this way: "All hail, ye angels and saints of the heavenly courts. Deign to intercede for our salvation and for the salvation of all mankind."

2. MEDITATION

Before offering up the Holy Sacrifice of the Mass, devote at least half an hour to meditation or mental prayer, a habit as vitally necessary to the soul of every Christian and of every priest as bread is to the body.

Acts Before Meditation

Prepare yourself for this holy exercise by the following acts:

Contemplate with the eyes of faith the infinite majesty and the immensity of God, Who is omnipresent and fills all creation, and Who is more in you than you are in yourself, according to the words of St. Augustine, *Intimo meo intimior*. Adore Him with profound humility. Realize how unworthy you are even to appear before Him, even to think of Him or have Him think of you or to suffer you in His presence.

Assure your Divine Creator that you are desirous of performing this act solely for His glory. Renounce yourself, your mind and your own self-esteem, giving yourself completely to Christ Our Lord. Enter into the holy dispositions which animated His continual prayer before His Heavenly Father. Unite yourself to those prayers constantly offered to God, not only by the saints in heaven, but likewise by all holy souls here below. Unite your prayers to those of the Blessed Virgin, the angels and the saints to whom you have special devotion. Beseech them to make you share in their fervor.

Give your mind and heart to the Master. Beg Him to take full possession, and guide them in prayer according to His holy will, in thought and affection pleasing to Him.

Acts After Meditation

You should conclude this exercise by thanking God for all the graces He has bestowed upon you, asking pardon for any carelessness you have manifested, imploring our Saviour to supply any defects and to offer in your place a continual prayer before His Heavenly Father.

Then make a summary of the principal thoughts and inspirations given you by God so that you may think of them during the day. In order to refresh your memory, select a text of Scripture or some aspiration to recall the subject of your meditation. Repeat this ejaculatory prayer frequently during the day.

Beware of relying only on your own thoughts and resolutions. Rely wholly upon the infinite mercy of God, placing in His hands what He has bestowed upon you in prayer, that He may grant you the grace of putting your resolutions into practice.

Beg the Blessed Virgin Mary, your guardian angel, your patron saint and all the angels and saints in heaven to continue your prayer before the Almighty.

Foresee those faults into which you usually fall and the occasions of sin which are the most dangerous for you. Be vigilant in the observance of the virtues you are especially required to practise, asking God for the grace to avoid pitfalls and to have the strength to be loyal to duty. Keep constantly before your mind the obligations of your state in life, what good you can accomplish this day, what evil you must avoid, what benefits you can reap for the honor and glory of God and the salvation of souls.

3. The Holy Sacrifice of the Mass

Preparation

Before celebrating Holy Mass, spend some time in recollection, considering the infinite importance of what you are about to do. The Mass is certainly the loftiest, the holiest and the most divine act ever accomplished in heaven and on earth. You should then endeavor to arouse within yourself lively sentiments of devotion and preparation that you may perform this noble action in the most worthy manner possible.

Humble yourself before God, recognizing your own incompetence and unworthiness, except through His mercy and favor.

Thank Him for the infinite goodness He displays towards you in permitting you to offer the Holy Sacrifice.

Protest to Him that you seek only His glory. Purify your soul by true contrition of sin, or even, if necessary, by the reception of the Sacrament of Penance.

Surrender yourself completely to the Eternal Father, to the Son and to the Holy Ghost. Pray that they may destroy within you whatever is displeasing to them and may adorn your soul with graces and virtues necessary for the offering of Holy Mass. Give yourself entirely to Jesus that you may enter with Him into His holy dispositions and intentions as He sacrificed Himself on Calvary and again sacrifices Himself daily on the altar. Offer yourself to the Blessed Virgin Mary, to all the holy priests and all the angels and saints in heaven that they may plead with God on your behalf, and make you share in their holy dispositions as they offer Jesus in perpetual sacrifice to His Eternal Father in heaven.

Offer Holy Mass for the following five reasons: 1. In honor of all that God is in His divine essence, in His divine perfections, in the Three Eternal Persons, in His Sacred Humanity and in all the mysteries; in His Blessed Mother, in the Church Triumphant, Militant and Suffering, in the visible and invisible world. 2. In thanksgiving for all the favors heaped upon His Son, Jesus Christ, upon His holy Mother, upon His Mystical Body, which is the Church, upon all creatures, even upon the demons in hell. 3. In satisfaction and reparation for any dishonor rendered Almighty God by the sins committed by sinners of the whole world, and particularly by yourself or your friends. 4. To obtain from God all the spiritual and temporal graces necessary to all creatures, especially to the Church, to its pastors and priests, to yourself and to all those for whom you are obliged to pray.

5. For the fulfilment of all the providential designs of God for you, for the Church and for the whole world.

Thanksgiving After Mass

After Mass prostrate yourself body and soul before our Lord truly present within you, adoring, thanking, loving and revering Him, and asking His pardon for all your ingratitude and offenses.

Consider that while He is within you, He performs the same function that He exercises in heaven, namely, He adores, praises, thanks and loves His Eternal Father, and sacrifices Himself to His greater honor and glory. Surrender yourself to Christ that you may be united with Him in His adoration, His love, His praise and His sacrifice, that therein you may glorify the ever Blessed Trinity, immolating yourself with Jesus, your Head and Master.

Even as Jesus Christ gives Himself all in all, with infinite love, so in union with the same love give yourself entirely to Him, imploring Him to possess you completely and thus destroy in you anything that is displeasing to Him. Ask Him to establish the reign of His glory and of His love in your heart and in your life.

4. THE DIVINE OFFICE

Preparation

Look upon this function as one of the greatest and most important in the life of a priest. Think of it as an action truly saintly, wholly angelic, completely divine. Through it you become one with the angels, with the saints, with the Blessed Virgin, with Christ our Lord, and with the Three Divine Persons of the ever Blessed Trinity, united in continual glorification and praise of one another. Consequently, let your resolution be to perform this duty well, with all respect and external modesty, and with the most perfect interior devotion.

Humiliate yourself before God, realizing that you are unworthy to undertake so holy a function and unable of yourself alone to discharge it becomingly. Try to make an act of contrition that your soul may be purified from every stain of sin. Offer to God your tribute of praise and prayer, mindful of the words of Sacred Scripture: "Praise is not seemly in the mouth of a sinner" (Ecclus. 15, 9).

Unite yourself to our Lord, reciting in unison with His praises your own poor efforts, joining in all that He offers or will ever offer to His Father in heaven and on earth. Thus, you will become associated with all those saintly souls on earth as well as those of the Church Triumphant and the Church Suffering. Endeavor to unite your soul with the holy dispositions of love, humility and devotion with which they offer their prayers to God.

Beg the Blessed Virgin Mary, the angels and saints to perform this holy action with you and to make you share in the devotion with which they pray perpetually in heaven.

Acts After the Divine Office

At the end of the divine office thank God for all the graces He has imparted to you through the recitation of the breviary. Ask His pardon for any faults you may have committed during its reading. Beg Him to atone for your transgressions in this particular matter, reciting the following prayer:

O clementissime Jesu, gratias ago tibi ex toto corde meo. Propitius esto mihi vilissimo peccatori. Ego hanc actionem offero divino Cordi tuo emendandam atque perficiendam, ad laudem et gloriam Sanctissimi Nominis tui et beatissimae Matris tuae, ad salutem animae meae totiusque Ecclesiae tuae. Amen.

5. READING OF SACRED SCRIPTURE

Following the completion of the exercises suggested above, kneel and read with great devotion and attention a chapter of the New Testament with the following dispositions:

Adore Our Lord in this manner: "O Jesus, I adore Thee as the Eternal Word of the Father and as the Source of all holy words contained in this book. I adore Thee in all Thy providential designs for Thy Church and for myself in particular in pronouncing these blessed words and in inspiring Thy sacred writers."

Thank Our Lord for having given you so precious a treasure, so holy a relic of Himself as His Divine Word, and for all the graces and light communicated to the Church through the instrumentality of Sacred Scripture.

Make a fervent act of humility, realizing how unworthy you are to read or even to touch the holy books, asking God's pardon for any negligence you may have shown or any improper use you may have made of them in the past. You should revere Sacred Scripture as the very heart of God containing all the secrets and the principles of the life of His children, according to St. Augustine's interpretation of Psalm 21, 15: *Factum est cor meum tanquam cera liquescens in medio ventris mei.*[2]

Recall the incident in the Gospel of St. Luke (4, 16) when Our Lord in the synagogue at Nazareth took up the book of the Scriptures and, opening it publicly, read therefrom. *Surrexit legere.* In memory of this episode of Our Saviour's life, give yourself to Him to share the admirable dispositions and intentions with which He read the Holy Book. Unite yourself also with all the great saints of the Church who read with such devotion the works of Scripture and sanctified themselves greatly by their inspired reading.

Give yourself completely to the Divine Spirit who dictated the Sacred Writings. Pray that He may engrave them on your heart, and make your soul and body living gospels and books in which is inscribed the exterior and interior life of Jesus Himself.

After your reading of Sacred Scripture, thank God for the light given us through His inspired Word. Give yourself anew to Him and beseech Him to imprint upon your heart the truths you have just read so that you may express them in your life. Memorize a few passages for meditation during the day.

6. Spiritual Reading

Spend some time daily in pious reading that you may be instructed in spiritual things according to the words of St. Paul: *Attende lectioni* (1 Tim. 4, 13). *The Following of Christ* and the lives of the saints, especially the lives of holy bishops and priests, are recommended.

At the beginning of the reading period, elevate your mind to God,

[2] Enarr. II Ps. 21.

assuring Him that you undertake this exercise solely for His glory and begging Him to grant you the light and grace necessary to do it well.

While reading, let your mind be lifted constantly on high. Make various acts of faith, hope, charity, confidence, humility and hatred of sin.

In reading the life of a saint, bless God for the glory which accrued to His divine majesty through the life and works of the particular saint in question. Rejoice with the saint for the many favors which he received from Almighty God and the happiness he now possesses in heaven. Be humbled in realizing how remote you are from the holiness the saint practised. Cultivate a great desire to imitate his virtues, praying for his intercession on your behalf that you may obtain that grace.

At the end of the spiritual reading, thank God for the light which He just gave you, as you perused this work of devotion. Then, pray that the fruits which have come to you may be used to His greater honor and glory.

7. Study

Adore God as the beginning and end of all science and learning, seeking nothing more than His glory, for Sacred Scripture says: "The Lord is a God of all knowledge and to Him are thoughts prepared" (1 Kings, 2, 3).

Avoid idle curiosity, and study only the subjects that are necessary for your state in life. Banish vanity, protesting to God that you wish to study and to learn not for any vainglory, not for worldly honor or praise, but simply that you may be enabled better to edify your neighbor and to glorify God by teaching men to save their souls. "Glorify ye the Lord in instruction" (Is. 24, 15). St. Bernard speaking on this subject says: *Alii sciunt ut sciant, et est curiositas: alii sciunt ut sciantur, et est vanitas: alii sciunt ut aedificent, et est charitas.*[3]

Humiliate yourself, recalling that of yourself you are nothing, as St. Paul says, "Not that we are sufficient to think any thing of ourselves, as of ourselves: but our sufficiency is from God" (2 Cor. 3, 5).

[3] *Sermo 36 sup. Cant.*

Remember that you are unworthy that God should give you any further enlightenment because you have already abused what knowledge He has imparted to you, and you have turned your back upon Him through sin to follow the prince of hell; therefore, you certainly have merited to know only eternal darkness.

Adore Christ as the Eternal Wisdom given to us by Almighty God to be our teacher and guide, our light and director. "I am the light of the world" (John 8, 12).

Give yourself to Jesus Christ to be taught by Him according to these words, "And they shall all be taught of God" (John 6, 45), or again "Blessed is the man whom thou shalt instruct, O Lord: and shalt teach him out of thy law" (Ps. 93, 12). Beg Him to grant you His divine light that you may be guided and directed in your studies; that you may be participators in that divine Spirit with which He made use of the knowledge given Him by His Eternal Father. Finally, throw yourself completely at His feet and beseech Him to be your director and sanctifier in your study, and ask Him for holy dispositions which prompted the words of St. Paul, "For I judged not myself to know any thing among you, but Jesus Christ, and him crucified" (1 Cor. 2, 2).

Pray to God unceasingly for deliverance from the three harmful effects often produced by learning.

The first is vanity, pride and arrogance. "Knowledge puffeth up," says Sacred Scripture (1 Cor. 8, 1). Consequently, you should constantly beg of God great humility and modesty of spirit that you may always remember that it is charity, not knowledge, which renders you acceptable to your Maker. Knowledge without piety leads to hell. The serpent used knowledge to tempt man to his downfall: *Eritis scientes* (Gen. 3, 5). Thirst for learning was to a great extent the cause of original sin and of all the other crimes that resulted from it. The necessity of study should make you remember that you are rebellious subjects of the Omniscient Creator. If our first parents had not sinned, you would have been endowed with all necessary knowledge without work and study. Consequently, the very fact that you must study to learn should remind you that the human race is still doing penance for the sin of Adam and Eve, who were condemned to earn their bread in the sweat of their brow. The word "bread" in this condemnation applies to knowledge, the bread of the mind, as well as to the material bread, which nourishes the body.

Thus, you should undertake study with the proper realization that it is part of your penance, and sanctify it in all humility, remembering that, when you become conceited about science learned the hard way, you are ridiculous. You are little better than the branded criminal who boasts of the prison stripes he wears. Finally, do not forget that the wisest man who ever lived recognized only too well that all knowledge, all science and learning are but vanity. For the creations of man, his arts and science will pass away. "Knowledge shall be destroyed" (1 Cor. 13, 8).

The second effect customarily produced by learning is that it kills devotion. "The letter killeth" (2 Cor. 3, 6). It makes man lukewarm and lazy in spiritual exercises and in works of charity and zeal. Consequently, you should not become too deeply absorbed in study, lest it cool your ardor for the service of God. During study periods, you should frequently detach yourself from the actual task before you, and lift up your soul to God, in order to fill your mind and heart with thoughts and affections of piety and devotion.

The third effect is the danger of becoming self-opinionated, or conceited, causing a tendency to belittle others, their views or expressions of opinion. From these faults there develops contention, against which St. Paul warns, "Contend not in words, for it is to no profit, but to the subverting of the hearers" (2 Tim. 2, 14). "Fulfil ye my joy, that you be of one mind, having the same charity . . . let nothing be done through contention, neither by vain glory" (Phil. 2, 2-3). These arguments often offend against charity, creating bitterness which rankles and dispels charity which is indeed the worst loss one could sustain. For St. Paul says: "If I should have prophecy and should know all mysteries, and all knowledge, and if I should have all faith, so that I could remove mountains, and have not charity, I am nothing" (1 Cor. 13, 2).

It is obvious, therefore, that you should not sacrifice the slightest degree of charity even if in doing so you should become famous for learning. Likewise, your opinions are better sacrificed, for their retention may become the cause of wounding the feelings of others. The prime obligation of the Christian is to love his neighbor as himself, and not to seek to get the better of him, but rather to master himself and to cultivate mutual understanding.

Prayer Before Study

Mitte, Domine, sapientiam de caelis sanctis tuis et a sede magnitudinis tuae, ut mecum sit et mecum laboret, ut sciam quid acceptum sit apud te. Sensum autem tuum quis sciet, nisi tu dederis sapientiam et miseris Spiritum sanctum tuum de altissimis? Da mihi intellectum, et scrutabor legem tuam. Da mihi, Domine, sedium tuarum assistricem sapientiam, et noli me reprobare a pueris tuis; quoniam servus tuus sum ego, homo infirmus, et minor ad intellectum judicii et legum. *Da mihi intellectum . . . * Gloria Patri . . . * Da mihi intellectum . . .

8. The Sacrament of Penance

Preparation for Confession

Adore Jesus Christ in His spirit of penance. He was charged with the burden of your sins, and He undertook to make satisfaction to Divine Justice. Consequently, He practised a most rigorous penance.

Surrender yourself to Him to enter into the true dispositions of penance. Beg Him to make you worthy participators in the divine light which illuminates all your faults and failings, that you, too, may see them. Beseech your loving Saviour to help you to know and share His humiliation and contrition and His intense hatred for sin. Likewise, let it be your constant aim to study His love for His Heavenly Father, a love which constrained Him to choose His Father in preference to Himself, so that, being charged with your transgressions, He might bear them Himself and satisfy the divine wrath.

Examine your conscience seriously. Judge and condemn yourself without mercy, that God may judge you with justice and mercy.

Cry out to God and beg through the merits of His wounds and sufferings, by His Precious Blood and Death, that you may understand the real spirit of penance. Likewise invoke the assistance of the Blessed Virgin Mary and the saints, that you may detach yourself from sinful habits, from the world and from yourself, and give yourself completely to Our Lord.

Make frequent acts of contrition. Formulate resolutions to avoid sin and the occasions of sin and to follow Christ in accordance with your baptismal promises.

Approach the tribunal of penance as if you were about to face judgment. Think of the priest as taking the place of Jesus Christ Himself. Confess your sins as if you were speaking to the Master in person and as if you were about to die. Receive with humility and thankfulness the instruction given by your confessor. Accept and discharge as soon as possible the penance imposed upon you, uniting it with that penance undergone by Jesus when, scourged and crowned with thorns, He died on the cross to save your soul.

Thanksgiving After Confession

After confession, thank our Saviour for the grace of pardon you have received, realizing that the smallest transgression is a greater evil than the worst temporal injury or misfortune. Remember that the pardon extended to you by God is a greater favor than if He had cured you of the most grievous physical illness. Thus, it is well after confession to say the *Gloria Patri* several times, in special thanksgiving to the Blessed Trinity. Also recite the *Qui natus est de virgine* as a gesture of gratitude towards God the Son, and an *Ave* to thank the Blessed Mother through whom all graces flow to us.

Say your penance with the most perfect dispositions of Christ as He completed the divine task of redemption. Offer it up in union with the penances of all holy men and women on earth.

Give yourself anew to Our Lord with a fervent desire to keep the resolutions you have taken, placing your complete confidence in the mercy and goodness of Christ Himself and begging Him to be more faithful in the future.

Recommend yourself again and again to the Blessed Virgin Mary, to the angels and saints.

9. Evening Exercise

Adore God as the beginning and the source of every good and thank Him for all the benefits which have come to you especially to-day. Thank Him, too, on behalf of the countless creatures who never think of giving thanks to Him for His infinite graces.

Adore Christ as your sovereign Judge, and offer yourself in submission to His holy will. Bless Him in that judgment which one day He will pronounce upon you. Beg Him to infuse into your heart the celestial light you need to see your sins and transgressions.

Examine your conscience carefully; endeavor to discern every thought, word or deed by which you may have displeased God, especially in matters concerning the good resolutions taken at meditation in the morning.

Ask God for a true spirit of penance, and of humility, similar to His own. Beseech Our Blessed Saviour to make you hate sin as He does, to have the courage to confess your offenses and receive absolution after having made genuine acts of contrition and amendment.

Offer to the Eternal Father the life, virtues, Passion and Death of His Only-Begotten Son, with all the merits of His Holy Mother and of the Universal Church in expiation for your offenses.

Pray to the Blessed Virgin Mary, to St. Joseph and St. Gabriel, to all the angels and saints, begging them to obtain His forgiveness for you, and the grace of true conversion.

Offer to God the night's rest you are about to take, in union with the repose of Our Lord and His Blessed Virgin during their life on earth.

Unite yourself with the praise which will be offered to the Blessed Trinity this night, on earth and in heaven, and for all eternity. Lovingly protest to the Creator that you wish every breath and every heartbeat of your sleeping hours to be so many acts of praise for His divine majesty.

Try to fall asleep with the dispositions and in the state in which you would like to be at the hour of death. Give yourself to Our Lord that you may enter into the dispositions with which He His Blessed Mother and the saints awaited the hour of death.

Ask the blessing of Christ and of His Holy Mother. Say with great devotion: *Benedictum sit Cor amantissimum et dulcissimum nomen Domini nostri Christi et gloriosissimae Virginis Mariae Matris ejus, in aeternum et ultra. Nos cum Prole pia benedicat Virgo Maria.*

While undressing, pray God that He may put away from you the old man and clothe you with the new, saying the words of the Psalmist, "Deliver me, O Lord, from the evil man: rescue me from the unjust man" (Ps. 139, 2). Make use of other ejaculations or meditate upon a text of Sacred Scripture.

Before getting into bed, bless yourself with holy water; make the sign of the cross with it upon your bed and renew your baptismal promise. *Abrenuntio tibi, Satana. Adhaereo tibi, Christe.*

Before falling asleep, listen to the voice of the Holy Ghost which says, "In all thy works remember thy last end, and thou shalt never sin" (Ecclus. 7, 40).

Repeat Christ's last words, "Father, into thy hands I commend my spirit" (Luke 23, 46). Try to say these blessed words as if they were your last. Give yourself to the Lord wholly that you may enter into the dispositions with which He and all the saints used these very words.

Try to fall asleep with these thoughts in your mind, and with the sweet names of Jesus and Mary upon your lips.

If you awake during the night, make use of some ejaculatory prayer such as, "Enlighten my eyes that I never sleep in death: lest at any time my enemy say: I have prevailed against him" (Ps. 12, 4-5). Or say these words, "For though I should walk in the midst of the shadow of death, I will fear no evils, for thou art with me" (Ps. 22, 4).

Bless and thank God for watching over you while you sleep. "Behold he shall neither slumber nor sleep, that keepeth Israel" (Ps. 120, 4). "I will fix my eyes upon thee" (Ps. 31, 8).

Realize, too, that, while you have been resting so peacefully, there are many poor souls in misery; there are countless others in agony, in prison, in peril upon land and sea. Recommend all these persons to the mercy of God.

Think also of those countless souls which suffer torments in purgatory. Go down in spirit into hell where countless souls suffer eternal torments. Humiliate yourself with the thought that by your sins you, too, have merited to be their companion, and that only the goodness of God has saved you from this fate.

Adore the Trinity, with the angels and saints and all the heavenly court. Say the *Gloria Patri*. Beg Mary's intercession. Recite an *Ave Maria*. Repeat *Avete omnes angeli et omnes sancti et sanctae Dei: benedicti sitis in aeternum et intercedere dignemini pro nostra omniumque salute.* Ask Jesus and Mary to bless you with the words: *Nos cum Prole pia benedicat Virgo Maria.*

CHAPTER V

THE APOSTOLIC LIFE OF THE PRIEST

1. General Dispositions for the Administration of the Sacraments

CULTIVATE a high esteem and respect for all the sacraments, looking upon them as the most efficacious means of God's infinite power, wisdom and goodness. Realize that the Heavenly Father employs them continually to give birth to Christ in the souls of His people. Realize also that through the sacraments He sanctifies the holy and restores to life the sinner whose soul is dead. Thus, St. Peter, the Prince of the Apostles, says: "Sanctify the Lord Christ in your hearts" (1 Peter 3, 15). Moreover, the Saviour uses the sacraments to multiply the numbers of His subjects on earth, to extend His Kingdom and consummate His love in each individual soul.

Think of the sacraments as the fountains of the Saviour in whose waters Christians find grace and strength to attain eternal salvation.

Know that the sacraments are the divine instruments of the Holy Spirit through which are applied to souls the fruits of the Life and Death of Jesus, supplying what is needed to complete the Passion of Our Lord, namely its application to those for whom it was offered.

Treat the sacraments as treasures of God's house which contains infinite riches hidden from the wise and prudent of this world, but manifested to the lowly and humble. Revere them as sacred vessels in which the Church preserves the Precious Blood, the Holy Spirit and the divine grace of her Spouse for the nourishment and sanctification of her children.

Seek to instil in the hearts and minds of Christians these sentiments of esteem and reverence for the sacraments.

Treat them with the utmost veneration, keeping particularly neat and clean all things used for their administration. When a sacrament is given, show the utmost respect, gravity, modesty and devotion.

Instruct the faithful fully regarding the sacraments. Point out that their origin depends on the goodness and mercy of God, and that their merits come from the Passion and Death of our Saviour. Explain their significance and their effects. Let it be understood that through the sacraments are accomplished the sanctification of the Church, the destruction of sin and the establishment of the reign of God on earth.

Impress upon your congregation that the sacraments are so noble and so lofty in themselves, that they should be shown the utmost reverence. Consequently, they should be received only with complete purity of body and soul. From them should be drawn fruits for spiritual advancement. All things that might profane them should be avoided. Worldliness and dangerous amusements should, therefore, be eradicated from one's life, particularly at the time of the reception of the Sacrament of Marriage. Certainly there are many who, entering into that holy state and receiving that sacrament, act as if they wished to disavow their baptismal promises and to contract marriage like pagans rather than Christians. Priests, therefore, must be on guard to preserve the sanctity of so great a sacrament as Matrimony: *Sacramentum magnum in Christo et in Ecclesia* (Eph. 5, 32).

Besides these general dispositions, teach your parishioners the meaning, the effects and the dispositions for each individual sacrament. Above all else, be sure that they understand Baptism and its obligations. Unfortunately in our day, many Catholics have forgotten the meaning of the solemn promises made at the time of the reception of that first and all-important sacrament.

When you are about to administer Baptism or any other sacrament, adore Our Lord Jesus Christ as the author who instituted that particular sacrament. Thank Him for all the glory He has brought to His Eternal Father and for all the blessings granted to the Church through the sacrament. Ask Him to forgive all the sins committed against Him through its unworthy reception. Prostrate yourself humbly before God, realizing that being a sinner you are unworthy to administer this sacrament.

Give yourself wholly to our Lord to formulate within yourself the holy dispositions with which He was filled as He instituted the sacrament you are about to administer, so that you may capture the spirit of worthiness He would have you bring to the treatment of His sacraments and all holy things. Unite yourself also to the whole heavenly company of those saints who, like yourself, were entrusted with the administration of Christ's sacraments.

Offer to Our Lord, to His Blessed Mother, to the guardian angels and patron saints, the souls of those to whom you are about to give the sacraments, praying that they may receive them worthily and be preserved in grace through their merit.

After you have administered the sacrament, thank God for His goodness in permitting you to be His minister and pray that the recipients may persevere in His divine grace.

2. General Disposition for the Administration of the Sacrament of Penance

Consider the grandeur and the importance of the action you are about to perform. You are to take the place of Christ, representing Him, acting in His name, clothed with His authority, continuing His office as Saviour, exercising His power as judge, pronouncing judgments in His sacred name. Hence, the Holy Spirit cries: "Take heed what you do: for you exercise not the judgment of men, but of the Lord: and whatsoever you judge, it shall redound to you" (2 Par. 19, 6). Moreover, by this action you blot out sin, spread the grace of God and pour it into the hearts of the faithful. You apply to them the merits of the Precious Blood of Jesus Christ. This function is, therefore, so great and holy that it must be exercised with the utmost care.

Adore all the divine plans of Our Lord embodied in this holy sacrament and thank Him for the mercy He displays through it. Humiliate yourself at the remembrance of your unworthiness and the realization that you cannot perform so holy a function unless you are aided by God's grace and help. Purify your mind, your heart and your soul, protesting that you desire only the glory of God and the salvation of souls.

Give yourself completely to Christ as Supreme Judge and Saviour that you may enter fully into the holy dispositions with which He Himself exercises these sacred offices, praying for the light and graces necessary to discharge your responsibilities according to His holy will.

Invoke upon yourself and upon the souls to whom you will administer the sacrament the powerful assistance of the Blessed Virgin Mary and all the saints, especially the patron saint of the church in which you are receiving your penitents.

3. THE PRIEST IN THE CONFESSIONAL

Try to observe the spirit of piety and concentration of mind upon God and His works. Lift up your heart to Him especially as you begin to hear each individual confession, meditating on various pious thoughts connected with the liturgical season or feast day to be observed.

For example, the first confession you hear on entering the confessional should be sanctified by elevating your heart to the Eternal Father, offering Him what you are about to do in union with the great love which prompted Him to give His Only-Begotten Son to all mankind, but especially to the person whose confession you are about to hear. In union with that great love, you shall give your heart, your soul and your mind, as well as your time, to the soul before you, to cooperate in his salvation by every means at your disposal.

As you hear the second confession, give yourself to the Son of God to share the holy dispositions of love and charity which prompted him to shed His Precious Blood for the soul of the penitent entering the confessional. In union with our Saviour's love, you shall not spare yourself in giving your penitent whatever instructions you can to save his soul.

The third confession will impel you to give yourself to the infinite love of the Holy Ghost for all souls, but particularly for that of your penitent.

At the fourth, offer yourself to the Heavenly Father in honor of the Incarnation of His Divine Son and in union with the infinite love whereby God effected this mystery for souls. The realization of His great love will serve as an impelling motive to help you to accept with patience and meekness whatever crosses you may have to bear, whatever pains and hardships you may endure in your work of saving souls, and particularly this soul now before you.

At the fifth, let your soul be filled with the memory of Our Lord's Birth, His Circumcision, His Presentation in the Temple and the other mysteries of His life on earth.

Offer yourself likewise to the Blessed Virgin and pray thus:

"O my God, I offer Thee this confession I am about to hear in honor of and in union with the great charity the Blessed Virgin Mary cherishes for the soul before me. O Mother of Fair Love, make me share in thy charity. Virgin most merciful, show thy great mercy towards this sinner and to thy humble servant."

It is useful to have a crucifix in the confessional to show the hardened sinner when occasion demands. It is an invaluable help in leading the sinner to understand Christ's unbounded love for every soul, and likewise it serves as a most potent means of reminding yourself of the zeal you should have for souls.

Besides the above mentioned dispositions, the confessor should have three other qualities on entering the tribunal of penance:

1. He should be clothed with mercy and compassion that like his Divine Master he may have pity on those who come to him.

2. Cognizant of his own nothingness and sinfulness, he should humble himself profoundly with the realization of the fact that but for God's grace he, too, would be guilty of all the sins that are committed throughout the world. So, he should see in the penitent at his feet an image and reflection of himself as he would surely be if it were not for Christ's infinite mercy. The priest, like every man, has within himself the roots of sin and is saved from falling only because God became man for us and saved us by His grace. Therefore, he should say with St. Augustine: *Domine, videam te in omnibus bonis, videam me in omnibus malis.*

3. The priest should be adorned with justice that he may render to God His just due and to the penitent that which is appropriate. He should be fortified with zeal, inflamed with hatred against sin and fired with the determination to help the penitent to use the means to avoid sin.

On leaving the confessional, thank God for the favor of having heard the confessions you have listened to, and for the graces imparted to yourself and to your penitents.

Ask Our Lord's pardon on behalf of yourself and your penitents for the sins committed by each in the past, begging Him to act as mediator in satisfying the divine anger.

Offer to God all the souls that have had recourse to you in the sacred tribunal, beseeching the Master to turn their hearts and minds from sinful ways to the knowledge of Himself and the love of His holy grace so that they may seek to die rather than offend Him.

Offer them to the Blessed Virgin Mary, St. Joseph, St. Gabriel and all the saints, especially the guardian angels and patron saints of the penitents.

Do not be satisfied merely to pray for these souls at this time, but all through life cultivate a special place in your heart for your penitents, remembering them constantly at the Holy Sacrifice of the Mass.

4. Administering the Blessed Eucharist

In addition to the general dispositions pertaining to the administration of all the sacraments, the Holy Ghost will inspire you with particular devotion and lofty sentiments concerning the Blessed Eucharist.

Enumerated here are certain dispositions suggested as being efficacious in your distribution of the Bread of Life to God's chosen ones.

To the first person you should give Holy Communion in honor of and in union with the infinite love of the Eternal Father in giving us His Divine Son.

The second communicant will personify the immense love of God the Son giving Himself to us as our spiritual food and drink.

The third communicant will represent the incomprehensible love of the Holy Spirit, forming the Flesh of the Son of Man within the womb of Mary Immaculate that we might be nourished thereby.

The fourth will symbolize the unutterable love which prompted the divine humanity of the Son of God to give Himself to us from the first moment of the Incarnation, continuing to give Himself daily to us in this Sacrament.

The fifth will recall the ardent love with which the Blessed Virgin

Mary gave us Jesus, her beloved Son, at the moment of His birth, and still gives Him to us in Holy Communion.

To the sixth communicant, you shall give Christ's Body and Blood in union with the great devotion, the purity and the sanctity with which the holy Apostles Peter and Paul, John, James and the others administered this Holy Sacrament.

As the seventh communicant receives Our Lord from your hands, you shall unite your soul with the blessed dispositions of all the saintly pontiffs, priests and deacons of Holy Church who, like yourself, administered this Sacrament during their lifetime.

Finally, you should unite yourself to the love of the Eternal Father, of the Son and of the Holy Ghost.

You may also follow another method in administering the Blessed Eucharist. In giving the Precious Body and Blood to the first communicant at the altar railing, you may offer to Jesus the infinite love of the Eternal Father in satisfaction for the sins committed by the person before you, for any defects in his reception of the Blessed Eucharist, and for a more perfect preparation for the coming of Christ into his heart may be more perfect.

In giving Holy Communion to the second communicant, you may offer God His infinite love for His own All-perfect Self.

As you approach the third recipient, you may offer up to Jesus the all-consuming love of the Holy Ghost.

The fourth person will be a signal to offer Christ the love and holy dispositions with which the Blessed Mother received Him at the moment of the Incarnation and many times after His Ascension.

St. Joseph, St. Gabriel, St. Michael, the Seraphim and the Cherubim and all the orders of angels in heaven will join you as you offer their love when the fifth soul receives the Body and Blood of the Saviour.

The Patriarchs, the holy Prophets, St. John the Baptist, and all the saints of the Old Testament will walk beside you and offer their love to Jesus as you continue your priestly ministration at the holy table.

Then you shall offer up the devotion and holy dispositions with which Our Lord was received in Holy Communion by the Apostles, by the Martyrs, by saintly pontiffs and priests, confessors and virgins, as well as by the holy souls now in heaven, who received with so much love and piety when they were on earth.

5. Visiting the Sick

Offer this priestly function to our Lord Jesus Christ, in honor of and in union with His abiding love for His children. Give yourself to Him that you may enter into that sublime spirit of love wherewith He bore in His Sacred Heart all our infirmities, our maladies and our afflictions. "He took our infirmities and bore our diseases," says St. Matthew (8, 17). Join yourself in spirit to the sentiments which filled the Heart of Christ as He visited the sick and the infirm. Join also with the saints in doing this act with the same holy dispositions and intentions with which they did this same act.

Greet the sick with charity, remembering that they are members of the Body of Christ and your brothers. Show them compassion and sympathy. Speak to them with discretion, cordiality and gentleness.

Try to make them understand the two causes of all mankind's afflictions.

The first is the Providence of God and His holy will, disposing and ordaining all things, for the best, if we will but accept them in the proper spirit, which we can do with the assistance of His holy grace.

The second cause of suffering is sin. In this regard, three things should be done in time of sickness. 1. We should humble ourselves in the presence of the offenses by which we have merited hell and the tribulations of this life. 2. We should give ourselves with confidence to the will of God. 3. We should suffer with patience for the love of our Saviour, who endured all for us, and offer ourselves and our sufferings in union with Him.

Having gently reminded the sufferer of these truths, teach him to put them into practice, thus:

"Try, my child, to follow my advice. Do you not wish really to humble yourself before your Maker? Do you not realize that even though you had never committed a single sin, God could send you sufferings and ills just the same and you would have absolutely no cause to complain?

"Will you try to adore His divine will for sending this sickness and give yourself completely to Him, even blessing and thanking Him for this affliction?

"Surely, you are willing to suffer for Him, who suffered so much for you? Will you not try to offer to Him the pains you are undergoing in return for all the torments He endured for you, so that He may reward you in heaven?

"Will you not offer to the Blessed Virgin Mary all your sufferings, asking her to offer them in turn to her Son, supplying any defects, substituting them for the duties you would be performing if you had your health and strength? Will you not likewise lay your heart and will before her?

"Will you not offer yourself to your Guardian Angel, and to all the angels and saints for this same purpose?"

Endeavor to incite in the soul of the sick man the proper dispositions for the Sacrament of Penance, and, if necessary, recall to his mind the conditions necessary for a proper reception of this sacrament. Help him to make a worthy preparation, if necessary, questioning him regarding his past confessions, his relations with his neighbors; whether or not he has always been careful to make restitution, and if he be found wanting in these respects, urge upon him their necessity. Make careful inquiries regarding the occasions of sin with which he may have to contend, suggesting means of avoiding them. If he has fallen into the sad plight of living in continual mortal sin, seek to point out to him the hideousness of his state and encourage him to make a firm purpose of amendment, suggesting means to assist him.

Help him in his preparation for Holy Communion. After he has received the Body and Blood of Christ, encourage him to try in the future always to render to God a full meed of willing service. In this respect, recall to his mind that as a creature he is obliged to give to God complete adoration, praise, thanksgiving, love and penance. Likewise, he must stand ready to sacrifice himself, his life, his will and inclinations and everything the world offers for the glory of the Creator.

Teach the sick person, if necessary, how to elevate his soul to God, to His Divine Son, to His Blessed Mother and to the saints through acts of faith, hope and charity, patience, humility and submission. Also instil in his heart a lively sense of contrition.

Open to his soul the significance of devout aspirations and recommend their frequent use. Suggest the following as most helpful:

"O my God, to Thee I give my heart and my soul."

"May Thy holy will be done."

"O Heavenly Father, not my will but Thine be done."

"O my God, I realize that by my sins I have deserved thousands of chastisements. Here cut, here burn, but spare me in eternity."

"O Jesus, I give myself gladly to Thee, and sacrifice my all for Thy sake."

"O Jesus, draw me to Thyself in Thy divine sacrifice that I may offer all with Thee for the glory of Thy Father."

"O Jesus, I wish to suffer for love of Thee, everything Thou mayest ask and in the degree that Thou mayest require of me."

"O good Jesus, I give myself to Thee that I may enter into those holy dispositions that marked Thy great suffering."

"O Jesus, be Thou my Saviour."

"O Jesus, be my strength and my patience."

"O my Saviour, render to the Eternal Father on my behalf a full measure of all that is required of me. I give Thee my will in all its entirety for this intention."

"O dear Jesus, I offer Thee all my sufferings which are so insignificant when compared to Thine. Unite them with the truly intense sufferings Thou didst endure for me. Bless and sanctify them; offer them with Thine own to the Heavenly Father."

"O Mother of God, be my mother, unworthy though I am. Unite my sufferings with thine. Offer them to thy Beloved Son. In my name do for me what I am unable to do; sanctify for me this sickness which I am undergoing."

"O my angel guardian, O St. Joseph, O all ye angels and saints, pray for me, help me, love and praise God for me, and in my stead offer up all that I owe to God."

When the sick person's illness is accompanied by great suffering and pain, suggest different episodes in Our Lord's Sacred Passion, that these may be honored at different times, in the following manner:

"My child, try to consecrate this day or night, this morning or afternoon, this very hour to Our Lord in honor of the first mystery of the Passion, His Agony in the Garden. With the eyes of faith endeavor to know the depth of the sufferings He endured for you at that awful time. Thus, you will find strength to suffer with Him. Thus, too, you will be able to consecrate the day or night, the morning or evening, in honor of those sufferings He knew as Judas betrayed Him.

"Unite your own misery to that which He experienced as He was led as a criminal before Annas, Caiaphas, Pilate and Herod, or was subjected to unspeakable ignominies during His Sacred Passion. In this manner, hour by hour, day by day, from place to place, from mystery to mystery, from suffering to suffering, uniting your comparatively small pains with His overwhelming burden, forgetting your own in thinking of His, thanking Him for the privilege of sharing His agony, you will know perfect imitation of and conformity to His Divine Passion."

Urge the sick person to adopt the suggestions outlined above, not all at once, of course, but by degrees, using great discretion and care not to tire the patient, letting the tone of your voice reflect your sincere desire to assist him in bearing the sufferings of life.

Intersperse your recommendations with prayer, kneeling at his bedside, reciting with the family or friends who may be present such prayers as the Litany of the Passion, of the Holy Name, or of the Blessed Virgin Mary. The "Hail, Holy Queen" or a decade of the beads may also be said with much profit.

Enjoin upon the patient obedience to the doctor's orders and conformity with the instructions of the nurses, offering up this tribute in honor of the obedience of the Master, and accepting medicine or treatments in the spirit of humble surrender with which Jesus Christ drank the gall on Calvary.

6. Assisting the Dying

Try to induce the dying person to give himself entirely to God, abandoning himself completely to His holy will. With great patience and gentleness prepare him to be ready to offer his life willingly to our

Lord who sacrificed for us His whole life, one moment of which is worth infinitely more than the lives of all men and angels.

Tactfully direct his thoughts to the realization of the fact that this life is transitory and a vale of tears, and that real happiness will be found only in heaven. There all our pains will be turned into joy, all our troubles will disappear and we shall know at last that this world is but a prison and place of banishment whence we escape through the portals, opened by death. Point out again and again that heaven is our true home. There reside our Father and Mother, Jesus and Mary; there are our brothers and sisters, the angels and saints; there await us the blessed company of the elect.

Let the patient be filled with the understanding of the fact that by our sins we have deserved to die a thousand deaths, and, in consequence, he should be reconciled to accept whatever death Christ may send, wherever and whenever it may come.

Even if Eve had never lost our original innocence and we were not children of Adam, we would still be the property of God our Sovereign Lord, who could do with us what He would. Thus, we should understand the meaning of complete submission to Him in all things, and the offering of our life to Him.

Even though we were not subject to death at all, nevertheless, in imitation of our Lord Jesus Christ, the Eternal Life, who willingly suffered death for us, and His Blessed Mother, the Mother of life, who likewise died, we should willingly accept death as a tribute of our devotion and love to them.

When the sick man's mind has become reconciled to the will of God concerning death, suggest to him the duties of a Catholic about to close his eyes on this world and face God. These duties are: 1. To thank the Blessed Trinity with Christ and the Church for all the favors received from their infinite goodness. 2. To ask pardon for all the sins committed during life and to offer one's death in union with that of Christ. 3. To adore, praise, glorify and love God, admitting that we are in this world only for that purpose, and that we should terminate our life in the fulfilment of the end for which we were created. 4. To beseech Jesus Christ to accomplish these things in our name, and likewise ask the intercession of the Blessed Virgin Mary, St. Joseph and all the saints. 5. To adore, honor and praise our Saviour, asking His pardon and forgiveness, praying to the Blessed Mother and all the angels and saints also to offer in our place our tribute and praise.

Outline to the sick man the duties of a Catholic towards the Blessed Virgin Mary, St. Joseph, his Guardian Angel and all the angels of heaven, and the saints of the celestial court, especially those he should honor particularly, exhorting him to thank them, ask their pardon, offer them the loving Heart of Jesus in satisfaction, and invoke their prayers and assistance especially at the hour of death.

Recall the Catholic's duties towards his fellow man. He should ask pardon of those whom he has offended or disedified, and forgive those who have offended him, saying with Our Blessed Lord: "Father, forgive them" (Luke 23, 34). If the sick person be a father or mother, a master or mistress, or a superior of a religious community, let him enjoin upon his subjects or children a wholesome fear of God and give them his blessing. Rather, let him ask God to bless them for it is not the place of a sinner to bless, but to pray God to bestow His benediction.

Remind the sick person to dispose of his worldly goods in a spirit of Christian charity, not forgetting the poor, the Church and spiritual works. Especially, counsel him to make his will with all the necessary legal formalities so that his children and heirs may be spared the bitterness of litigation.

Dispose him to receive Holy Viaticum, forming his intention in union with that of the Blessed Virgin and the saints communicating for the last time.

Try to have him gain what indulgences he can, especially those applicable at the hour of death. To assist him in doing so, excite in him a great desire in this respect. Urge him to affirm that he desires only the glory of God; help him to acquire a true spirit of penitence, making acts of contrition and determination of amendment, after he has gone to confession. Place on his person blessed and indulgenced medals. Have him repeat again and again, *Jesus, Mary, Jesus, Mary,* always remembering that he should have the intention of pronouncing these holy names in union with the pure love which is and will always be evoked in heaven at the mere mention of these gracious names.

Early in his sickness dispose him to receive Extreme Unction, with the intention for which Christ instituted that sacrament, namely, to efface sin and destroy its effects, and to perfect in the Christian soul God's love and grace. Let him dwell upon the fact that this last of the sacraments is meant to strengthen the soul against the final onslaughts of the devil, and to help him to die a truly Christian death. Likewise, remind him that Extreme Unction can restore health if it be God's holy will to do so.

Help the patient achieve the proper dispositions for the reception of this Extreme Unction, of which the first is really to desire that the designs of Christ in its institution may be fulfilled. The second is to adore Him who instituted this consoling sacrament, thanking Him for all the glory our loving Saviour has rendered His Eternal Father, and all the graces communicated through its instrumentality to the souls of the faithful.

The third disposition is humbly to confess one's sins again. The fourth is to offer to God the Father all the honor His Son has brought Him through this efficacious means, in atonement for the dishonor heaped upon Him by its improper use by sinners. The fifth disposition is for the sick soul to unite himself to all the holy dispositions of the saints when they received Extreme Unction. The sixth is to give himself to Christ that He may prepare the soul to receive the sacrament worthily. The seventh is to pray to the Blessed Mother, the angels and saints to supply any defects within him and to take his place in the presence of God, interceding for him that he may receive all necessary graces and dispositions.

Help the sick person to renew his baptismal promises. For this purpose: 1. Encourage him to thank God for having been privileged to receive Baptism. 2. Urge him to ask God's pardon for any misuse of baptismal grace, offering in satisfaction the life and death of His Divine Son, with all the merits of Mary our Mother and of the saints. 3. Say with him these words, "I renounce thee, O Satan; I renounce all your works and pomps; to Thee I cling, O Jesus, my Lord, my God, my King. I wish for Thee and nothing more. Be thou King of my heart now and forevermore."

7. Consoling the Afflicted

Remember always that the Son of God has said that whatever is done to the least of His little ones is done to Him. Be assured that consolation offered to those who are afflicted is given likewise to Our Lord and His Blessed Mother for whosoever consoles the Son certainly consoles the Mother. Consequently, when God gives you the opportunity to assuage the misery of some troubled soul, He surely bestows a very special grace. Your approach to this duty therefore, should be serious, mindful that you should do unto others as you would have them do to you.

Thus, you should cast the eye of your faith upon that great love with which our Saviour came into this world to console the afflicted, remembering the inspired words: "He hath sent me . . . to comfort all those that mourn" (Isa. 61, 1-2). Regard your neighbor who is in trouble as a child of God and as your brother, extending to him that charity which consumed the Merciful Heart of Jesus. Approaching him with great kindness and understanding, talk to him with compassion. Then endeavor to impress upon his mind the seven following truths, which are truths of faith founded upon divine infallibility.

1. Providence guides and governs the world. "But thy providence, O Father, governeth it" (Wisd. 14, 3). Nothing on earth happens by chance but by the divine will or by God's permission. Whether He permits or wills a thing to happen to us, it is always for our good, if we on our part make use of it. Consequently, we should accept whatever comes to us as having been sent by the hand of God and emanating from the loving Heart of our Creator.

2. God is our true Father, loving us far beyond the degree of our love for ourselves. He is a Father having only thoughts of love and peace, not of affliction and harshness. "I know the thoughts that I think towards you, saith the Lord, thoughts of peace, and not of affliction, to give you an end and patience" (Jer. 29, 11). He loves us with such devotion and takes such infinite care of us that He has assured us that even the hairs of our head are numbered. If then He has such regard for the simplest details of life, what must be His devotion in the important matters, such as our reputation, our health or life? He is in-

deed a Father who is so powerful and wise and good that He knows how to take care of those who love and serve Him. We must always live in the fear of God, fulfilling the words of Sacred Scripture, "No evils shall happen to him that feareth the Lord" (Ecclus. 33, 1). "To them that love God, all things work together unto good" (Rom. 8, 28).

3. God bestows a signal grace upon us when, instead of treating us with the severity of an exacting judge, He accords us the kindness of a merciful father, punishing us not by the harshness due to an enemy, but with the paternal chastisement suitable to children. He often makes us suffer temporal punishment in expiation for our sins, thus ensuring for us the eternal rewards we have merited in heaven. The sufferings He sends us in this world should be looked upon as being permitted here below so that we may not have to undergo torments in purgatory, where their severity would be multiplied a thousand fold. Consequently, we have every reason to thank God for adversity as the least of the punishments He could visit upon us, as the most merciful means He could employ to chastise us for sins. We should be like the prisoner at the bar who thanks his judge for a commuted sentence.

4. One of the greatest favors Our Lord can grant us is to send an affliction which enables us to share His cross. Thus, we learn to drink His chalice of bitterness; we come to know the meaning of the cross which He chose as His instrument for the destruction of sin, the source of every evil. Through affliction He brings us closer to His Sorrowful Mother. Those who are dear to God have known the most suffering. "All that have pleased God, passed through many tribulations" (Judith 8, 23). "Because thou wast acceptable to God," said the Archangel Raphael to Tobias, "it was necessary that temptation should prove thee" (Tob. 12, 13).

5. Sacred Scripture proclaims the cross as the glory, the treasure, the supreme good of the Christian on earth. "But God forbid that I should glory, save in the cross of Our Lord Jesus Christ," cries St. Paul (Gal. 6, 14). And again in his Epistle to the Romans he says, "We glory also in tribulations" (Rom. 5, 3). St. James reminds us to "count it all joy, when you shall fall into divers temptations" (James 1, 2).

Truly, it may be said that, when a great affliction comes upon us, we actually receive a treasure of priceless value. If we bear the cross patiently, it will pay unlimited dividends. The greatest consolations in this world, even the spiritual and divine consolations, are merely little flowers which bloom and die. A great affliction is like a golden treasure, solid and enduring. It may be compared even to a precious stone of inestimable value, or to a fertile field which, being carefully cultivated, will enrich its possessor with an infinity of spiritual and heavenly returns.

6. Nothing purifies the soul like suffering. Nothing embellishes it more, nothing renders it so pleasing to God. True Christian nobility which makes us like unto our Crucified King, is acquired only through suffering and affliction.

7. Finally, we must turn afflictions to holy advantage. First of all, he who bears them in a true Christian spirit renders supreme homage to God because the Son of Man, who came on earth to honor His Father and repay the ravages of sin, chose the cross and suffering as the most efficacious means at His disposal. Secondly, he acquires treasures of grace on earth and glory for eternity. On the other hand, the Christian who does not accept afflictions willingly deprives God of the glory He otherwise would have received, and inflicts on himself such a loss that if he could estimate its worth, he would be inconsolable.

Having outlined these principles to the person whom you wish to comfort, you must teach him how to derive real profit from adversity and recommend the following practices:

1. He should make an act of faith in all these truths because no true Christian can doubt them.

2. He should make his peace with God by a good confession. Remind him that a person who suffers while in the state of mortal sin loses all the merit he would otherwise gain. He becomes like the impenitent thief; he is miserable in the sight of God and man alike. He is miserable in this world and will be infinitely more miserable in the next, if he does not repent.

3. He must humiliate himself before God because of his sins, the cause of all his sufferings, realizing that he is worthy of hell and the eternal wrath of his Maker. He must strive to realize also that, even if God should send him the most awful afflictions and if all the forces of earth should rise up to crush him, he could not rightly complain,

because a single mortal sin merits the most dreadful punishment, the everlasting torments of hell, one moment of which surpasses the most ghastly torture life can inflict. Consequently, the sufferer on earth should accept gladly whatever affliction comes to him in requital for his offenses; he should remember the words of Sacred Scripture, "Thou art just, O Lord: and thy judgment is right" (Ps. 118, 137). "For we have sinned, and committed iniquity, departing from thee . . . and we have not hearkened to thy commandments . . . Everything that thou hast done to us, thou hast done in true judgment" (Daniel 3, 29-31). Humility inclines the heart of God towards His erring creatures. "Be you humbled therefore under the mighty hand of God, that he may exalt you in the time of visitation" (1 Pet. 5, 6).

4. The afflicted person should adore the holy will of God, making an act of submission, resignation and self-annihilation in all things, seeking only that the Kingdom of God be established in his own and in all hearts. Make him repeat the words of Christ in Gethsemani: "Not my will, but thine be done" (Luke 22, 42). Recall also St. Gertrude's prayer: "O Lord, I beg Thee and desire with all my heart that Thy adorable will be done in me and in all creatures."

5. Let him bless and thank God in affliction. "I will bless the Lord at all times" (Ps. 33, 2). Certainly, this should apply in time of suffering more than at any other time for it has been truly said that affliction is a proof of God's goodness. Should not he who owes a great debt and is forgiven by his creditor, make some gesture of his gratitude? How much does the sinner owe, who is indebted for the remission of eternal punishment and who is made to undergo temporal sufferings instead of these torments of hell which he has so justly deserved!

6. He ought to adore our crucified Lord covered with wounds from head to foot, called so aptly by the Prophet Isaias, "A man of sorrows" (Isa. 53, 3). He ought to surrender himself to the boundless love that nailed his Redeemer to the cross, and in union with it accept with perfect love and resignation every cross sent to him.

7. If Divine Providence should employ certain individuals to become the cause of suffering, the person who is harassed or hurt should not seek vengeance nor let his heart be filled with bitterness towards them. He should rather exert towards them great charity and forgiveness, in

imitation of the Master who said, "Father, forgive them" (Luke 23, 34).

8. If suffering be caused by the tragic illness or death of someone dear and cherished, the person thus afflicted should remember that Christ gave His own life for us, a life so precious that one moment of it was worth more than an infinite number of lives of men and angels. Consequently, in the hour of sorrow, let each one give himself to Jesus in union with the incomprehensible sacrifice made on Calvary, offering to Our Lord the life of our friends and even our own, in satisfaction for his offenses and in return for Our Lord's offering of His own life for us.

9. Though it is permitted and expected that a person should use every legitimate means to recover and restore his health, he must never make the mistake of placing all his faith in human expedients. Rather let him have supreme confidence in God and in prayer. As evidence of Our Lord's pleasure in the trust we show in Him, the sick person ought to ponder these words spoken to St. Gertrude by the Saviour: "When a soul torn by pain or affliction places himself firmly under my protection, that soul so touches my Heart, that to it the words of Sacred Scripture are applied: 'One is my dove, my perfect one is *but* one. . . . the chosen of her that bore her' (Cant. 6, 8). It so transfixes my Heart that, if I were to know I could not succor the soul in its misery, my own Heart would suffer (were that possible), and its sufferings would be so great that not even the infinite delights of heaven could assuage its misery. The glance of my dove which transfixes my Heart like an arrow of love is the firm and unshakable confidence that I can and will assist it in all things. And so strong is that confidence in its impelling force that I could not disregard it" (*Legatus Divinae Pietatis* lib. 3. c. 7).

10. The afflicted person ought to picture the innumerable army of the saints and martyrs in heaven, who while they were on earth knew so many sufferings. He must remember that they, too, were once human beings like himself, beset with all human weaknesses. He should find encouragement in their example, and beg them to make him participate in their patience and their love for God.

11. He ought to think of all the thousands of people on earth who

suffer in every conceivable way without the consolations he has or the spiritual helps and graces. This thought should urge him to bless God and to bear patiently the trials of life.

12. He must have recourse to the Mother of God, the true consolation of the afflicted, whose heart is filled with compassionate mercy especially for those who suffer. "O clement, O loving, O sweet Virgin Mother," cries the Church. Never has the Blessed Virgin Mary been found wanting by those who have confidence in her. Her Divine Son gave her power in heaven and on earth over His creatures. She was given to us as our refuge, our help and our consolation in all our necessities.

In the recommendation of these acts of virtue remember three things:

1. Do not suggest their use all at once, but encourage the sick person to employ these spiritual helps on different occasions.

2. You should assist the patient to put them into practice, especially if he is unable to do so himself. Make the following suggestion: "Tell Almighty God that you renounce your own will and wholly accept His."

3. Kneel and pray with the patient from time to time. The prayers, "We fly to thy patronage," "Remember, O most Blessed Virgin" and others to Our Lady will be very helpful and consoling.

8. Preaching and Catechizing

Before undertaking the duty of preaching and catechizing, adore God as He is manifested in the mystery, the saint or the virtue which is to be the topic of the sermon or instruction. Thus, if you are to speak on a mystery of Our Lord's or Our Lady's life, or if you are to preach about a saint, you should adore God in the mystery or in the saint. When preaching on a virtue, you should adore Our Lord Jesus Christ in His perfect observance and practice of it while He walked on earth with men. When speaking against any vice, you should adore God in His great hatred for that particular sin.

Realizing your nothingness, prostrate yourself before God, begging His forgiveness for any negligence which may have crept into your preaching or catechizing.

Renounce all vanity or pride, making a renewed protestation of your undivided desire to please God alone.

Adore Jesus Christ as the light of the world, the sovereign Preacher, and beseech Him to infuse into your heart His inspiration, that your preaching may in some small measure reflect His divine teaching.

Pray to the Blessed Virgin Mary, to your Guardian Angel and the Saints, particularly those whose lives mirror the virtues you are explaining. Beg the holy preachers who are now in heaven to assist you in the worthy preparation of your subject matter.

Let no unsuitable or unbecoming topics enter into your sermons or instructions. "My speech and my preaching was not in the persuasive words of human wisdom, but in showing of the Spirit and power" (1 Cor. 2, 4). Confine yourself to the necessary truths of the Gospel, the examples of Sacred Scripture and the works of the Fathers of the Church. Let it never be said of you that you preach your own thoughts, but rather the word of God.

When you have studied your subject and prepared your instruction thoroughly, thank God and place your knowledge in the Sacred Heart of Jesus and of His Blessed Mother.

Pattern yourself on the great Preacher Himself of whom it was written that He was "mighty in work and word before God and all the people" (Luke 24, 19), and that He "began to do and to teach" (Act. 1, 1). Implement the words of St. Paul: "Carefully study to present thyself approved unto God, a workman that needeth not to be ashamed, rightly handling the word of truth" (2 Tim. 2, 15). Endeavor to realize in yourself the words of Sacred Scripture, "As from God, before God, in Christ we speak" (2 Cor. 2, 17), that is, endeavor to draw your thoughts from God and to make Him your only desire and end, preaching in His name and solely for His honor and glory.

Before delivering a sermon or teaching a class in Christian doctrine, kneel down and pray humbly to Him in whose name you are about to speak.

Adore Christ the great Preacher and Teacher in the holy dispositions which He brought to this noble function. Try to cultivate similar dispositions, asking Him to make you participators with Him in this divine work, avoiding any suggestion of vanity.

Humble yourself at the Master's feet, protesting your unworthiness, begging Him to take up His abode within you, so that He will speak through your lips and mouth, since He alone is worthy of so lofty a task.

Give yourself to the Eternal Father, pleading with him to eradicate in you anything which is not of Himself, and to establish Christ within your heart.

Invoke the Holy Ghost, praying Him to take full possession of you, with His guidance and direction, that He may open wide the hearts of those to whom you are going to preach.

Offer yourself to the Blessed Virgin Mary, to your Angel Guardian and all the angels, as well as to the patron saints and protectors of those you are to address. Beseech them to obtain from God the grace required for your task, that it may be Christ Himself who will speak through you. Let it be your fervent prayer that He may open and dispose the hearts and minds of your hearers to a worthy reception of the divine Word.

After the sermon or catechetical instruction, thank Our Lord for the glory He has rendered the Eternal Father; for all the effects He has produced and the grace He has given mankind through His own preaching as well as by the mouths of His prophets, teachers and doctors through whom He truly spoke. Thank Him especially for the grace He has brought you through your own preaching and catechizing.

Ask pardon for the faults you may have committed while discharging this duty. Invoke the help of the Blessed Virgin Mary, the angels and saints, for this same purpose.

Do not make your sermon the topic of conversation after it has been delivered, lest in seeking to hear complimentary remarks, vanity may rob you of whatever merit you have gained. Fear, too, that, after you have taught and instructed others, it might well be said of you, "Lest perhaps, when I have preached to others, I myself should become a castaway" (1 Cor. 9, 27). Remember the rebuke of St. Paul to the Jews of his day: "Thou therefore that teachest another, teachest not thyself" (Rom. 2, 21).

CHAPTER VI

THE ANNUAL RETREAT

NOTHING is more useful or necessary to a Christian, and especially to a priest, than the annual retreat. It represents the most powerful and efficacious means for the purification and sanctification of the soul. So, too, it is of paramount importance for our advancement in grace and our preparation for a happy death.

For your annual retreat to be well made, five things are required: 1. Purity of intention; 2. Dispositions; 3. Proper disposal of time; 4. Subjects of meditation; 5. Retreat books.

1. PURITY OF INTENTION

You should make the retreat for three principal reasons:

1. To please God and in memory of the sublime seclusion and retreats Our Blessed Lord observed, as well as those of His Holy Mother who was always united with Him. He observed a long retreat in the stable at Bethlehem, in Egypt and later at Nazareth. For forty days He lived in the silence of the desert; and now He hides Himself in the bosom of the Eternal Father as well as in the Blessed Sacrament. You should choose one of these periods of Christ's retreats to honor Him during your own annual retreat.

2. Offer the retreat as an atonement for the innumerable sins and offenses committed in the past.

3. Make it with the intention of disposing yourself for the worthy reception of new light and graces for the future.

2. Dispositions

To make your retreat with required dispositions, you should make seven preliminary acts.

First, humble yourself because of your great unworthiness. Secondly, enter into the spirit of true solitude, with utter renunciation of all worldly ties. Relinquish your study or any other kind of work. Do not leave the place of retreat unless it be absolutely necessary. Keep rigid silence except during recreation periods. Give yourself wholeheartedly to Our Blessed Lord with those sentiments which animated His own Sacred Heart, and the hearts of Mary and Joseph and of all the saints who practised mortification in solitude.

Thirdly, be faithful to every exercise of the retreat. Fourthly, make use of each moment of your time as if this retreat were to be your last and were given to you as a final opportunity of making reparation for all your unworthiness and sins. In every act of your retreat, or at least in the principal acts, have this thought in mind, "I wish to perform this particular act so well, with God's grace, that I may fully atone for my past sins, and I desire to perform it in the same manner that I would if this were my last day on earth, and if I knew this would be the last opportunity I should ever have of performing it."

Fifthly, follow the guidance of the retreat master and be docile to his injunctions. Sixthly, make a complete renunciation of your own desires, will and self-love, abandoning yourself entirely to the will of God. Let Him guide and direct you during the days you will spend in this holy duty. Seek no human consolation. Trust alone in God.

Seventhly, invoke the assistance of the Blessed Virgin Mary together with the prayers of St. Joseph, St. Gabriel, your Guardian Angel and all the angels and saints of heaven. On the day before you go to make your retreat, spend at least an hour in prayer, preferably in the presence of the Blessed Sacrament.

3. Proper Disposal of Time

A. *Morning*

Arise promptly at the sound of the bell, pronouncing the blessed names of Jesus and Mary. Make the sign of the cross and renew your baptismal promises in these words, *Abrenuntio tibi, Satana; adhaereo tibi, Domine Jesu.* Then, say with great devotion: "I will rise, and . . . I will seek him whom my soul loveth" (Cant. 3, 2).

While dressing, recite some vocal prayers or recall passages from Sacred Scripture or from the previous day's spiritual reading, or concentrate on the meditation which you are about to make.

Then, kneeling beside your bed, honor and salute the Blessed Trinity by reciting the *Gloria Patri.* Adore Christ Our Lord, saying, *Adoramus te, Christe, et benedicimus tibi, quia per sanctam crucem tuam redemisti mundum. Qui passus es pro nobis, Domine Jesu, miserere nobis.* Recite the *Ave Maria* to salute the Blessed Virgin Mary. Invoke your Guardian Angel saying, *Ave, Sancte Angele, qui custos es mei: benedictus sis in aeternum, et intercedere digneris pro mea omniumque salute.*

Address all the angels and saints in heaven thus: *Avete, omnes Angeli, et omnes Sancti et Sanctae Dei: benedicti sitis in aeternum, et intercedere dignemini pro nostra omniumque salute.* Ask Jesus and Mary to give you their blessing: *Benedictum sit Cor amantissimum et dulcissimum nomen Domini nostri Jesu Christi, et gloriosissimae Virginis Matris ejus, in aeternum et ultra. Nos cum Prole pia benedicat Virgo Maria. Amen.* At the Angelus bell, recite the words of that beautiful prayer; then, begin the meditation period.

If the retreat is to be made in common, the schedule will be followed as set forth by the director. But, if the exercise is to be private, it might be well at this point to recite the *Little Hours.* Then you may say Mass if it is convenient at this time. After Mass, a period of profound thanksgiving is a prime requisite.

After breakfast you should spend a half hour reading the New Testament. The rest of the morning should be devoted to the exercises as prescribed for a retreat in common, or if it be in private the beads and litany should be recited, followed by a period of spiritual reading and a thorough examination of conscience.

B. *Afternoon*

After noonday meal, some time will be assigned for recreation in which all the retreatants will participate. During the remainder of the afternoon, there will be various exercises, lectures, spiritual reading, visits to the Blessed Sacrament, recitation of the Divine Office and the rosary, until dinner or supper time.

C. *Evening*

The evening meal will be followed by recreation in silence, preparation of the points for next day's meditation and a sermon. The day will be brought to a close by night prayers and the reading of the points of meditation.

Sometime during the retreat, the retreatant will prepare his soul carefully and devoutly for the most important exercise of the retreat, namely, Confession.

4. Subjects of Meditation

Ordinarily these will be outlined by the Retreat Master.[1] They should be adopted wholeheartedly, with the fullest spirit of cooperation and with the help of God's grace and guidance. Before meditation, the *Veni Sancte Spiritus* should be said.

5. Retreat Books

The only books you need for the retreat are the Bible, the Breviary, the *Following of Christ,* and the Lives of the Saints. There are, however, numerous excellent spiritual writings which might be read most profitably at your own discretion or upon the advice of the Retreat Master.

[1] See Part VI, for a series of excellent retreat meditations.

When it is a question of reading the Scripture, the parts which might be chosen with most profit are the Four Gospels, especially chapters five, six and seven of St. Matthew, and chapters eleven to seventeen of St. John. Then the Epistles of St. Paul and the other apostles may also be read with great benefit.

Part II

THE APOSTOLIC PREACHER

Part II

THE APOSTOLIC PREACHER[1]

CHAPTER I

EXCELLENCE AND IMPORTANCE OF THE OFFICE OF PREACHING

THE PREACHER should keep constantly before him the realization of the importance and sublimity of his noble work, not as a matter of conceit or complacency, but rather as a humbling reminder of his unworthiness and incompetence. Consequently, it should be his constant aim to neglect nothing which can be of assistance in qualifying himself for his task.

Before undertaking to preach, the preacher should always remember the truly great excellence of his work, as well as its lofty origin and divine purpose.

He should never forget that his office is higher than that of the Prophets of the Old Law, for the teachers of the Old Testament taught only the letter and not the spirit, while the exponent of the Gospel of Christ breathes the very spirit of God if his hearers will open their minds and their hearts. "Who also hath made us fit ministers of the new testament, not in the letter, but in the spirit. For the letter killeth, but the spirit quickeneth" (2 Cor. 3, 6). The Apostle St. Paul also refers to the ministry of preaching as *ministratio spiritus* (*Ibid.* 3, 8). In the Acts of the Apostles, we read that "while Peter was yet speaking

[1] Two chapters in the original French edition have been omitted in the English version and short chapters dealing with similar material have been combined into one chapter.

73

these words, the Holy Ghost fell on all them that heard the word" (Acts 10, 44).

The work of preaching is a labor shared with the great saints of the New Law, namely the apostles and disciples of Our Lord Jesus Christ.

The preacher should bear in mind that the office of preaching is so lofty in character and so pleasing to God that Our Blessed Lord promised that He would reward and love those who received His ministers, as though they had received Him personally. "He that receiveth you, receiveth me: and he that receiveth me, receiveth him that sent me" (Matt. 10, 40). On the other hand, on Judgment Day God will condemn and punish those who refused to give ear to the exponents of His doctrine, in a manner more terrible than that experienced by the inhabitants of Sodom and Gomorrha: "It shall be more tolerable for the land of Sodom and Gomorrha in the day of judgment" (*Ibid.* 15).

By preaching and exhortation were idolatry and the tyranny of Satan destroyed. Through this instrumentality, the Church was established in spite of the powers of hell.

Preaching is giving God's children the bread of life to nourish them in this vale of tears and to perfect in them the divine life they received at baptism. "Lord, to whom shall we go? Thou hast the words of eternal life" (John 6, 69).

Preachers of the Gospel of Christ are incarnate angels of the Lord, messengers of heaven, seraphim of the Church, heralds of the Blessed Trinity. Consequently, the priest always begins his discourse with the words: "In the name of the Father and of the Son and of the Holy Ghost. Amen."

Priests are the veritable mouthpieces of the Eternal Father, the ambassadors of the Son of God. "For Christ therefore we are ambassadors, God as it were exhorting by us" (2 Cor. 5, 20). They are active cooperators with God in the salvation of souls.

As precursors of the Lord, they exercise an office similar to that of St. John the Baptist, preparing the ways of the Lord. They are spiritual parents of Christ, forming Him in the lives and souls of their flock. They are saviours of the world. "And saviours shall come up into mount Sion," says Sacred Scripture (Abdias 21).

The mouth of the preacher is the mouth of Jesus Christ who came on earth to speak to men, to instruct and guide them. Through His ministers He wishes to continue till the end of time the divine work He founded. "Christ speaketh in me" (2 Cor. 13, 3). The tongue of the preacher is the instrument and the voice of the Holy Ghost used to announce to mankind the eternal verities spoken by the tongue of Christ Himself.

Preaching is truly making God speak, who having of old spoken by His prophets, and in the New Law through His Divine Son, now wishes to speak to His children through the living members of that same Son.

Preaching had its origin in the bosom of God Himself, from which emanated the Word Divine, Christ, the First Preacher. Thence flowed, too, all those eternal truths still proclaimed on earth.

The end and purpose of this heavenly office is to form Christ in the hearts of the faithful that He may reign there; to dispel the darkness of hell and illumine the light of heaven in men's souls; to destroy sin and open the floodgates of grace; to destroy the tyranny of Satan on earth and reestablish the Kingdom of God. Preaching aims to reconcile men with their Maker, transforming them into His children, deifying them as it were, according to the words of Sacred Scripture: "He called them gods, to whom the word of God was spoken" (John 10, 35). In a word, it means perfecting here below that great work Christ came to effect for He says to all preachers, "As the Father hath sent me, I also send you" (John 20, 21).

So noble and great is this holy duty that it should be carried out with the greatest exactitude, inspired by the holiest of dispositions and intentions. Preachers should unite themselves to the prophets, the apostles and all the saints in heaven in order to learn to imitate them and practise their virtues.

Likewise, as God's heralds and ambassadors, preachers should be clothed with His qualities, possessed with a burning love, fired with the all-consuming zeal of the Holy Spirit. The lips of the preacher, being consecrated to the Gospel, should never utter anything save the words of God. "If any man speak, *let him speak,* as the words of God" (1 Peter 4, 11).

Preaching emanated from the bosom of God and through it He

speaks to mankind. Its only purpose is to establish His reign in men's hearts, and to lift them to the very throne of the Father that they may abide eternally with Him. Preachers, therefore, should always speak in a manner worthy of God's infinite majesty, making Him truly speak through them. They should study and practise what St. Paul says, "As from God, before God, in Christ we speak." *Sicut ex Deo, coram Deo et in Christo loquimur* (2 Cor. 2, 17).

Sicut ex Deo means that the preacher should not depend upon his own thoughts or ideas, but his matter should be founded on Scripture, theology, prayer and the reading of devotional works. *Coram Deo* means that the preacher should have no other aim, no other thought or object in mind than God, His glory and the salvation of souls. For these things represent the sole purpose for which Christ established His Church and the office of preaching.

In Christo loquimur means that he should make a complete renunciation of self and become one with Christ absorbing those dispositions and intentions which animated the Saviour when He preached here on earth.

Finally, be assured that to undertake and carry out the office of preaching, according to the directions outlined, is more praiseworthy in God's sight than the most profound contemplation. Nothing pleases Him more than the salvation of souls, which is accomplished more efficiently by preaching than by contemplation. St. Bernard expresses this thought very strikingly in a beautiful metaphor: *Noli nimis insistere osculo contemplationis, quia meliora sunt ubera praedicationis.*[2]

[2] *In Cantic. sermo 9, no. 8.*

CHAPTER II

INTERIOR DISPOSITIONS FOR PREACHING

WHOSOEVER would preach the word of God in an apostolic spirit should endeavor to acquire the interior dispositions that filled the Divine Preacher and the apostles when they preached the Gospel to the world.

He should so live that he would rather die a thousand deaths than ever be guilty of a deliberate sin, no matter what its nature. Moreover, before daring to speak in the name of the Saviour, he should purify himself from every blemish either by going to confession or by making an act of contrition. He should dwell in constant fear that the words of the Psalmist might be applied to him: "To the sinner God hath said: Why dost thou declare my justices, and take my covenant in thy mouth? Seeing thou hast hated discipline; and hast cast my words behind thee" (Ps. 49, 16-17).

Banish every shadow of self-love, pride, ambition or vanity. Have no other thought than to please God and to save souls. Satan was damned because he envied God's glory[1] and sought to become like unto Him. "How many great preachers have been lost eternally," exclaims St. Francis Xavier, "because they were consumed with vanity and self-esteem."[2]

---

[1] "Beware of vanity, you who go to preach missions or speak in public . . . Seek only the glory of God, for which end alone you should strive to work and labor. Yes, let His glory and the salvation of souls be your only aim. Otherwise, you will be preaching yourselves, not Jesus Christ. And what can be said of one who preaches solely that he may be applauded, praised and acclaimed? What is he doing but committing a sacrilege? Yes, a sacrilege. To use the word of God and divine things to enhance his own reputation and acquire honor for himself, is surely a sacrilege. O God, grant that no member of this little company may fall into such a terrible sin. Believe me, we shall never be able to do the work of God unless we have profound humility and learn to despise ourselves." Saint Vincent de Paul, quoted by the Abbé Maynard in *Vie de Saint Vincent de Paul*, Vol. 2, p. 393.

[2] Epist., lib. 4, ep. 16.

Avoid negligence and the seeking of easy ways, instead of embracing wholeheartedly the hard work entailed in preaching. Study with care and diligence. Prepare your sermon or instruction well in advance. Never go into the pulpit without being thoroughly familiar with the subject for otherwise you are merely tempting God.

Do not rest your entire dependence upon your own feeble efforts. Rather depend on grace and the bounty of Our Lord Jesus Christ. Before beginning even to outline a sermon, kneel down and beg God's help. Seek light and strength before the Blessed Sacrament, adoring there the incomprehensible love which prompted God to send His Only-begotten Son into the world to instruct and teach mankind. Adore the infinite goodness and the charity which moved the Holy Ghost to speak through Jesus, His apostles and saints.

Thank the Father, the Son and the Holy Ghost for all these favors, and ask pardon for any misuse made of your talents, ability or opportunities. Be humbled before the divine majesty of God and mindful of your own insignificance.

Renounce self-love and self-esteem. Avoid vanity and pride under any guise. Surrender yourself to the love of the Father, the wisdom of the Son and the charity of the Holy Ghost. Beg them to put in your mind inspiring thoughts so that your sermon may produce abundant fruit in the soul of your listeners.

Adore Christ as the beginning and end of all everlasting verities. Unite your intentions to those which animated the God-man, thanking His bounty for all His manifestations of truth to mankind, and for the great privilege of being associated with Him in the holy work of preaching. Beg divine forgiveness for being unworthy of the great trust bestowed upon you.

Cultivate humility, learning to plumb the depth of your own nothingness, realizing that the preacher speaks only through the goodness of our Saviour, in His name and for His cause. Affirm vigorously that even if you did possess the ability of making the most eloquent human orations, you, nevertheless, would refrain from this display of learning and would choose to proclaim instead the undying truths of the Gospel.

Salute Mary Immaculate, Mother of the Eternal Light and Truth. Thank her and offer her your will, praying in return only for the great privilege of being able to continue doing the evangelical work of her Divine Son with merit and fruit. Salute your Angel Guardian and all the saints and protectors of the diocese and the parish where you are to preach. Invoke their prayers and assistance.

While studying, frequently elevate your heart to God. Before going into the pulpit, recall briefly the foregoing injunctions and then consider the importance of the action you are about to perform. Unite yourself with the holy dispositions which filled the mind and heart of Jesus as He preached to His disciples. Make an act of utter renunciation of self. Ask Our Lord to remove from your heart all that is not of Him, so that He alone will speak through your mouth since it is He alone who should speak the words of salvation. Tell Him that you are willing to accept any humiliation, nervousness or confusion which you may suffer while you are preaching. Offer to the Father your memory; to the Son your understanding; to the Holy Ghost your will.

Offer to God the hearts of your hearers, praying earnestly that they may be well disposed. Offer them to the Blessed Virgin Mary, the angels and the saints. Then, kneel humbly and say: *Veni, Domine Jesu, veni, veni.* "Come, Lord Jesus, come into my heart. Annihilate my own being that Thou alone mayest preach Thy divine word. Come into the hearts of all here present and dispose them to receive and practise whatsoever Thou dost desire them to do."

Standing before the congregation, raise your eyes to heaven and ask God to help you to seek His glory alone and to implore the saints to pray for you before the heavenly throne.

Make the Sign of the Cross with great devotion. Let its meaning penetrate the heart, mindful of St. Paul's words: "God . . . hath spoken to us by his son" (Heb. 1, 1-2). Try to enter into the sentiments of love which prompted the Eternal Father to give us His Blessed Son. Pray to the Holy Spirit, that His zeal and piety may abound in you as it did in the holy apostles and doctors of the Church.

During the sermon proper, a great spirit of recollection and piety should be maintained. Remember that, in speaking to sinners, you really speak to men like yourself encompassed with every temptation and sin. Do not show impatience at interruptions caused by the congregation. Never display displeasure. Do not scold harshly or rant. Use kindly words. Speak modestly, not boastfully. Let authority and humility be intermingled.

After the sermon, thank the Blessed Trinity, Our Lord and His holy Mother, the angels and saints, saying: *Gloria Patri, Gloria tibi Domine, Ave Maria, Avete omnes Angeli et omnes Sancti et Sanctae Dei, benedicti sitis in aeternum, et intercedere dignemini pro nostra omniumque salute.*

Likewise, ask pardon for any shortcomings and close your heart and ears against vanity or flattery. If your sermon has not measured up to standard or has been somewhat of a disappointment, offer this trial in a spirit of real faith.

Do not tolerate praise. When well-wishers congratulate or compliment you, humble yourself inwardly and direct to God all honor and glory: *Soli Deo honor et gloria* (1, Tim. 1, 17). Remember, too, that people who praise you to your face may despise you in their hearts, and that while you may enjoy the approval of a few, perhaps the great majority are indifferent to you, if not actually hostile. Yet, though you are openly acclaimed by all, you should still shun as poison the praises of men for flattery and adulation can kill Christ in your heart: "Woe to you when men shall bless you: for according to these things did their fathers to the false prophets" (Luke 6, 26).

When you are corrected, accept these admonitions in a spirit of humility and submission.

Learn to practise the sublime truths that you preach and apply them to yourself in actuality, lest it be said of you: "Thou therefore that teachest another, teachest not thyself" (Rom. 2, 21). Remember that the truths that you have expounded will be so many verdicts and condemnations against you at the hour of death unless you have tried to live up to them.

You must be mindful of these things, and in so doing you will be strengthened and fortified with a most potent weapon to protect you against conceit and false estimation of self. St. Prosper says: *Bene loqui et male vivere, quid aliud est nisi se sua voce damnare?*[3]

[3] *Praefat. in Job.* cap. 7.

CHAPTER III

EDIFICATION AND EXAMPLE TO BE GIVEN BY PREACHERS

PREACHING the Gospel is simply a continuation of the divine mission of Christ. Preachers, therefore, should imitate the great Master whom they represent. "Jesus began to do and to teach" (Acts 1, 1). "He was mighty in work and word before God and all the people" (Luke 24, 19).

Consequently, preachers should be living examples of devotion and virtue, especially humility, obedience and charity. Likewise, they should avoid as a plague anything that savors of vanity and ambition, and they should never show any signs of seeking the pulpits of large churches. They should be willing to go to the poorest parishes and the smallest, as well as to the wealthiest and most isolated churches in order to walk in the footsteps of the Divine Master who said: "He hath anointed me to preach the gospel to the poor" (Luke 4, 18), and one of the proofs of the divinity of His mission was: "The poor have the gospel preached to them" (Matt. 11, 5).

Preachers should always be careful not to put themselves forward, but should rather give place to other preachers, speaking of these latter always with esteem and affection. Each one should excuse and defend his confreres charitably whenever they are unjustly blamed, and guard at all times against jealousy. Nor should they excuse themselves from preaching when the congregation is very small, remembering always that even one soul created to the image and likeness of God and redeemed by Christ's Precious Blood is well worth the labor and effort of all the theologians, the preachers and even of all men and angels. Indeed, the salvation of a soul is of infinite value, as Christ Himself demonstrated when He took special care to instruct the poor Samaritan woman at the well, thus proving that He would gladly have come into the world if there had been only one soul to instruct and save.

Likewise, if your audience is not so attentive as it should be, you must not show displeasure, which would be a proof of vanity.

Nothing should be said in a sermon simply for effect or self-glorification, to show one's erudition or wisdom, nor should any personal touch be permitted to enter into the theme. The words of the Apostle St. Paul should be kept always in mind: "We preach not ourselves, but Jesus Christ our Lord" (2 Cor. 4, 5).

Make your life conform to your preaching, and let your actions speak as loudly as your words, so that like St. John the Baptist you may be *lucerna ardens et lucens,* "a burning and a shining light" (John 5, 35), burning before God, shining before men; burning in prayer, shining in action; burning from within, shining from without; burning in words, shining in deeds.

Be particularly devoted to the virtues of temperance, frugality and abstinence. Give a true example of abstemiousness when visiting in another parish, so that this spirit of mortification may be a silent lesson to those about you. In visiting, too, you should be careful to give every evidence of sobriety.

Avoid familiarity with seculars, especially women, lest suspicions be engendered in the minds of others: *Ut non vituperetur ministerium nostrum* (2 Cor. 6, 3).

Your whole deportment should place you beyond the faintest or least suspicion of avarice or greed and show clearly your detachment from temporal things and your devotion only to the eternal. Consequently, you should ask no recompense for your services, but you should receive thankfully whatever the charity of the people will offer out of the goodness of their hearts.

Never discuss the faults and shortcomings of other priests or religious. Show a great respect for parish priests and never undertake any activity without their sanction. Incite the faithful to love and respect them.

Try to be kind and accessible to all. Be ever ready to do good to every person without exception, in imitation of the charity of the Master, "who went about doing good, and healing all that were oppressed by the devil" (Acts 10, 38). Be especially kind to the poor, visiting them rather than the rich, in their homes, in prison and in hospitals. Have a tender solicitude for the afflicted, consoling them and urging them to turn their sufferings to spiritual advantage.

Endeavor to reunite families and members of broken homes, being always careful not to take sides, showing to both factions that your only interest is the promotion of God's glory and the salvation of souls.

Let your conversation be modest, gentle and edifying, taking advantage of every opportunity to speak of things eternal. Bear the good odor of Christ everywhere, but especially in consecrated places where your Christian conduct should be an inspiration. This will apply especially to the church, where by silence and piety you will show the faithful the great respect due to the house of God.

Finally, you should be in imitation to St. John the Baptist, *vox clamantis* (Matt. 3, 3), that is, you should act and live in such manner that everything about you will be a continual proof that you are a man of God. Let the world see in your actions, your walk, your person, your gestures, your attire, your daily habits, the reflection of your interior life, which will prove beyond doubt that you are a priest, not only at the altar and in the pulpit, but in every place and in every thing you do and think and say. Thus, you will always preach piety, modesty, humility, simplicity and all the other virtues.

CHAPTER IV*

BOOKS FOR SERMON MATERIAL

THE FIRST and most important book for preachers is Sacred Scripture, especially the New Testament. In the Old Testament, the Book of Wisdom, of Job, and of the Prophets are especially recommended.

Some time should be devoted each day to the reading of Sacred Scripture and it is suggested that this be done kneeling, in imitation of St. Charles Borromeo. Parts of Scripture should be memorized, certainly the most impressive passages. Spiritual commentators, too, should be read with care, especially Cornelius a Lapide and Barradas.[1]

Next in importance after Holy Scripture come the writings of the Fathers of the Church, foremost among them St. Augustine, St. John Chrysostom, St. Gregory the Great and St. Bernard. The *Summa Theologica* of St. Thomas Aquinas is, of course, an indispensable reference book for any preacher of Catholic doctrine.

There are also the works of Louis of Granada, a Spanish Dominican, renowned for his virtue and erudition. St. Charles Borromeo made extensive use of the writings of this learned man, using them as his sole manual of theology. Certainly Granada's *Guide of Sinners* should be studied and read with special care.

There are also Father Saint Jure's *Knowledge and Love of Our Lord Jesus Christ*, William Peraldus's *De Vitiis et Virtutibus*[2] and the *Catechism* of St. Peter Canisius.

---

* This chapter has been considerably curtailed by the omission of several works no longer available and by the elimination of long footnotes included in the original French edition, *Oeuvres Complètes,* Vol. IV, p. 29 ff.

[1] Barradas, a Portuguese Jesuit (1542-1615), published *Commentaria in concordiam et historiam Evangeliorum,* in four *volumes.*

[2] William Peraldus, a French Dominican, died in 1260.

The Lives of the Saints must be the handbooks of any preacher who wants to perform his duty with success and devotion. Other good books in the preacher's mother tongue must be read attentively and studied in order to perfect his style and to acquire clarity and fluency of speech.

Frivolous and worldly books should not be used nor should the mind of the priest be sullied with the contents of such useless works. Such volumes are often part of Satan's library, completely opposed to the maxims of the Gospel.

CHAPTER V

SERMON TOPICS

PREACHERS should remember that it is their duty to preach the word of God. They would be criminally guilty if they should distribute ordinary bread instead of the Sacred Host; so also they cannot be excused if their sermons are merely worldly dissertations instead of well-digested discourses on the eternal verities.

Consequently, preachers must be on guard lest they preach their own thoughts rather than those of Sacred Scripture and tradition, lest they expound a human doctrine rather than the deep truths of Christ, so amply explored in the writings of the Fathers of the Church.

Likewise, preachers, especially the young and inexperienced, should beware of falling into the error of thinking that they must seek unusual topics, use new unconventional expressions and propound extraordinary ideas. By so doing, they make a great mistake because the common subjects are always the most useful and most appealing, not only because they convince listeners, but because God imparts a blessing and a particular efficacy to the words of those who preach the Catholic doctrine with simplicity and humility.

Subtle questions, which are better suited to gratify curiosity than to edify and touch hearts, should be omitted. The preacher should confine himself to a simple and lucid exposition of the Gospel and reject anything superfluous, useless or of little merit so that he will speak only thoughts that will help men to know and honor God and spur them on to work out their eternal salvation.

The principal sermon topics are the following:

The Epistles and Gospels read at Holy Mass, or any part of Sacred Scripture.

The perfections, mysteries, works and gifts of God.

The Ten Commandments of God and the Six Commandments of the Church.

The Life, Excellence and Mysteries of the Blessed Virgin Mary.

The Holy Sacrifice of the Mass, the Sacraments, Ceremonies and Liturgy of the Church.

The life and virtues of the Saints.

Sin and the particular vices.

Evil customs which are the causes of numberless sins, such as bad books, pictures, dancing, plays, fashions and harmful games.

Christian virtues, such as faith, hope, charity, humility and patience.

Good works, such as prayer, fasting, almsgiving, the corporal and the spiritual works of mercy.

The duties and obligations of one's state in life, whether one be rich or poor, a workman or an employer, a father or mother, married or single, master or servant.

The four last ends of man and purgatory.

These and similar topics are always most suitable for the preacher who is eager to preach the word of God with success.

In all his sermons and instructions the preacher should endeavor to make Almighty God better known in His mysteries, His works and His benefits. He must also strive to make divine goodness better loved and appreciated by the faithful. Likewise, he should exhort them to greater love for their Creator, make them sorry for sin and determined to amend their lives. He should urge them to fear God's justice and His punishment, to hope in His promises, to have confidence in His goodness, His grace and His help. So he should encourage his hearers to offer to God their entire being and their all. He should strive constantly to make the Saviour better known and loved by all men, inducing them to follow Him as true disciples of the great Leader. Into their hearts, too, he should infuse a profound and tender love and respect for the ever Blessed Mother.

The preacher should also make his people understand that they, as well as priests and religious, are called upon to live holily and follow in the footsteps of the saints. For this purpose, he should be assiduous in his efforts to make them love the Church and everything associated with it. This means that they should be taught reverence and veneration for consecrated places such as churches, chapels and cemeteries. Likewise, they should insist upon the sanctification of Sundays and holy days of obligation.

The importance of Baptism and its obligations should be impressed upon the faithful. The dignity and sanctity of Confirmation and the other sacraments should be thoroughly explained, their origin and purpose, their institution and the proper dispositions with which they should be received. Likewise, their efficacy should be made clear and their frequent reception urged, especially the Sacraments of Penance and of Holy Eucharist.

Marriage, being one of the most important events in the life of most Christians, should be held up to highest esteem and its sacramental character made thoroughly clear. Its far-reaching effects in time and eternity should be the topic of many sermons by the preacher who is devoted to his task.

Young people considering wedlock should be reminded of their duties, particularly that of consulting their parents. They should be encouraged to pray to Our Lord, to His Blessed Mother and to St. Joseph to guide them in the choice of a suitable partner, who will be a help and not a hindrance in the performance of their Christian and Catholic duties. Their preparation for this Sacrament of Matrimony should be such as to guarantee the graces and blessings of God. Like the young Tobias, they should resort to prayer and be firm in continence, and on their wedding day stand, in God's presence, purified by Confession and Holy Communion.

Enjoin upon parishioners and all Catholics a wholesome respect for Holy Matrimony and especially seek to banish from marriage celebrations any unseemly and unbecoming conduct. Fulminate against the pagan customs which sometimes accompany these wedding feasts, when sinful excesses of eating and drinking are committed and sinful dancing indulged. Also, urge parents to prevent as far as possible prolonged courtships which often lead to evil.

Let married persons learn that wedlock does not permit them to use the holy state as a cloak for sinful practices and immoral license. Let them remember, too, that their duties as parents are most serious; that their obligation of bringing up their children and educating them is binding before God.

Teach them to offer their children to Our Lord at the hour of birth, and to have them baptized as early as possible. Then, when the children come to the age of reason, the parents should instruct them faithfully in their Christian duties, watching over them at all times, helping them to decide their state in life when the moment comes for that important decision.

Preachers should point out the hideousness of sin in general and of particular vices, causing evil to be shunned and detested. They should urge the faithful to cultivate a great respect and love for our Holy Father, the Pope, the Bishops of the Church and for all priests. Likewise, too, preachers should remind Catholics of their duties towards the civil law and their obligations to obey its mandates. Those who are in high places of authority should be exhorted to remember the sacred trust they hold. They should be encouraged to govern with justice and wisdom, treating those under their jurisdiction with kindness and consideration. Their example should be a shining light for their subordinates.

The rich should be reminded that the things on earth are merely passing; therefore, they should not attach too much importance to them, seeking rather to lay up treasures for eternity. The poor should be helped to bear their lot with submission, remembering that theirs was the lot of Jesus, of His Blessed Mother and of the great majority of the saints. The Master who possessed all riches became poor for us.

Teach masters and servants, employers and employees to have mutual respect, using every means at their disposal for the betterment of their spiritual condition. Guide mothers and fathers in their imitation of the Eternal Father, the perfect example of love, kindness, patience and zeal. Give the child Jesus as a model to the children, pointing out His loving obedience and devotion to Mary and Joseph.

Finally, there are four topics which can never be preached too often:

1. Veneration of holy places and of holy days of obligation.
2. Frequent use of the Sacraments of Penance and the Holy Eucharist.
3. Charity towards God and one's fellow men and reconciliation with one's enemies.
4. Restitution.

CHAPTER VI

FURTHER SUGGESTIONS ON SERMON TOPICS

In ADDITION to the topics suggested in the preceding chapter, the following rules should be observed by those who are called to the divine ministry of preaching.

They should have a sufficient knowledge of the doctrines they preach, though it is not necessary for them to be outstanding theologians. They should be careful not to discuss or preach any subject with which they are insufficiently familiar. "A preacher knows enough," says St. Francis de Sales, "when he does not pretend to know more than he really does." [1]

Too many quotations from Scripture or from the Fathers of the Church should be avoided; likewise, lengthy scriptural texts which merely confuse the listener. Let quotations be short and to the point. Interpret the Scriptures faithfully according to the teachings of the Catholic Church, the Fathers and the Doctors of the Church. If there is diversity of opinion on any point, do not include this in your sermon because the pulpit is not the proper place for theological disputation.

Examples from the lives of the saints make excellent sermon material, for the deeds of the saints represent the Gospel in action. Short stories drawn from nature can be most helpful, for the world brought into being by the Creator's fiat proclaims the greatness of the word of God. This world of nature was St. Anthony's great book, from which he preached the glories and perfections of the Maker. Similes and other comparisons also can be very helpful if they are appropriate. Logical reasoning is an excellent adjunct. This can be found in abundance in the *Summa Theologica* of St. Thomas Aquinas. Profane

---

[1] *Letter to the Archbishop of Bourges.*

authors should be quoted sparingly if at all. So-called miracles and visions should never be mentioned unless officially accepted and ratified by the Church.

The truly humble preacher will not seek his own glory, nor will he hesitate to preach on subjects that have been treated time and time again by other preachers of the day.

A preacher should not indulge in idle descriptions and irrelevant details. If he is discussing the sacrifice of Abraham, for instance, it is useless to waste time describing Isaac's comeliness, Abraham's sword or the topography of the place of sacrifice. Similarly he should not introduce imaginary conversations between people involved in a Biblical narrative unless these be well-founded and to the point. It would be far-fetched, for instance, to describe Isaac weeping at the altar and plaintively imploring his father's compassion, or to picture Abraham arguing with himself in the act of doing God's will.

If ideas come suddenly to the preacher while he is preaching, ideas which he has not studied and digested beforehand, he must be wary of giving utterance to them. It is possible that the devil may be seeking to delude him through vanity and lead him into the trap of making statements that he may regret. If spontaneous thought suggests well-founded principles and truths which he had not included in his preparation but which are obviously apt, he should by all means make use of them.

When addressing an ordinary congregation, it is useless to discuss contemplation or other stages of exalted perfection which they seldom attain. On the contrary, such topics may serve only to discourage souls for, finding themselves so far from the suggested goal, they are tempted to cease to lead an ordinary Christian life.

A preacher, therefore, should select topics that the ordinary Christians can understand and practise; he should give utterance to principles and maxims that can be followed; he should make virtue loved and vice detested. He must always avoid extremes, saying neither too much nor too little. He must neither be too strict nor too lenient. He must never indulge in prophecies concerning the coming of the Anti-Christ. He should not promulgate new indulgences unless they have been authorized by the Ordinary.

He should at all times encourage the faithful to pray for our Holy Father the Pope, for the Bishops and Priests, for the civil rulers and for all fellow Christians and Catholics.

Nothing provides a better ending for a sermon than a good story, provided it is not too long and has a definite bearing on the subject matter of the discourse. Biblical stories are excellent. A preacher who would draw the greatest fruit from his labors would be well advised to make frequent use of such stories.

The preacher should avoid making the sermon too long, lest he tire his congregation and render God's word fruitless.

CHAPTER VII

SERMON PLANS

I. *The Mysteries of Religion*

THERE ARE various ways of treating the mysteries of religion:

A. FIRST PLAN

1. Point out the effects of the power, wisdom, love, charity, justice and mercy of God towards men as made evident in the mystery under consideration.

2. Outline the duties owed to God because of this particular mystery, namely, adoration, praise, love, thanksgiving, reparation and satisfaction for offenses and the oblation of self to Him.

3. Explain the light and motives to be derived from this mystery, to lead man in the ways of God.

B. SECOND PLAN

1. Relate the Scriptural account of the mystery.

2. Show the reasons why this particular mystery should be honored, setting forth its dignity and excellence. Recall the glory given to God through its instrumentality together with its fruits and spiritual advantages.

3. Suggest the means to honor the mystery in their interior and exterior life.

C. THIRD PLAN

1. Show the external aspects of the mystery as made evident in the persons concerned, the words said and the virtues practised in connection with it.

2. Explain the interior spirit of the mystery, that is, the interior virtues of the persons associated with it, their thoughts and affections.

3. Stress the fruits to be drawn for the instruction and edification of the congregation.

D. FOURTH PLAN

Choose two or three particular circumstances connected with the mystery and build your sermon around them.

E. FIFTH PLAN

Take one or more virtues which shine forth from the mystery of which you are to speak, or single out some Christian truth founded on it. Make this the topic of a sound thoughtful discourse.

F. SIXTH PLAN

In each mystery consider three aspects and make them the points of your sermon. Who? Why? How? Take, for example, the Nativity of Our Lord. Answer three questions. Who was born? Why was He born? How was He born? Then show how the Son of God came to save mankind and a poor, naked baby in a stable, was born of the Blessed Virgin Mary.

II. *The Gospels and the Epistles*

A. FIRST PLAN

Paraphrase and explain the particular passage of Scripture, point by point. At the conclusion of each point, draw a particular application. This is not, however, as useful as the other plans suggested, because little time can be given to any part of the discourse.

B. SECOND PLAN

Concentrate on two or three necessary or important topics. This is a better plan than the preceding one.

Choose one point alone and develop it fully, drawing from it some particular truth or some practical application to certain virtues or vices. This plan is strongly recommended.

III. *The Sacrifice of the Mass*

There is such a wealth of material for use when preaching on this sublime mystery that many sermons may be delivered on this topic without repetition. I shall merely suggest the following plan:

1. Show what the Holy Sacrifice of the Mass is.

2. Point out the obligations owed Our Lord for having given this sublime proof of His love for the Church. Impress upon the faithful the great love, veneration, devotion and respect they should have for the Mass, wherein Christ immolates Himself anew daily for mankind.

3. Insist on the interior and exterior dispositions the Catholic should have when assisting at this august sacrifice.

IV. *The Commandments of God and of the Church*

1. Having explained what is enjoined by each particular commandment under discussion, point out what it forbids, and give the reasons why one should conform to its dictates.

2. Make known the various sins committed against the commandment in question by word, thought and action. When treating of the Sixth Commandment, however, use great discretion and care.

3. Give the means whereby one may obey the Commandment and show how sins against it may be avoided.

V. *The Blessed Virgin Mary*

Since the Blessed Mother is in herself a veritable wellspring of virtue, grace and holiness, many plans could be given for sermons about our Lady. One very useful plan is included herewith, containing two points.

1. Show the reasons why she should be honored and served, dwelling upon her shining excellence in relation to God and to us.

2. Teach the people how to honor and love her with devotion worthy of their most admirable Mother.

VI. *The Saints*

In a sermon for the feast day of a saint, or on any occasion when a saint is honored, the following plans are suggested.

A. FIRST PLAN

1. Show how the saint lived in relation to God.
2. Point out how he fulfilled his duties to himself.
3. Portray his dealings with his fellow men.

This plan might be based on St. Paul's words: *Sobrie et juste et pie vivamus* (Titus 2, 12). *Sobrie* towards himself; *juste* towards his neighbor; *pie* towards God.

B. SECOND PLAN

1. Recount the remarkable periods and events of the saint's life: his childhood; his youth; middle age; old age, if he grew to advanced years; his death and the events following it.
2. Draw a salutary lesson from each period; the first for the children, the second for the young men and women, and the third for the older members of the congregation.

C. THIRD PLAN

Show how the saint overcame the three vices enumerated by St. John: "For all that is in the world is the concupiscence of the flesh, and the concupiscence of the eyes, and the pride of life" (1 John 2, 16). These vices are avarice, lust and pride.

D. FOURTH PLAN

1. Demonstrate why we should honor each particular saint, and what fruit should be gathered from his virtues.
2. Give practical suggestions as to how the saint should be honored on his Feast Day by devotion, good works, prayer and, above all, by imitation of his virtues.

E. FIFTH PLAN

1. Explain the graces that God bestowed upon the saint.
2. Mention the holy and practical use the saint made of these graces, and counsel imitation.
3. Select two or three particular virtues for emulation.

F. SIXTH PLAN

Take one virtue only and develop it, for example, by selecting a personal or intimate detail about his life.

G. SEVENTH PLAN

1. Give reasons why we should try to practise this virtue which the saint practised in so perfect a manner.
2. Give the marks by which this chosen virtue may be distinguished and the means by which it may be acquired. Then show how the saint made use of these particular means.

All the plans outlined are excellent and can be used to great advantage. Do not make comparisons between one saint and another. Render to each the respect, praise and honor due him for his particular merits.

VII. *Controversial Matters*

Public controversies with ministers of other creeds are often useless and must be avoided if at all possible. Usually these controversies are not actuated with the intention of learning about the Catholic Faith, but rather are used as an excuse for publicity.

Do not discuss controversial matters except in communities where Catholics come into contact with non-Catholics, or when heretics and lukewarm Catholics are present in the congregation.

If these topics must be discussed, use discretion and charity, avoiding any semblance of giving offense to anyone.

Explore thoroughly the subject to be explained. Point out the truth, then give the errors concerning it, explaining why they are errors. Answer the common objections usually advanced in support of these heresies. Leave no doubt in the minds of the faithful.

Use one of the following plans.

A. FIRST PLAN

Show the truth of the Catholic religion as proved by Scripture, the Councils of the Church and the writings of the Fathers. Show the falsity of the objections brought against Catholic doctrine by the enemies of the Church, using the very texts they quote to confound them.

For example, if it be a question of our using the Bible in the vernacular, explain the belief and teaching of the Church in this matter.

It is said that we deprive the faithful of the Word of God, which is the soul's daily bread. We may answer this falsehood by stating that while, indeed, the Scripture is our soul's daily bread, Mother Church proportions it to our needs. Just as parents do not give the whole loaf to their children, or the knife with which to cut it lest they injure themselves, so it is the duty of the Church, of the priest or the preacher, to distribute the spiritual bread of the Word of God to his people in portions suited to their requirements.

It is said that the Word of God is the light of the world. Well indeed do we admit this truth. But, we do not place a lighted candle in a child's hands, lest he burn himself.

B. SECOND PLAN

Establish the unswerving certainty of the Catholic doctrine. Then, dovetail with it the mysteries being discussed, for example, how Our Lord is present in the Blessed Sacrament, or how the saints hear our prayers.

C. THIRD PLAN

Let the discourse be an explanation of Scriptural passages often questioned by those outside the Church, proving from these same passages the truth of the Catholic position.

VIII. *The Maxims of the Christian Life*

Sermons on these truths are most practical, since they concern the principles of religion, the virtues, vices and last ends of man. It might be well at this point to enumerate some of these Christian maxims.

"Without faith it is impossible to please God" (Heb. 11, 6).

"If any man will come after me, let him deny himself and take up his cross and follow me" (Matt. 16, 24).

"Flee from sins as from the face of a serpent" (Ecclus. 21, 2).

"So likewise every one of you that doth not renounce all that he possesseth cannot be my disciple" (Luke 14, 33).

"Love not the world, nor the things which are in the world" (1 John 2, 15).

"He that saith he abideth in him, ought himself also to walk, even as he walked" (*Ibid.* 6).

"Blessed are the poor in spirit: for theirs is the kingdom of heaven" (Matt. 5, 3).

"Blessed are the meek: for they shall possess the land" (*Ibid.* 4).

"Blessed are they that mourn: for they shall be comforted" (*Ibid.* 5).

"Blessed are the merciful: for they shall obtain mercy" (*Ibid.* 7).

"Many are called, but few chosen" (*Ibid.* 20, 16).

"Wide is the gate, and broad is the way that leadeth to destruction . . . narrow is the gate, and strait is the way that leadeth to life" (*Ibid.* 7, 13-114).

"Every one that exalteth himself, shall be humbled; and he that humbleth himself shall be exalted" (Luke 14, 11).

"They that will become rich, fall into temptation, and into the snare of the devil, and into many unprofitable and hurtful desires, which drown men into destruction and perdition" (1 Tim. 6, 9).

"No evils shall happen to him that feareth the Lord (Ecclus. 33, 1).

"To them that love God all things work together unto good (Rom. 8, 28).

Preaching on these and other Christian principles, you should: 1. Explain the words and their meaning; 2. Show why they should be followed, quoting examples from the life of Our Lord or of the saints; 3. Give practical suggestions for a rule of life founded upon these inspiring maxims.

IX. *Virtues*

Here is a practical plan:

1. Give reasons and motives why we should love the virtue which forms the topic of the sermon.

2. Explain the virtue, pointing out the qualities whereby it may be known.

3. Show how virtue is acquired and how easy it is to practise when the proper means are used. Give examples of the lives of other persons who have succeeded in doing so. Chief among these should be the example of Our Lord, of His Blessed Mother and of the saints whose virtues exalted them to such high places in heaven.

X. *Sin and Vice*

1. Demonstrate the hideousness of sin in general; then particularize about various vices.

2. Arouse a great hatred of anything which is sinful and urge a real determination to eradicate anything which is displeasing to God in the lives of your hearers. Reasons suggested for this are: a) the injury and dishonor caused God; b) the hatred of God for sin as demonstrated by the terrible chastisements He has heaped upon malefactors, even hurling the fallen angels into hell; c) the punishments to be expected in time and eternity.

3. Suggest means to destroy evil in the soul and to avoid its occasions. For example, Christians should remember their own unworthiness and impotence to avoid evil; make a determined resolution to do all in their power to cooperate with God's grace, throwing themselves on His mercy and invoking His constant assistance; avoid occasions and everything that may lead to sin; pray always; make a good examination of conscience in the morning to foresee what pitfalls may await them and in the evening to review their transgressions; assist at daily Mass and pay frequent visits to the Blessed Sacrament; cultivate a lively devotion to the Blessed Virgin Mary, especially by saying the Rosary every day; read good books; listen attentively to the sermons; fast and practise mortification; give alms to the poor; go to confession and receive Holy Communion frequently.

XI. *The Four Last Ends and Purgatory*

DEATH

A. FIRST PLAN

Show the difference between the death of the just man and the death of the unrepentant sinner.

B. SECOND PLAN

1. Show the motives and reasons which should impel us to pray for a happy death.
2. Give the signs of a happy death.
3. Point out the means of dying a Christian death.

C. THIRD PLAN

Preach on the preparation for death. To prepare for death one must:
1. Purify one's soul by a good confession and communion, making a firm purpose of amendment.
2. Try to die to sin, the world and oneself.
3. Submit to the will of God.
4. Give oneself completely to Our Lord.
5. Fall asleep nightly in the same state that one would like to be at the hour of death.
6. Set aside a little time each year to make a preparation for death.[1]

JUDGMENT

A. FIRST PLAN

Paint for your hearers a picture of the awe-inspiring scene of the general judgment, and what will take place. Outline the various signs that will precede it, the qualities of the Judge, His coming, the resurrection of the dead, the separation of the good and evil, the opening and reading of the Book of Life, the account of each one's stewardship which must be made and the terrible sentence that may be pronounced.

[1] There is an excellent exercise for the preparation for death in St. John Eudes's work on Christian perfection, *The Kingdom of Jesus* (New York, 1946), p. 312-344.

B. SECOND PLAN

Give an instruction on each of these points and the lessons to be learned from them.

C. THIRD PLAN

Suggest various means whereby the dreadful consequences of the last judgment may be avoided.

HELL

1. Describe the pains of hell, particularly as they will affect the senses.
2. Show how eternal torment may be avoided.

HEAVEN

1. Describe the infinite good and happiness God has prepared for those who love Him.
2. Point out the means whereby we may reach heaven.

PURGATORY

1. Show that purgatory is founded on the justice and mercy of God.
2. Stress the reasons why we should have pity on the souls in purgatory, helping them by our prayers so that they may reach heaven and glorify the Eternal Father.
3. Explain the means of helping the holy souls.

CHAPTER VIII*

COMPOSITION OF THE SERMON

IF THE PREACHER has studied the subject thoroughly, the words will come easily. At all costs, he must endeavor to be clear and simple, avoiding learned words and abstruse expressions that may not be understood.

The truly devoted priest, who is actuated only by the desire of preaching in the simplicity and spirit of Our Lord and His Apostles, *sicut ex Deo, coram Deo, in Christo* (2 Cor. 2, 17), will sedulously follow St. Paul's admonition to Timothy: "Keep that which is committed to thy trust, avoiding the profane novelties of words, and oppositions of knowledge falsely so called" (1 Tim. 6, 20).

The preacher should never use vulgarisms and improprieties; on the contrary, his language should be correct and precise. The discourse should never be over the heads of the people. Rather the sermon should be such that it will appeal to the hearts of the faithful, persuading and touching them in its simplicity. St. Paul refers to those who are fastidious about the choice of words, while sacrificing the sermon itself, as "adulterating the word of God" (2 Cor. 2, 17). The Fathers of the Church and the saints avoided that type of discourse as more appropriate to worldlings and profane orators. Their aim was to preach Jesus Christ Crucified. In the words of St. Francis de Sales, *non sectamur lenocinia rhetorum, sed veritates piscatorum.*[1]

The following rules will be helpful for the composition of the sermon:

---

* In this chapter we have transposed and combined chapters 21 and 22 of the French edition, *Oeuvres Complètes*, Vol. IV, p. 65 ff.

[1] *Letter to the Archbishop of Bourges.*

1. Choose with great care the subject to be treated, selecting a topic that will be useful and well-suited to the congregation.

2. Have in mind the aim of the particular sermon which is, of course, to make God loved, honored or feared, or to destroy some vice and establish a particular virtue in its place. So dispose the sermon material that your discourse will make your purpose clear and rightly dispose the congregation to the results you have in mind.

3. Study the subject matter in prayerful meditation.

4. Make a clear plan and follow it carefully. There is nothing which can be of greater assistance to a preacher than a well-thought-out and well-divided discourse, which the faithful can follow easily. It is well to state clearly the subject to be discussed and to enunciate the method which is to be used in treating it.

For example, if you choose humility for your subject, you will state that it is your intention to implant in the hearts of the faithful a great love for this virtue and an ardent desire of practising it. "It is my intention to make you love and embrace humility. Consequently, I shall suggest to you three points which will be helpful: *a.* What is humility? What are its marks and how do we recognize it? *b.* What are the motives which should induce us to practise it? *c.* What means should be used to acquire humility?"

5. Let the discourse be full of sound doctrine, short scriptural texts, natural comparisons and short anecdotes.

6. Do not quote too many passages of Scripture, or give too many expository reasons, for it is better to elucidate a few than to confuse the faithful with a bewildering number of illustrations.

7. Have the subject logically organized for what belongs to one part of the sermon may lose its value if introduced where it will be irrelevant.

8. Place striking passages from Sacred Scripture or comparisons at the end of the sermon. Reserve speculative or general motives for the beginning.

9. Do not pass from point to point without the proper transition or connective. Let there be smoothness and coherence in the composition, so that the whole discourse will hold the attention of the faithful.

10. Avoid monotony in diction and structure. Use variety in words and expressions.

11. Make the introduction to the sermon fairly short, delving at once into the main body of the subject.

12. Draw a moral lesson from each point. Let the conclusion be striking and moving.

13. This conclusion may be a summary or recapitulation. A text from Scripture makes a very effective ending; a prayer or aspiration may also be very apt.

14. Having very carefully thought out the plan of the sermon, you should write it down. Some speakers write merely the principal points or headings. Some write the entire sermon and memorize it. Others again make a skeleton outline, memorizing some portions, and relying on the various headings which they develop as they go along. There is another method which is particularly good. It consists in composing, ordering and possessing in the mind every part of the discourse, namely, exordium, division, various points, proofs, texts, stories and conclusion. After having studied, meditated upon and considered these points, one could even preach without writing a word, and the subject would be so imprinted upon the mind that the sermon could be used at any time in the future.

CHAPTER IX*

DELIVERY OF THE SERMON

THE MOST BEAUTIFUL thoughts and the most carefully written discourse if poorly delivered may represent a waste of time, whereas a very ordinary sermon if delivered with fluency, sincerity and warmth may produce the most efficacious results. These qualities contribute in no small measure to the preacher's success.

Pronunciation and correct use of language constitute a most important part of the office of preaching. No priest can afford to be negligent in these matters.

One of the most efficacious means at the disposal of the preacher is to play on the listeners' hearts, affections and emotions by the use of the human voice. He should spare no trouble to learn to modulate and inflect his voice properly, suiting it to the subject, now speaking softly, now forcefully, as occasion demands, with affection when speaking of virtue and with animation when preaching on sin. Never let the sermon become sing-song nor monotonous, sounding like a school-boy reciting a lesson by rote. Let the words flow naturally and simply, without affectation or studied attempts at oratory.

The preacher should be careful not to speak too slowly for fear of boring the faithful, but, on the other hand, he must not speak too fast as if he were trying to rush through the sermon. Otherwise, the whole discourse will have failed in its purpose.

On going into the pulpit, he should pitch his voice according to the size of the church, speaking neither too loudly nor too softly but so as to be heard by all.

_____
* This chapter includes the most practical suggestions as found in the French edition, *Oeuvres Complètes,* Vol. IV, p. 71 ff.

In order to speak with fluency and feeling, the speaker must care-fully learn the sermon, especially the beginning of each successive topic; otherwise he will stumble or grope for words and will not hold the attention of his hearers.

Though inflections of the voice must be made as the sermon pro-gresses, the speaker should never drop it so low as not to be heard nor reach such a pitch as to end in a scream.

When using such terms as *O my God, O Mother of God* and longer aspirations, let the warmth of the preacher's tone bespeak the fire of love in his heart.

Inexperienced preachers should give great attention to the matter of gestures and train themselves not to give the appearance of being wooden or stilted. On the other hand, the opposite extreme of affectation must be avoided. All gestures should be simple and natural as those used in ordinary conversation.

Do not use the same gestures throughout the sermon. Do not beat on the pulpit or play with a book that may happen to be there. Do not drop your head so low that the words are lost on your breast. Do not roll your eyes continually or raise them to heaven, but look at the congregation in general and at no individual in particular. Do not wave your arms or cross them on your bosom. Do not preach with your arms folded or with one hand holding the other. In a word, do nothing that is unbecoming to so holy and divine a function as the preaching of the word of God.

St. Francis de Sales says: "Let gestures be free, noble, generous, strong, holy, grave and measured. They should be free from restraint; noble as opposed to those of an uncultured person or a novice; generous as one who would speak to one's children; strong in the sense that they are convincing; holy, not seeking self-glorification; grave, not given to worldliness; measured and not used to cause ridicule or amusement." [1]

[1] *Letter to the Archbishop of Bourges.*

CHAPTER X

FAULTS TO BE AVOIDED IN PREACHING

IN ADDITION to several faults already mentioned, the following should be carefully avoided:

1. Guard against affected eloquence which can tend only to corrupt the Word of God. Do not seek to parade a knowledge of worldly subjects, but be concerned only with the spiritual. Do not transform the pulpit into a theatrical rostrum.

2. Avoid long-drawn-out preambles to excuse one's incapacity or unworthiness. Do not expound the difficulty of the subject to be treated, but get to the point at once. Do not make excuses and say that one has not had time to prepare. These things are childish and destroy whatever impression the priest might make.

3. In discussing grave and important matters, use only expressions and phrases which have been carefully thought out. Be sure, too, that they would bear the scrutiny of the most rigid theologians. If by chance you let slip a remark which might be misinterpreted, correct or explain it at once, lest it engender doubt or misunderstanding among the faithful.

4. Do not exaggerate. Stick to the plain unvarnished truth.

5. Do not use humor. Christ never sought to amuse his audience.

6. Do not forget to bow the head when the name of Jesus is mentioned.

7. Do not recite or talk in a sing-song manner, but naturally, warmly and forcefully. In this connection, one can school himself to avoid this fault by teaching catechism for then one must speak in a natural tone, by listening to other pulpit orators, by practising

alone, by preparing the material carefully, by watching the inflections, and by using questions often, such as, "How can you prove this truth?" "Do you recall what St. Paul says?" In this way you will acquire fluency and naturalness, and will avoid any semblance of sing-song and declamation.

8. Do not discourage the faithful, but rather, after pointing out the horror of sin, lift them up to new heights of hope by showing how they may practise and acquire virtue by serious and continued efforts. Show them, too, that, if they are willing and cooperative, God will give them graces of conversion and perseverance, and that it is far easier to be saved than to be lost. Likewise, they should be inspired with the means to avoid evil and to put their trust in God. "Tribulation and anguish upon every soul of man that worketh evil . . . but glory, and honour, and peace to every one that worketh good" (Rom. 2, 9-10).

9. Do not imitate those false preachers who are steeped in worldliness, who inject into preaching the spirit of the flesh and motives of avarice and vanity, who preach themselves and not Christ Crucified, using eloquence only for their glory and gratification, who fill the holy office of preaching simply as a means of livelihood and seek only flattery. Never stoop to imitate those who preach not Christian virtues but the vanities of earth, making the road to heaven sound easy and attractive by permitting laxity while minimizing the dangers of hell. Do not imitate those who never use Scripture but depend upon profane authors, who refer to secular sciences rather than to the truth of the Gospel and utter honeyed words which contain no food for thought nor grace of conversion.

10. Finally, do not follow those whose sermons merely arouse expressions of opinion concerning the preacher himself, such as, "What a learned man! What an eloquent speaker!" If listeners who praise in these words were asked what the priest said, they would be at a loss to give the slightest idea of his sermon for it was empty and devoid of substance. Whosoever would work for the salvation of souls, and not be reproved for failing in his duty, should never fall into these faults of misguided preachers, who endanger their own and the faithful's salvation.

11. Again I repeat, there is nothing against which a priest should guard himself more assiduously than vanity for through it many a preacher has fallen. If the great St. Paul avers that he feared he himself might become a castaway after he had preached to others, which of us should not tremble? Which of us should not be humbled? Should we not, indeed, employ every means at our disposal to banish vanity from our lives and preserve within our hearts a Christ-like humility? Should we not crush the slightest thought or feeling of self-love or complacency, mindful of our nothingness? Should we not shun the praises of men as a veritable poison, remembering that honor and glory are due God alone, begging Him to destroy pride within us, that our souls may know true humility?

CHAPTER XI*

FURTHER ADVICE TO PREACHERS

THE EXORDIUM should be short. Then, enter into the discourse at once, telling the faithful very plainly what the subject of the sermon is. Do not waste time describing the plan, but get to the point immediately.

If there be present a distinguished personage, such as a Cardinal or a Bishop, let the mark of respect paid him be short and without flattery, as becoming one who preaches Christ Jesus.

In proving some truth, put the strongest proofs at the beginning and at the end; keep the less important ones for the body of the sermon. If you use the device of making God speak directly to the people, do not employ words or terms unworthy or unbecoming. Likewise, this applies to the Blessed Virgin Mary and the Saints. In apostrophes to Our Lord, His Blessed Mother or the Saints, speak with the utmost respect.

When hurling maledictions upon sinful practices or describing the horrors of evil or the punishment of sinners, do not forget to inject a note of mercy and forgiveness lest the faithful be discouraged. When preaching about a Saint, make the discourse truthful and simple, showing forth his wonderful virtues, his works and his claims to spiritual greatness.

Let funeral sermons be restrained and pious, not flattering discourses to please the relatives of the dead person. Use these occasions to give particular emphasis to the inevitability of death and the nothingness of earthly things.

Finally, have no other aim in preaching than to enlighten men's minds, touch their hearts and make them better Christians. Remember

* This chapter has been slightly shortened.

that, if God demands an account of every idle word that man shall speak, how strictly will He judge those who while preaching made use of the divine word to please their own vanity, tickle the ears of their hearers or as means of parading their own knowledge and erudition. There are many priests in hell because on earth they thus profaned the word of God while preaching.

No matter who offends you or hurts you, say nothing from the pulpit which might cause the faithful to notice that you harbor spite or bitterness. If you have been the victim of calumnies or lies and have suffered them sufficiently long, and fear that your work may be hindered thereby, then it might be well to justify yourself in the pulpit, calmly and modestly.

CHAPTER XII

TOUCHING THE HEARTS OF THE FAITHFUL

In order to impress your hearers, put into practice what has been written in "Chapter II" concerning the interior and exterior dispositions required and the exemplary life that you should lead. The word of God is all the more effective when it is reflected in the life of the preacher.

Preach solid doctrine, using texts of Scripture and passages from the writings of the Fathers. Give good and convincing reasons in support of your theme and, since nothing moves more than the truth, your hearers will be won to Christ.

Observe faithfully the suggestions on pronunciation and gestures in Chapter IX.

Be assiduous in prayer and meditation. Therein you shall find food for sermons and light to understand the beauty of the Christian truths. If you are animated with the truth of what you preach, you cannot help animating others. When your heart and your mind are enlightened by the Eternal Father, you will be more able to give forth His doctrines than if you simply culled them or studied them from books. There will be almost the same difference between these doctrines as there is between raw food and well-cooked viands.

Hence St. Gregory the Great[1] and St. Thomas Aquinas[2] say that preaching should proceed from the fulness of contemplation, and that

---

[1] *De perfectis viris post contemplationem suam redeuntibus, dicitur* (Ps.44): *Memoriam suavitatis tuae eructabunt* (Homil. 5 in Ezech.).

[2] *Unum quidem (opus vitae activae) ex plenitudine contemplationis derivatur, sicut doctrina et praedicatio (Sum. Theo.* I^a II^{ae}, q. 188, art. 6).

preachers should be as nearly as possible perfect men, filled with God's goodness, which they pour out from the fulness of their hearts.

The truly apostolic priest will need no other medium to touch the hearts of the faithful than to prepare, accompany and follow his sermon with prayer, asking God for the light to draw from the Divine Word the help he himself needs to move those to whom he speaks. *Res quae in se ipsa non arserit, alium non accendit,* says St. Gregory.[3] There is no heart that is so cold that it will not be inflamed by a good meditation: *In meditatione mea exardescet ignis* (Ps. 38, 4).

The priest being himself convinced and inflamed with the doctrine he is preaching, should pronounce with love and devotion the words of his discourse. He will not indulge in vehement language nor give vent to anger and indignation, but rather will make his sincerity and fervor manifest in his every word and gesture. Thus, his congregation will know that he speaks from a heart full of compassion and love for sinners, and that he is fired with zeal for God. His words will be like living coals which will inflame even the hardest hearts. Although the lips may speak to the ears, the heart always speaks to the heart.

He will dispose of his time so that he will be able to prepare for the divine office of preaching. Whenever he is to preach in the morning, he should allow himself enough time for the celebration of Holy Mass. St. John Chrysostom says that the tongue which has received the Sacred Body and Blood of Christ, is a terror to the devil and is consequently a most powerful instrument to touch the hearts of hardened sinners.[4]

Before going to the church to preach, the speaker should make one last rapid survey of his topic to make sure that he is fully prepared. Consequently, he should avoid other work or conversations which might distract him. There is nothing more unbecoming than to see a priest about to speak the word of God talking frivolously with others before mounting the pulpit. It is well to kneel before the Blessed Sacrament for a few moments before the sermon and to proceed to the pulpit with his eyes cast down and his whole being giving evidence of the seriousness of what is to be done.

[3] *Moral.* 91, cap. 28.
[4] St. John Eudes does not give the reference for this statement.

Use Sacred Scripture, especially the words of the Prophets and of Our Lord Jesus Christ, which are particularly effective.

Do not be too long or yet too short. Put vigor and force into every part of the discourse, but especially in the conclusion.

After the sermon, go down from the pulpit modestly with a devout and humble deportment.

CHAPTER XIII

TEACHING THE DISPOSITIONS REQUIRED
FOR RECEIVING THE WORD OF GOD

To MAKE the preaching of the Word of God effective and fruitful, the faithful, as well as the priest, must do their part; therefore, you must teach the people how to profit by sermons. When you are going to deliver a sermon in a parish, you might first point out to the people the best methods for profitable cooperation. These may be summed up in five points: 1. Dispositions regarding the Word of God; 2. Dispositions regarding God Himself; 3. Dispositions regarding the house of God; 4. Dispositions regarding the preacher; 5. Dispositions regarding the hearers themselves.

Explain these dispositions very clearly to the congregation.

1. They should have a great respect for the Word of God, and regard the assistance at a sermon, not as a commonplace act but as one of the most important and necessary for the preservation of their faith. "Faith then cometh by hearing; and hearing by the word of Christ," says St. Paul (Rom. 10, 17). The Sacred Scripture classifies those who know no God with those who lack preachers. "And many days shall pass in Israel, without the true God, and without a priest a teacher, and without the law" (2 Par. 15, 3). The law of God, which is the basis of our faith, comes to us through preaching.

Make the faithful understand that assistance at a sermon is of such importance that St. Augustine compares it to Holy Communion. He assures us that the person who listens carelessly to the Word of God is just as guilty as he who allows the Sacred Host to fall to the ground. *Non minus reus erit qui verbum Dei negligenter audierit,*

*quem ille qui corpus Christi sua negligentia, in terram cadere
permiserit.*[1]

It follows, then, that even as the Christian should not approach
the Holy Table without preparation, so he should not hear a sermon
without the proper dispositions. There should be a desire to listen
attentively and with profit, and a fixed determination to make use of
the knowledge required. There should also be the realization that
one is not listening to the harangue of an orator or demagogue, but
rather to the exposition of the Word of God, which is to be preserved
in one's heart and practised as a sure means of salvation.

2. The faithful should realize their great debt of gratitude to God
for the grace bestowed upon them in the gift of the priest, Christ's
representative, to show them the way to heaven. They should never
leave the church without saying a prayer of gratitude to God for the
sermon to which they have listened. If they fail to thank God for the
spiritual nourishment, they are guilty, to say the least, of gross ingratitude.

3. The faithful must remember the sanctity of the church where
the sermon is to be preached. They must respect and reverence it as
the house of God, where noise and useless conversation are out of
place. As the dwelling place of Him in whose presence the very
angels tremble, nothing untoward or unseemly must be tolerated or
countenanced.

4. For the preacher himself they must entertain much respect and
charity. *Respect* for he is God's messenger and Christ's ambassador,
taking the Master's place, clothed with His authority and speaking
in His name. Well, indeed, may we say that he is the instrument
through which Christ Himself speaks: "For it is not you that speak,
but the Spirit of your Father that speaketh in you" (Matt. 10, 20).
"Christ . . . speaketh in me," says St. Paul (2 Cor. 13, 3), "God as
it were exhorting by us" (*Ibid.* 5, 20).

Charity for the faithful must not censure or judge rashly him who
is preaching, nor misinterpret his words or intentions. *Charity* in
that they must not find fault because the preacher repeats and stresses
the same truths others before him have taught. After all, there

[1] *Lib.* L. *Homiliarum*, Homil. 26.

is no better food then wholesome bread taken frequently; good medicine used continually may effect a cure; music played often brings unalloyed pleasure. *Charity,* not despising those preachers who, because of their mediocrity of talents, are not so forceful or eloquent as their more gifted brethren. It should be borne in mind that it is not the preacher half so much as the preaching which counts. Should we receive a letter from the king, we would cherish and treasure it, without considering the talents or character of the messenger who delivered it.

5. The faithful should have *purity of intention,* for which two things are necessary: the first is a complete renunciation of all that is not proper, for instance, to hear a sermon for amusement or pastime, out of curiosity or from some selfish motive. The second is an act of protestation to Jesus Christ that they wish to hear His word in order to learn the truths of eternity.

They should *purify their conscience* by an act of contrition so that nothing may hinder God's grace from operating in their souls.

The faithful must also practise *humility* and *docility* by a) dispelling any trace of vanity and feeling of superiority to the priest; b) remembering that no one is so learned that he does not need further instruction, as St. Ambrose[2] and St. Augustine[3] point out; c) recalling that the words of the priest are meant for each listener. If some vice is mentioned, let no one make the mistake of thinking the remarks are intended only for others. If perchance they have no application for particular individuals, let those favored souls thank God in a spirit of deepest humility.

The faithful should receive God's word with edification and piety. Teach them to read their prayer books while awaiting the sermon, thus using the time they are in church for their soul's advantage. When the priest has entered the pulpit, let them give all attention and respect, seeing in him the person of Christ the Saviour. They should make the sign of the cross with him, with devotion and reverence, and during the sermon proper, they should give their concentration to the priest,

[2] *De Officiis,* L. I, cap. I.
[3] *Epist. ad Mercatorem.*

banishing every profane thought or distraction. They should be taught not to turn around or gape at their neighbor, but to keep their minds fixed on the subject being treated and their hearts united to God.

After the sermon, the faithful should not leave the church without thanking God for all the benefits received from the sermon and praying for the grace to cooperate with the truths exposed; meditating upon what the priest has said, singling out certain points or passages for further reflection; beseeching Our Lord's help for the preacher, that his work on this and all future occasions may be fruitful of good. Even as one thanks ordinary teachers who instruct in profane subjects, so, too, one should be grateful to him who nourishes with the words of life. *In Christo Jesu per Evangelium ego vos genui* (1 Cor. 4, 15). What ingratitude would the faithful show, indeed, if after the sermon they criticize the priest, or, instead of thanking God for the help given them, merely find faults with the efforts of the preacher?

These, then, are the dispositions required that the faithful may hear the Word of God with profit, which every priest must seek to instil into them. To which I would add that the priest should preach, not only by word and example but also by prayer. At Mass, during the Divine Office and at all times, his constant entreaty to God should be that his words will be efficacious for good. *Det voci suae vocem virtutis* (Ps. 67, 34). He should pray that he may be able to destroy in the minds and hearts of his hearers all that is not in conformity with the divine will, or whatever may impede the fruitful reception of the Word of God.

CHAPTER XIV

THE TEACHING OF CATECHISM

CATECHISM is most useful and necessary, not only for children but also for adults who are often ignorant of the faith. Priests, therefore, should give as much attention as possible to this part of their sacerdotal duty and should see that their flock is properly instructed. Pastors especially should look upon the teaching of catechism as one of their most important tasks.

There is, however, a common fault which priests must avoid at all costs, which consists in thinking themselves so far above the simple teaching of catechism that they make of it a lecture in theology, which no one understands. This smacks of vanity and pride and destroys whatever spiritual good their work might accomplish.

The priest who would teach catechism well should make it a point to explain the simple matter of faith as set forth in the catechism, and employ his time, not in preaching nor in long instruction, but in questioning and instructing the children.

Naturally, teaching catechism will not demand the same type of gravity and seriousness as preaching; nevertheless the priest must preserve a certain dignity while at the same time trying to make himself one with the children. He must treat them with cordiality and gentleness, yet not give way to levity. Above all else, he must not tolerate any irreverence on their part in the church, but enjoin upon them due respect for the sanctity of the house of God.

If his youthful charges are inclined to be unruly or irreverent in any way, he should rebuke them gently at first, and then with becoming severity. Failing to see any improvement from this type of children, he should advise their parents.

Before beginning the catechism class, a short prayer should be said. The *Veni Sancte Spiritus* is recommended. Then, the children should be taught to pray aloud with the teacher, asking the blessing of Christ and His holy Mother. Before the first class, a short instruction may be given to show the necessity and excellence of learning about God and His holy law.

As the sign of the cross is most important, and yet so many persons persist in making it irreverently and carelessly, no catechism class could begin better than by insisting on the correct use of this blessed act of faith.

To make the children repeat either singly or in pairs the answers contained in the book being used, is an excellent manner of impressing upon their youthful minds the necessary truths of religion. A new subject may be broached by saying: "Today we shall take up such and such . . . ." It may be very helpful to have the children question one another. Make them speak distinctly, but do not let them talk in a babble of confusion. Do not give them too much to memorize at one time. A short instruction or moral lesson may be drawn from each one of these catechism classes.

When the Incarnation is discussed, do not use words and expressions to cause wonder or arouse curiosity, but simply explain that the little body of Jesus was formed in the Blessed Virgin Mary and His soul was made out of nothing like our own. The body and soul are united in the person of the Son of God.

Teach the children the excellence of serving Mass. See that the boys learn how to pronounce the Latin and serve at the altar in a becoming manner. Point out the holiness of this function and how privileged they are to be admitted within the sanctuary.

Little stories and anecdotes may be used with profit and serve as a fitting conclusion for any catechism class. They should, however, be prepared in advance.

Do not be content merely to teach catechism, but endeavor to make your children good sturdy Catholics. Teach them to have the love of God in their hearts and a salutary fear of breaking His commandments. Impress upon them a profound hatred of sin and a tender devotion towards Jesus Christ and His Blessed Mother, St. Joseph, their guardian angel and their patron saint. Urge them to go to confession and Holy Communion very often. Guide them in the ways of obedience to their parents and the civil law. Enjoin upon them charity, modesty and devotion. Infuse into their young hearts real respect for the church and the cemetery.

Preparation for First Communion is the most important event in their lives; therefore, the subject should be explained with special care. The Sacrament of Penance will have to be treated well lest their tender consciences be formed falsely. Everything which concerns Our Lord in the Blessed Sacrament should be outlined clearly.

Do not make exceptions in dealing with the children, singling out certain brighter ones, but treat all alike and even go out of your way to be kind to the backward ones. Prizes may be helpful to encourage them to learn their catechism.

After catechism class is finished, a hymn may be sung and a prayer said, perhaps the *Our Father*, the *Hail Mary*, or the *Creed*.

Do not keep the children too long for they tire easily and lose interest in coming again. It is good to spend a little time in recreation with the children after the class.

It need hardly be added that, since morning and evening prayers are so important, the teaching of them should occupy a considerable portion of every priest's time. If the pastor is not able to discharge these duties himself, he may select some devout Catholics to assist him.

A set hour for the classes is imperative, and one that will be convenient for all. Teach the children to come to the church and take their places at the hour fixed. Then, kneel down and say a little prayer. They must understand that the church is a holy place; hence, it must not be profaned by talking and misbehavior.

While the children are in class, nothing else must be considered or talked about except the lessons for the day. Do not let them whisper among themselves; do not permit them to play or act lightly. Teach them to regard one another as brothers and sisters, not shunning this one or that one or having hard feelings towards any other child.

Teach them obedience to parents, love for God and His holy Mother, devotion to the Rosary. They should say the beads daily to obtain the favor of living and dying in the state of grace.

Part III

THE GOOD CONFESSOR

Part III

THE GOOD CONFESSOR[1]

CHAPTER I

EXCELLENCE AND IMPORTANCE OF THE OFFICE OF CONFESSOR

JESUS CHRIST has made every priest His associate in the infinite power of His Divinity. He has given the priest a power greater than any other in heaven and on earth except that of His Blessed Mother. He has bestowed upon His earthly representative a power unequalled by that of any human prince or king; a power denied even to the Prophets of old; a power strong enough to destroy Satan, erase sin and infuse divine grace. St. John Chrysostom rightly says: *Omnis potestas caelorum sacerdotibus commissa est; quaenam potestas major esse quaeat?"* [2]

The Son of God has made the priest judge with Himself, giving him the power to pass sentence, to forgive or to condemn others. "The Father hath given all judgment to the Son" (John 5, 22). "The Son gave all powers of judgment to the priest," says St. John Chrysostom.[3] Elsewhere the same saint adds that the throne of the priest is in heaven. *Sacerdoti thronus in caelis collocatus est.*[4] St. Clement, disciple of St. Peter, declares that the priest holds in his hands the keys of life and

---

[1] This work was originally published as a separate volume with opening paragraphs discussing all the powers of the priest. Some of these have been omitted to focus the reader's attention on the powers of the confessor.

[2] *De Sacerdotio*, lib. 3, c. 4.

[3] *Idem.*, loc. cit.

[4] *Homilia 5 in illud Isaiae: In anno quo mortuus est rex Ozias.*

death, God having given him the power of condemning or delivering the sinner.[5]

Thus, O priests of God, you are one with the Sovereign Priest in a most intimate association. To you He communicates His own divine qualities. Guard carefully the talents He has bestowed upon you lest in neglecting them you be cast into exterior darkness. Use them for the glory of God and the salvation of souls.

Do you want to learn how to exercise these divine powers usefully and efficaciously? Then make proper use of the Tribunal of Penance. There you exercise the role of mediator, redeemer, physician and judge. There you continue the work of the redemption; there you should act with humility and patience like unto Christ's. Though the task be hard, remember how Our Lord Jesus Christ suffered for souls and for the destruction of sin. Recall the prolonged torments endured by our Saviour to redeem mankind, and so discharge your duty as confessors unhurriedly without display of irritability or weariness.

In the Tribunal of Penance you are the living image of the power and majesty of the Son of God. There you are as it were little gods, vested with the powers of God, doing what belongs by right to Him alone, blotting out sin, communicating the grace of the Holy Ghost to souls. Consequently, in the Sacred Tribunal you should serve the interests of God, thinking only of Him, desiring only to establish His kingdom in the hearts of men.

As a judge representing the Supreme Judge, yours is the power of bestowing or refusing absolution. God communicates to you His power of judge in a more excellent manner than He does to the judges of earthly courts. They judge bodies; you judge souls. They judge temporal affairs; you judge eternal ones. Their power is a passing one; yours reaches beyond to eternity. What you absolve or condemn on earth is absolved and condemned in heaven. Their judgments are recorded on paper; yours are written with the Blood of Christ in the eternal books of divine justice.

These reflections show you the importance of your duties as confessor. If you discharge them well, sin will be destroyed and grace will be infused into men's souls. The devil will be expelled and the Holy

[5] *In Constitutionibus apostolicis* c. 37.

Ghost will be imparted to souls, so that they will become a terrestrial paradise instead of an abode of Satan. Men will be reborn spiritually. The fruits of the Passion will be applied in their fulness. The Blood of the Lamb will wash and purify and the words applied by the Sacred Writers will be fulfilled in souls: *Quam pulchra es, amica mea, quam pulchra es* (Cant. 4, 1). Finally the children of Satan will become children of God; the members of the devil will become the members of Jesus Christ.

I say "if you discharge your duties well," for a confessor who does not act as he should, may be guilty of grave wrongdoing. Instead of destroying sin he merely establishes the soul more firmly in its grip. He ensnares the sinner in a net of evil and gives him a false sense of security. "Peace, peace, and there is no peace" (Jer. 6, 14). Instead of driving out the devil he merely strengthens Satan's hold on the unhappy penitent. Instead of raising the sinner to life he kills him; instead of giving life to Christ in souls, he crucifies the Redeemer anew. Instead of cleansing souls, he soils them; instead of beautifying souls, he renders them more hideous; instead of filling up what is wanting to Christ's Passion (Col. 1, 24), he renders the sufferings of the Saviour vain and useless.

These things are said for the priest's enlightenment in the administration of the Sacrament of Penance and to make him realize the importance of his holy office. The confessor, who is fired with zeal and filled with prudence, is a treasure in the Church of God. Following as he does the teachings of the Gospel and the guidance of the Church, he is a spiritual physician, an equitable judge, a charitable mediator, and a merciful saviour among men.

But the bad or careless confessor, who is ignorant, imprudent, lazy and negligent, is a plague in Christ's holy Church. He is not an emissary of God, but an agent of the devil. He is not a doctor of heaven but of hell, for as God has his patriarchs so the devil has heresiarchs. As God has His prophets, apostles and martyrs, so, too, the devil has his prophets, apostles and martyrs.

The unworthy confessor is not a divine judge, but another Pilate pronouncing sentence upon Christ and the souls that the Son of God died to redeem. He is not a mediator for God, but for the devil, not a dispenser of heavenly blessings but a profaner of divine mysteries and sacraments. In a word, instead of being another Christ, he is a very devil.

No tongue can tell the evil the bad confessor commits. He does great harm to the Church, persecuting it more cruelly than Nero, Diocletian and the tyrants of history. Would to God that all priests who administer the Sacrament of Penance might meditate seriously on these truths! Would to God that they might consider the inestimable good that they would accomplish if they were animated with the same spirit and if they followed the same maxims! They would completely overthrow the devil's tyranny and snatch souls from perdition. Would they might open their ears to the words of the Holy Spirit: "Take heed what you do: for you exercise not the judgment of man, but of the Lord" (2 Par. 19, 6). Take heed in very truth for what you do is not temporary, but eternal. What you perform does not concern an earthly kingdom, but the Kingdom of God. You handle the treasures of heaven; you are responsible for the salvation or the damnation of souls. *Videte quid faciatis.* Remember to bring to your task the care and application demanded; have the necessary qualifications. Otherwise, the absolutions you give may become so many damnations for you. Never forget that when you say the words, *Ego te absolvo,* the Eternal Judge may reply, if you are unworthy, *Ego te condemno.*

If you were to ask what are these necessary qualifications, I would answer that they are six, namely: zeal for souls, science, charity, prudence, piety and fidelity to the secrecy of confession. To each of these qualifications an entire chapter will be devoted.

CHAPTER II

ZEAL FOR THE SALVATION OF SOULS

THE FIRST and most important obligation of the priest is to labor for the salvation of souls. For that purpose Christ established the priesthood in the Church. For that end should a young man embrace holy orders. When he enters the priesthood, his soul should be so filled with grace that he is able to sanctify and save the souls of others.

Thus, priests are called "saviours" in Sacred Scripture (Abdias 1, 21). Christ came into this world to effect the salvation of souls, and for thirty-three years He devoted every thought, word, action, suffering, and even His very life for that purpose. Then, He returned to His Heavenly Father, but before departing He appointed successors to take His place. Who are these successors? They are His priests, who must seek always to imitate the ineffable love and ardent zeal of His Sacred Heart.

"He who is content with saving himself and neglects the salvation of others," says St. John Chrysostom, "cannot secure his own salvation." *Qui sua contentus salute, negligit alienam, nec suam consequi potest.*[1] If that is true of the ordinary Christian, how much more can it be said of priests and especially of confessors! Since the work of the confessional is difficult, they need special zeal for the honor of their Master and for the salvation of their brethren.

Thus to inflame your hearts with this holy zeal, it is well to ponder how pleasing it is to God to work with Him for the spiritual welfare of your neighbor. These considerations will apply to all priests as well as to confessors.

[1] *In cap.* 18 Matt. *homilia* 60.

What, then, does it mean to save souls created to the image and likeness of God and redeemed by the Precious Blood of His Divine Son? It is the great work of God, the task of the God-Man and His Holy Mother. It is the mission of the Church, the desire of the angels and saints and of all chosen souls on earth. In a word, it is the supreme work of all works.

1. *The Salvation of Souls is the Great Work of God*

First of all, the salvation of souls is the great work of God. *Domine, opus tuum* (Hab. 3, 2). Herein God employs all His thoughts, actions, mysteries, power, wisdom, goodness, mercy, and all His other divine attributes. All that God accomplishes in Himself from all eternity and outside Himself in time is directed towards this very end.

What does God do in Himself from all eternity? He gives birth to His Son, and from the Father and the Son proceeds the Holy Ghost. It follows that even as God gave being to His Son, it was His eternal design also to send Him into the world to save man. Likewise, it is clear that the Son, born from all eternity, had that same intention. And the Holy Ghost proceeding from the Father and the Son shared that same design for man's salvation. If one could speak of moments of time when referring to timeless eternity, one might say that at the very moment that the Holy Ghost proceeds from all eternity, it is His will to come into the souls of men and to transport them from earth to heaven. Thus it is apparent that all that God accomplishes within Himself is associated with the salvation of souls.

So it is, too, with all that God accomplished outside of Himself. If He created the world, it was that He might people it with beings who would by their good works fit themselves to enjoy the beatific vision; that He might make a place where men would battle against the enemies of their souls, disposing themselves to merit heaven by practising faith, hope, charity, humility, patience and all the other virtues. If God made a heaven, it was to share it with those who conquered the enemies of salvation. If He established a Church on earth, it was to give men easy and efficacious means of saving their souls through the sacraments. If He made a hell with frightful torments, it was to impress those who are actuated more by fear than by love to work out their salvation in fear and trembling; to chastise those who are so far spent in sin as to be willing to yield their souls to sin and perdition and to drag others to ruin with them.

From the foregoing we learn that the salvation of souls is the end and purpose of all the works of the power, wisdom and goodness of God. It is, therefore, the great work of His divine majesty.

2. *The Salvation of Souls is the Great Work of the God-Man*

Saving souls is likewise the great work of the God-Man. Listen to His very words: "As the Father knoweth me, and I know the Father: and I lay down my life for my sheep" (John 10, 15). St. Thomas Aquinas explains these words by saying that God the Son knows the inclinations of His Father; He knows what the Father loves most, namely the souls of men. Nothing is nearer to God's heart than their salvation; that is the reason why Christ gives His life for souls. A little later we read in the same chapter of St. John: "That which my Father hath given me is greater than all" (John 10, 29). According to the Angelic Doctor, this means that the God-Man holds in higher regard the souls His Father has given Him than anything else, even His own body and His own life, since He sacrifices them for the salvation of men.[2]

Thus does Our Lord speak and behold what He does for souls! See Him coming forth from the bosom of the Father, putting aside His glory to become one of us. See Him annihilate Himself at the time of the Incarnation: *Exinanivit semetipsum* (Phil. 2, 7). See Him reduced to the helplessness of a child, born in a stable and dependent on others for every single thing. See Him suffering every type of hardship, shedding His blood eight days after His birth, fleeing into Egypt, separated from the Chosen People, living seven years among strangers. See Him laboring in the carpenter shop with Joseph and doing penance in the solitude of the desert. Behold Him conversing and dwelling with men, eating and drinking with sinners, going about preaching, suffering the indignities of His terrible Passion, even kneeling before a devil according to Sacred Scripture, "One of you is a devil" (John 6, 71). Behold Him in the Garden of Gethsemani, overwhelmed with

[2] *Expositio aurea Sti. Thomae in Joannem* 10, 15.

anguish, sweating blood, His Heart oppressed with sorrow. Behold Him in the midst of His enemies, mocked as a common criminal before Annas, Caiaphas and Pilate, buffeted, spit upon and reviled, scourged and stripped of His garments. Behold Him crowned with thorns, placed on the same level as Barrabas, a notorious criminal, condemned to death, crucified and dying on the cross. Behold His Sacred Body laid in the sepulchre.

Seek to evaluate the all-consuming love with which He endured all these things for souls. You will find that His love was so perfect that He was ready to suffer still more if in doing so He might benefit individual souls. He loves them so much that He would be willing to suffer even eternally for them. That infinite love made Him willing not only to suffer in Jerusalem, but also in every place in the world, and even to accept atrocities much more humiliating and terrible than those of Calvary.

What does all this signify? Simply that all these things, these mysteries of the Incarnation, Birth, Circumcision, Passion and Death, are so many voices crying out to us: "Thus Jesus loved souls." Thus did He love and prefer them to anything else, even His own life. For that reason, He abandoned everything of His own, stripped Himself of all glory and happiness that He might insure their perpetual felicity in heaven. That was why He gave His most precious possessions, His Body and Blood, even His life, and was ready to endure an eternity of suffering, if such were the will of His eternal Father.

O my Saviour, who could conceive and express Thy love for men? O merciful Jesus, since Thou dost love souls so much, surely those persons, who cooperate with Thee in the work of redemption, must be very close to Thee. On Thy ministers surely Thou must lavish an abundance of grace and blessings.

3. The Salvation of Souls is the Great Work of the Mother of God

The salvation of immortal souls is also the great work of the Mother of God. Why did Almighty God choose the Blessed Virgin Mary to be the Mother of God? Why did He preserve her from original sin and make her holy from the very first moment of her life? Why did He shower upon her so many privileges, ornamenting her with grace and virtue? Why did He confer upon her so much wisdom, goodness, meekness and such great power in heaven, in hell and on earth? It was simply that she might be worthy to cooperate with her Divine Son in man's redemption. All the Fathers of the Church say clearly that she is co-redemptrix with Christ in the work of our salvation. I hear Our Lord and His Blessed Mother saying to St. Brigid, whose revelations are approved by the Church, that Adam and Eve lost the world by eating an apple, but that they saved it by a heart: *quasi uno Corde mundum salvavimus (Revel. extravag.* cap. 3), that is Our Lord and His Mother had but one heart, one love, one sentiment, one mind and one will with each other. As the Sacred Heart of Jesus was a furnace of love for men, so the heart of His loving Mother was inflamed with charity and zeal for souls. Christ immolated Himself upon the cross for the redemption of mankind, and Mary made a similar sacrifice in undergoing untold sufferings and sorrows.

What more shall I say? I would even go so far as to state that the Blessed Virgin Mary so loves souls that she was and is ready to undergo every torment of earth to save even a single soul. There have been many saints in history who have offered to do that very thing. How can we say less of the Queen of saints? Who can doubt that she would not willingly undergo a thousand hells, rather than behold her Son so afflicted? Yet she accepted this unspeakable sorrow in order to co-operate with her Divine Son in the redemption of the world. The salvation of souls is, therefore, the great work of the Blessed Virgin Mary, Mother of God.

4. The Salvation of Souls is the Great Work of the Church, of the Angels and Saints, of the Apostles

The salvation of souls is the great work of the Church, the reason for its establishment, the purpose of its sacraments and ceremonies. It is the object of the ministry of priests, bishops and supreme pontiffs. It is the aim of all the Councils, laws and functions of the Church.

It is also the work of the angels, for St. Paul says, "Are they not all ministering spirits, sent to minister for them who shall receive the inheritance of salvation?" (Heb. 1, 14).

It is likewise the great work of the Apostles and saints. Listen to St. Paul speaking to the Christians of his day: "I most gladly will spend and be spent myself for your souls" (2 Cor. 12, 15). To the Jews who had persecuted him and conspired against his very life he speaks thus: "I lie not, my conscience bearing me witness in the Holy Ghost; that I have great sadness, and continual sorrow in my heart. For I wished myself to be anathema from Christ, for my brethren, who are my kinsmen according to the flesh" (Rom. 9, 1-3). "These latter words suggest," says St. John Chrysostom, "that the great apostle was ready to sacrifice even the happiness of heaven on behalf of his brethren."[3] According to Cassianus St. Paul means that he would willingly suffer the everlasting punishment of hell to deliver the Jews from it, if that were possible and in accordance with God's will.[4]

Be not surprised at so great zeal in St. Paul for many great doctors say that Moses was inspired with the same thoughts and feelings when he prayed for the Chosen People: "Either forgive them this trespass, or if Thou do not, strike me out of the book that Thou hast written" (Exod. 32; 31-32).[5]

Speaking to his flock, St. John Chrysostom said: "I would willingly be a thousand times anathema for your salvation."[6] St. Catherine of Siena and other holy persons offered to suffer the pains of the damned for souls. And have we not met a holy person[7] so actuated by God's love

---

[3] *In cap. IX Epist. ad Rom.*

[4] *Collat.* 32, cap. 6.

[5] In this paragraph and the preceding one St. John Eudes simply paraphrases a passage from Cornelius a Lapide, *in Epist. ad Rom.* 9, 3:

"*Optat Paulus heroico quodam excessu quasi caesae caritatis, quae abstrahit, nec considerat an res sit possibilis, an secundum Dei ordinationem, necnon: vel si non abstrahit, optat sub tacita conditione, si Deus vellet et si fieri posset; optat, inquam, aeternam separationem, non a caritate, sed a beatitudine et gloria futura cum Christo, ut Judaei salventur. Imo optat, ait Chrysostomus, in aeternum perire; et, ut Cassianus ait Collat. 32, cap. 31, aeternis addici poenis, idque tum pro gloria Dei, ne scilicet Deus a Judeais blasphemetur, sed in aeternum laudetur, tum pro salute ipsorum Judaeorum. Optat ergo hic Paulus illud, idem quod in simili casu optavit Moyses (Exod. 32, 31), dicens: 'Aut dimitte eis hanc noxiam, aut, si no facis, dele me de libro tuo quem scripsisti.'*"

[6] *Hom. 3 in Acta Apostolorum.*

[7] The person to whom St. John Eudes refers is Marie des Vallees, a holy woman of Coutances in Normandy. See Father Joseph Mary Ory, *The Origin of the Order of Our Lady of Charity* (Buffalo, 1918), p. 95.

that she was granted the privilege of suffering unlimited torments which others had merited, merely to save these souls from perdition? Have we not heard her protesting her willingness to undergo the torments of hell rather than to have a single soul commit a mortal sin?

With these realities before you, be not surprised at the explanation of St. John Chrysostom of the words of St. Paul, "I wished myself to be an anathema from Christ, for my brethren" (Rom. 9, 3), for the zeal and love of the apostles transcended the charity and zeal of the saints and holy persons to whom reference has just been made.

This then is the great work of the apostles, of the saints whose only desire was to witness the fulfilment of the words of the Queen of saints in her Magnificat: "He hath filled the hungry with good things; and the rich he hath sent empty away" (Luke 1, 53). Who are the hungry? The saints who hungered and thirsted for souls. Who are the rich? The demons who have in their possession the treasure of countless souls purchased by the Precious Blood of the Lamb.

O my Saviour, when will these sacred words of Thy holy Mother be at last fulfilled? O Mary, my Mother, when will thy great prophecy come true? When will the devils be deprived of their spoils? When will the zeal of thy loving children be satiated? May every creature of heaven and earth prostrate himself before the throne of God to implore this grace!

5. *The Salvation of Souls is the Great Work of Priests*

To all the foregoing considerations permit me to add that the salvation of souls is the great work of priests, whose holy office was founded simply for man's salvation. How weighty are the obligations of priests! What a burden is laid upon their shoulders! Listen to the words of the Prophet Ezechiel, "I will seek that which was lost: and that which was driven away, I will bring again. And I will bind up that which was broken and I will strengthen that which was weak, and that which was fat and strong I will preserve: and I will feed them in judgment" (Ezech. 34, 16). Five things must be observed to discharge these sacerdotal obligations.

The first is for the priest to conduct himself so that his life may be a model of priestly devotion. "Be thou an example of the faithful in word, in conversation, in charity, in faith, in chastity" (1 Tim. 4, 12). "In all things shew thyself an example of good works, in doctrine, in integrity, in gravity" (Titus 2, 7). A priest should be such that he may say at all times, "For we are the good odour of Christ unto God" (2 Cor. 2, 15). Thus, he should be a living example of charity, purity, sobriety, humility and patience. He should be like John the Baptist, "A voice of one crying in the wilderness" (Luke 3, 4), that is, crying to sinners in the wilderness of the world: "Do penance."

Do you not know that the robe of the Great High Priest was adorned with little bells to show, as St. Jerome explains, that the priest should be *totus vocalis*,[8] all voice, and that everything about him should be a tongue preaching and instructing those who come in contact with him. *Universa vocalia sint: quidquid agit, quidquid loquitur, sit doctrina populorum*.[9]

Nothing is so potent as the example given by the priest be it good or bad. Thus, St. Gregory says that priests deserve eternal damnation as often as they give bad example to those confided to their care. *Pastores tot mortibus digni sunt, quot ad subditos suos perditionis exempla transmittunt*.[10]

The priest should be "a burning and a shining light" (John 5, 35), burning before God, shining before men; burning in prayer, shining in action; burning by example, shining by doctrine. "Let your light shine before men that they may see your good works, and glorify your Father who is in heaven," says St. Matthew (5, 16). And St. Bernard says that "the light shed by a priest must be so strong and so bright that the wind of vanity will not extinguish it."[11]

The second thing that the priest must do is to instruct the faithful on their Christian obligations. He must teach them to know and love God, to fear and serve Him through obedience to His commandments. He must lead them to know their Saviour, His principal mysteries, Jesus and Mary, the Church and the Sacraments. They must be made to pray in gratitude and petition for pardon and help. They should learn

[8] *Epistol. ad Fabiolam.*
[9] *Apud Corn. a Lapide, in Exod.*, 28, 35.
[10] *De cura pastorali*, p. 2, c. 3.
[11] *Serm. de Joan. Baptista*, Cf. A. Lapide, in Joan. 5, 35.

to recite their daily prayers with utmost care, the *Lord's Prayer,* the *Hail Mary,* the *Creed* and the *Confiteor.* Through exhortations from the pulpit and in catechism classes, the priest should encourage the faithful to cooperate to the fullest extent in their own salvation.

Thirdly, he should eradicate spiritual disorders from the lives of the flock. To do this he must know his people and their conduct. He should be unsparing in his pains to track down and root out evils which may exist; he should frequently visit the schools to instruct and guide the young in the way of salvation. He should enjoin great respect for the church and all holy places, insisting on proper deportment there at all times. He should keep everything pertaining to the altar in good order and see that the liturgical functions are carried out with the dignity becoming the King of heaven and earth.

Fourthly, the priest should practise charity. He should be affable and kind to all without distinction. He should be assiduous in visiting the sick, especially those in danger of death. He should console the afflicted and the needy, and be ever kind to the poor. He should advise those who seek his fatherly counsel, correct those who are wayward and seek to put an end to any quarreling among his parishioners.

Fifthly, he must administer the Sacraments with *holiness,* for the glory of God and becomingly lest through carelessness he neglect any requisite. Above all else, he should apply himself heartily to the administration of the Sacrament of Penance, for through it he will know the state of his people, their spiritual needs and weaknesses. Through it he will find the means of curing the ailments of their souls. He will open to them unexplored avenues of grace, will spread before them in his instructions and encouragements a banquet of heavenly delicacies.

These are the chief obligations of the priest and he must be ever vigilant lest even one soul be neglected or lost for the Sovereign Pastor will hold him responsible, and the price of Christ's Blood will be visited upon him. "I will require his blood at thy hand" (Ezech. 3, 20). I mention neglect for this makes him a murderer in God's eyes, a murderer of souls committed to his charge.

St. John Chrysostom observes that when priests allow themselves to fall into sin, the people quickly follow. Every soul will be held to a strict accounting of his own misdeeds, but the priest will also be held responsible for those of his flock who fall because of his example. *Sacerdotes non solum pro suis, sed etiam pro omnium peccatis reddituri sunt rationem.*[12]

"If each individual soul will find it difficult to render an account of his works on Judgment Day," says St. Augustine, "what must be said of priests, who must give an accounting of the souls committed to their care?" *Si pro se unusquisque vix poterit, in die Judicii, rationem reddere, quid de sacerdotibus futurum est, a quibus sunt omnium animae requirendae?* [13]

6. The Salvation of Souls is the Work of Works

Since the salvation of souls is the great work of God, of the God made man, of the Church, of the angels, the apostles and the saints, it is readily seen that it is the work of works, surpassing all others in time or eternity.

What indeed would be considered great human endeavors? Constructing great palaces or public buildings, raising armies and marching at their head into battle, being acclaimed as a mighty ruler? These would be great, no doubt, but remember the words of Sacred Scripture, "Vanity of vanities and all is vanity" (Eccles. 1, 2). All these things vanish and pass away. "That which is high to men is an abomination before God" (Luke 16, 15). To teach even a child to make the sign of the cross or instruct one of God's little ones, is a nobler work in the eyes of God than all human and natural undertakings.

Among the supernatural works there are five of paramount importance: 1. Fasting and mortification; 2. Works of mercy; 3. Prayer and contemplation; 4. Miracles; 5. Martyrdom. Yet, the saving of a soul is greater even than these works.

St. Chrysostom says: "The salvation of one soul is far greater than fasts or vigils or the austerities of the hermits; it is greater than to give most generous alms to the poor." [14]

Surely to ransom a soul from Purgatory is a marvelous act, but to

---

[12] *Homil. 38 in cap. XI. Matth.*
[13] *Lib. L. Homiliarum,* Hom. 7.
[14] *Orat. 5 contra Judaeos.*

snatch a soul from mortal sin is greater for theologians teach that the slightest sin is worse than all the evils of earth, purgatory and hell.

To spend one's time in prayer and contemplation is a very holy work, but St. Teresa says that while contemplation is pleasing to God, it is far more efficacious to leave prayer aside and go to the rescue of a soul in sin.[15]

Who shows the greatest love for God? St. Gregory answers this all-important question. *Ille in amore Dei major est qui ad ejus amorem plurimos trahit.*[16] And it is written that Our Lord revealed to a great saint[17] that it is more pleasing to Him for His faithful servant to instruct and lead a soul to salvation than to spend a year in contemplation.

Si separaveris pretiosum a vili, quasi os meum eris (Jer. 15, 19). "If thou wilt separate the precious from the vile, thou shalt be as my mouth," which means, according to St. Gregory, that, if you lead souls from evil by exhortation and example, you will be like unto Jesus Christ Himself, who is the mouthpiece of His Almighty Father.[18] St. John Chrysostom explains this same text thus: "If you use your words to convert and instruct others, you will be like the Master, who is the mouthpiece of His Father and who became Man and was crucified in order to redeem sinners."[19]

The greatest physical miracle is to bring a dead man back to life, but to raise a soul from sin is greater still. *Majus est miraculum peccatorem convertere, quam carne suscitare.*[20] The life of the soul is infinitely more precious than to raise up all the dead bodies of all men on earth. The resurrection of the dead is, therefore, but a shadow of the resurrection of the soul from sin.

If God gave a man power to create a new world, imagine how that man would be regarded by his fellow creatures. Yet, St. Augustine says that the conversion of a sinner is a work greater and more admirable than even such a deed for the soul is dearer to God than all

---

[15] *Exclamat.* 2.
[16] St. Greg. apud S. Bonav. *Pharetra* 1. 1, cap. 14.
[17] We are unable to say who this great saint is.
[18] *Moral.* 18, 23.
[19] *Orat. 5 contra Judaeos,* apud Corn. a Lapide, in Jerem., 15, 19.
[20] St. Greg. *Dialog.* lib. 3, cap. 17.

created things.[21] And St. John Chrysostom remarks that "nothing, not even the whole world, is worth a single soul." [22] Did not Christ say, "That which my Father has given me, is greater than all"? (John 10, 29) St. Augustine prays thus: "Thou hast made all things, O God, in the visible world for man's body, the body for the soul, and the soul for Thyself." St. John Chrysostom avers that man is the noblest of God's creatures, for all else was created for the use of man, heaven and earth, the stars and all that exists.[23]

What greater return could one make to God than to offer one's life for Him? Yet St. John Chrysostom says that to forego martyrdom in order to work for the salvation of souls is more acceptable to Almighty God. He states that this is not his own thought, but that of St. Paul. Writing to the Philippians, the great apostle says that though he desires to be with Christ, he feels it more advantageous to God's glory that he remain with them (Phil. 1, 23-24). St. Teresa envied those who worked for the salvation of souls, more than she did the martyrs. St. Catherine of Siena kissed the ground trodden by those engaged in apostolic ministry. Richard of St. Victor wonders whether it could be possible for heaven to grant a greater favor than to set men aside to work for the spiritual salvation of their fellow men.[24]

What more can I say? *Omnium divinorum divinissimum est co-operari Deo in salutem animarum,* writes St. Dionysius.[25] And St. Gregory adds, *Nullum omnipotenti Deo tale est sacrificium, quale est zelus animarum.*[26]

These things being so, who can measure the love of God for those who serve Him in ministering to souls? Who can plumb the depths of the graces that He pours upon them on earth? Who can envision the extent of the reward that He reserves for them in eternity? Who can conceive the horrors and punishments He has prepared for those guilty of leading souls to ruin? "I will meet them as a bear that is robbed of her whelps and I will rend the inner parts of their liver; and I will

[21] *Tract. 17 in Joannem.*
[22] In 1 Cor., *Homil.* 3.
[23] *Orat. 3 contra Judaeos.*
[24] *In Cant.* 1, 1.
[25] *De Caelesti Hierarchia,* Cap. 3.
[26] *Homil.* 12 *in Ezech.*

devour them there as a lion, the beast of the field shall tear them" (Osee 13, 8). Who does not tremble at such words; who does not shudder at the thought of causing the loss of a single soul; who will not give himself wholeheartedly to a work so dear to the heart of God?

O priests of God, what obligations are yours towards Him who called you to share His office of Saviour! How lofty is your calling, for you are the associates of God, of Jesus, of Mary, of the angels, of the apostles and the saints! Work unceasingly, courageously and constantly for Him! Let your only joy be to please Him! Accept whatever difficulties you encounter for His sweet sake!

Take pity on the souls created to His image and likeness, the souls of your brethren. Commiserate the sufferings of Our Lord, the agony He endured, the tears He shed, the blood He poured out, the miseries He bore. Compassionate the Blessed Virgin Mary in the grief she experienced for her Divine Son, and let no day go by without endeavoring to assuage that grief by laboring for souls. Obey the injunction of Sacred Scripture: "Deliver them that are led to death; and those that are drawn to death forbear not to deliver" (Prov. 24, 11).

Pray the Master of the heavenly harvest to send workmen into His vineyard. Imitate the apostles and the disciples, of whom it was said that they were occupied at all times, in public and in private, in preaching Jesus Christ. If your labors do not produce the results you hope for, do not be discouraged. Even if you should keep only one soul from falling into mortal sin, you would have done more good than if you had delivered the world from a universal pestilence.

If a great physician of antiquity[27] was given the title of divine for having rid his country of a physical plague, what term should be applied to the physicians of souls who cure men's spiritual ills? Think of a man afflicted with the worst human disease you can imagine, and then visualize the pains and torments of hell, the punishment of one mortal sin. Is there any comparison? Consequently, when by word or example or prayer, you prevent a soul from sinning, or rescue it from the grip of iniquity, you save it from punishment far exceeding the greatest torment possible on earth.

I can hear the Angel of the Apocalypse cry out: "Woe to the earth,

[27] Hippocrates, a Greek physician, 460-378 B.C.

and to the sea, because the devil is come down unto you, having great wrath, knowing that he hath but a short time" (Apoc. 12, 12), to appease his hatred for souls. Should you not love your brethren more profoundly than their enemy hates them? Should you not be more actuated by the desire to save them than he is to destroy them? If he in his rage deems the time permitted to him to seek their ruin as a mere *modicum tempus* "a short time," how ardently should you use every minute of your definitely short life to work for good?

Cease not, then, to work for so lofty a purpose, and the day will dawn when you will reap the rewards of your labors. "And in doing good let us not fail. For in due course we shall reap, not failing" (Gal. 6, 9), for even though you should not always succeed in drawing souls from evil, at least your earnest efforts will be rewarded.

Try, then, to save as many souls as possible and above all apply yourself with most fervent zeal to hearing confessions for in this way you can accomplish untold good, as I shall point out in the following section.

7. *Further Considerations*

All that has been said surely can inflame the heart of a priest, but I would repeat that, from all the duties of the priest, I would single out the hearing of confessions as the most useful and important. Nothing else even approaches it in its power for good and fruitful results.

Surely a good preacher can win souls, but so can a good confessor. Preaching is the soul of the priestly work, while confession is its heart. Preachers begin the work of salvation, confessors bring it to completion; preachers make known the will of heaven, confessors have it practised; preachers are doctors giving general principles, teaching the faithful to love and serve God, confessors are physicians imparting individual direction and treatment. Preachers pronounce what remedies will be effectual, confessors apply them. Preachers are the trumpets of God, confessors are the soldiers destroying sin; preachers direct the artillery of eternity from a distance and not always accurately, while confessors battle at close quarters.

Preachers are God's watchdogs, who drive away the ravening wolf;

confessors are His guardians who rescue souls about to be devoured. Preachers exhort, confessors reconcile; preachers are ambassadors of God, speaking in His name, confessors are like little gods, clothed with His power and doing God's work in men's souls. Preachers describe the terrors of His judgments, confessors apply those judgments; preachers are angels announcing the ire of the Creator, confessors are other Noahs saving men in the ark of penance.

Each preacher is an Aaron commissioned to address the Pharoahs of earth and soften their hearts with virtue; each confessor is a new Moses guiding the children of God to the Promised Land through the Red Sea of Christ's Blood.

The preacher is a faithful servant of Abraham, that is, of the heavenly Father, seeking another spouse for the only Son of God; the confessor is a wise Egeus of King Assuerus, adorning other Esthers, that is, immortal souls, with the ornament of divine grace to make them pleasing to the King of heaven and earth.

The preacher is a Saul mustering an army to battle against the Philistines, that is, the devils; the confessor is a David killing Goliath, that is, sin, with the sword of prayer when he gives absolution to the sinner.

The preacher is a prophet crying to those who enter the temple of the Lord: *Audite verbum Domini; haec dicit Dominus;* declaring to men the promises of the divine bounty and the threats of divine justice; predicting eternal reward for the good and an eternal punishment for the wicked. The confessor is a Levite slaying the victims of the sacrifice, that is, sinful souls; making them die to sin; washing them in the Precious Blood of the Lamb; placing them in the sacred hands of Jesus Christ, the Sovereign Priest, that He may offer them in sacrifice to His Heavenly Father.

The preacher is a forerunner of the Son of God, preparing the ways of the Lord; the confessor is a disciple cleansing, adorning, and making ready the upper rooms of men's hearts for the coming of Christ in Holy Communion.

Finally, the preacher announces the mysteries and sufferings of the Saviour, while the confessor applies them and their fruits to souls.

The preacher denounces Satan publicly without fear; the confessor drives the devil from men's hearts, delivering them from tyranny and placing them in the bosom of the Father.

From these considerations learn the excellence and importance of this great function of your priestly life. Know, too, how useful and necessary it is and how pleasing to Him who loves souls so much. Your zeal for its careful discharge should be all-consuming. If the angels know the meaning of jealousy, they would envy the priest who is privileged to share a ministry so pleasing to God, and so efficacious for the souls for whom the Saviour shed His Blood.

If, then, you have a spark of love for God, be assiduous in carefully discharging this part of your sacerdotal office. Cherish it and consider yourself honored to have been chosen by God for this divine work. Be zealous in discharging your work in the confessional; seek to acquire the ultimate of those qualities which will fit you to be an excellent confessor.

CHAPTER III

SCIENCE OF THE CONFESSOR

THE PRIEST who does not possess the science necessary to exercise the ministry of confession is culpable in the eyes of God and is incapable of discharging this great duty.

Imagine a doctor seeking to practise medicine without sufficient training. He would be a murderer, who, instead of healing his patients, would soon destroy them. Yet, the priest, who is in truth the physician of souls, can become their destroyer if he is not fitted for the work of the confessional.

As an ignorant judge would do irreparable harm in attempting to dispense the law, even more so the priest lacking a thorough familiarity with theology would be guilty of criminal negligence. He would cause innumerable sins, making false consciences, obliging people to make restitution when they are not bound, refusing absolution when it should be given, granting it when it should be withheld. Truly, the Scripture says: "If the blind lead the blind, both fall into the pit" (Matt. 15, 14).

Science is, therefore, the second qualification for the confessor, and this science supposes eight requisites:

1. The priest must be thoroughly familiar with the extent of his jurisdiction. 2. He must understand the matter and form of the Sacrament and must know what makes it valid or invalid. 3. He should have a complete knowledge of sins against the commandments of God and the precepts of the Church. 4. He must be able to distinguish between sins, mortal and venial, and must know the circumstances that change

---

* The chapter dealing with the judiciary power of the priest, which appears in *Oeuvres Complètes,* Vol. IV, p. 203 ff., is omitted in this edition.

the nature or increase the gravity of each sin. 5. He should know the ordinary censures and irregularities. 6. He should know the impediments of marriage. 7. He should be able to make sinners realize the horror of sin, and by his direction and guidance lead them to contrition and a firm purpose of amendment. 8. He must be able to suggest remedies for each soul; he must be able to point out the duties and obligations of every state in life and to give persons suitable penances.

To acquire this science, it is necessary that the priest study moral theology and that he be conversant with the best standard works[1] on the administration of the Sacrament of Penance.

---

[1] St. John Eudes recommends several works on confession that are not available today. Father Cousin, editor of the 1732 French edition of *The Good Confessor*, adds to the list of books given by the Saint "the second and third parts of the *Summa Theologica.*" There is undoubtedly no better handbook on moral theology than these parts of the *Summa.*

CHAPTER IV*

CHARITY OF THE CONFESSOR

CHARITY is a most necessary qualification for any confessor. He should be consumed with love for sinners. He should be filled with kindness and mercy. He may thunder and fulminate in the pulpit, but in the Sacred Tribunal of Penance he must speak only words of gentleness and encouragement. One catches more flies with a spoonful of honey than with a cask of vinegar.

The priest should enter the confessional with a heart consumed only with the desire of assisting penitents, and should receive, in a spirit of graciousness and helpfulness those who present themselves. No exception should be made. Rich and poor, great and humble, adults and children, all alike should experience the same spirit of understanding.

Remember that in the confessional the penitent addresses you as "Father." Treat him, then, with paternal kindness, overlooking any shortcomings he may have, impressing upon him the seriousness of what he does, while at the same time refraining from harshness. Avoid familiarity under any guise, but seek to banish unwarranted fear lest it interfere with a frank and open confession. Be spiritually helpful. Point out that Christ died for the sinner and extends complete pardon for sin to the soul whose sorrow is sincere and whose purpose of amendment is firm.

If you observe that the penitent is in a state of perplexity and needs help in examining his conscience, be ready to assist him. Urge him to make a complete and accurate confession of his sins, see that he avoid

---

* If the reader compares this chapter to that of the original French, he will find that it has been considerably shortened. Nothing important, however, has been omitted in the translation.

long and meaningless explanations; assist him in making a succinct picture of his wrongdoing, glossing over nothing, omitting, minimizing or withholding nothing, but making a full and clear accusation of every mortal sin of which he believes himself guilty. Console the afflicted, showing them how to turn their trials and sorrows into merit.

CHAPTER V

PRUDENCE OF THE CONFESSOR

BESIDES ZEAL, science and charity, prudence is also required, for without it you will encounter many pitfalls and cause grievous harm to your penitents. Study, therefore, the following rules that should carefully be observed in the confessional.

Examine the penitent according to age, sex and condition. Be careful not to arouse wrong thoughts or to suggest unknown sins. Do not interrupt him during his confession, but wait until he has finished. Treat each penitent individually. For example, if you notice that a person seems to be ashamed to confess his sins, encourage him by reminding him that priests are not angels but men who, being human themselves, understand the faults and frailties of others. Remind him, too, that although it is human to fall into sin, it would be positively diabolical to remain in that state; that whatever is revealed in the confessional becomes a really sacred trust because of the seal of confession. Recall to his mind the fact that God commands us to confess our sins to priests and that we should do so for love of Him and in honor of the shame which the God-man bore on the Cross because of our iniquities. It is far better to experience a little shame in confessing a sin to another man than to have it revealed before all the angels and men on the Day of Judgment.

With a bold or flippant person, however, adopt the opposite course. Remind him that he is actually kneeling at the feet of Christ, the Supreme Judge, as represented in the person of the priest; that he is not confessing his sins to a mere man, but to God whose place the priest occupies. Induce him to think of himself as a criminal who has merited punishment by his evil doing. With patience seek to have him understand that his soul's salvation is at stake, impressing upon him the gravity of making a bad confession. Point out to him that at the hour of death he will have to render a strict accounting to God for such a terrible sin.

Use great discretion regarding the Sixth Commandment. Pray to the Holy Ghost for wisdom so as not to ask too much or too little. Inquire cautiously concerning the sins confessed, but be careful not to destroy innocence or to disedify.

Likewise, approach the subject of restitution with great care, being mindful of the problems involved. This applies also to the breaking of sinful associations and the avoidance of the occasions of sin. If it is obvious that the penitent did certain things in good faith or invincible ignorance, use extreme tact in enlightening his mind.

Suggest remedies suitable to each particular soul. Give a penance which will be at once salutary and easy for the penitent. This requires prudence so that the penance imposed may not be an impossible task. Be lenient rather than harsh in this matter. In refusing or deferring absolution, be particularly careful to act in such a way that you will not attract the attention of persons near the confessional.

The confessor should imitate the wisdom of the serpent and safeguard his own soul lest in helping others he himself be lost. In this regard, four things are suggested.

First, learn to humble yourself by the knowledge of your own unworthiness and sinfulness, seeing your own image in the crime of your penitents, always being fearful that you, too, may fall unless sustained by divine grace.

Secondly, put into practice the injunction of Sacred Scripture: "Let your modesty be known to all men" (Phil. 4, 5), practising mortification of the eyes, giving an example of true priestly deportment at all times when administering the Sacrament of Penance. If you are careful to observe exterior modesty, God will protect you so that your interior life will not be destroyed and the beauty of your soul will not be contaminated. Yet, this can be done only by special grace from God, which will always be given to those who seek it with humility.

Thirdly, have a great horror of anything contrary to holy purity, observing the following seven recommendations: 1. In treating of the

Sixth Commandment, renounce everything that is contrary to the spirit of purity, begging God for an increase of his virtue He loves so much. 2. Ask nothing out of mere curiosity. 3. Concerning sins against purity, question the penitent only when necessary. 4. In the confessional, avoid anything approaching familiarity with those of the opposite sex. 5. Keep the eyes modestly cast down. 6. Close the heart and mind against every human affection. 7. If you should transgress in any of these matters, make a profound act of humility, and, correcting the fault, beg God's grace for the future and implore the assistance of our Blessed Lady to obtain it.

Fourthly, to preserve your own soul while working for the salvation of others, cultivate constantly the spirit of piety. The following chapter will treat of this important qualification.

CHAPTER VI

PIETY OF THE CONFESSOR

IT IS NOT without reason that the great Apostle, St. Paul, urges his disciple, Timothy, to practise piety, declaring it to be a great treasure, useful in all things (I Tim. 4, 8). A priest animated by the spirit of piety is a worthy instrument in God's hands to accomplish marvels for the salvation of souls.

In the sacred tribunal the confessor frees souls from the misery of sin and forms the Son of God within them anew. He inspires penitents with sentiments of purest devotion, makes them taste the sweetness of God's love, teaches them to know the meaning of true piety, helps them in the practice of the other Christian virtues and at the same time sanctifies himself.

What is piety? Do you wish to know it and to possess it? Practise mental prayer. I assure you that if you do not practise mental prayer you will never grasp the meaning of true piety, and, consequently, you will not be truly fitted to hear confessions. It is not sufficient for a priest to drive sin out of souls by absolution; he must form in them the Christian virtues, whose foundation, says St. Ambrose, is piety. *Pietas virtutum omnium fundamentum.*[1]

How can you infuse piety into a soul unless you yourself possess it? How can you nourish if you have no food to give? The more pious the confessor is, the more effectively he will work for the salvation of souls. Truly then, he should strive unceasingly to acquire and practise this indispensable virtue. For this end, three things are suggested. The first concerns what the confessor should do before entering the con-

[1] *In Psalm.* 118.

fessional; the second, what he should do while he is there; and the third, what he should do after leaving the confessional.

1. Before entering the confessional, he should spend some time in recollection before the Blessed Sacrament to recall the importance of what he is about to do. In the Sacrament of Penance he must be a saviour of souls, destroying sin and opening heaven by the infusion of grace. He must remember that he is about to apply to men the fruits of the Redemption, to fill up in souls those things that are wanting of the sufferings of Christ (Col. 1, 24), and to make Jesus live and reign in them. These considerations should arouse within him a great desire to discharge his duty in a fitting manner. He must make an act of humility in view of his unworthiness and incapacity, and must be filled with mistrust of self lest he become like the torch that consumes and destroys itself while bestowing light on others.

He must put his entire confidence in Our Lord, protesting that his only desire is to serve and to please His Master, begging for the light and graces he needs. If necessary, he must go to confession or at least make an act of contrition, so as to have his own soul pure and holy. He must pray to the Blessed Virgin Mary, the angels and saints for guidance. He must recall that many saints now in heaven heard confessions with holy dispositions and he must ask the Holy Ghost to grant him the same dispositions. Thus he will dispose his soul in such a way that he will not deprive God of the honor and glory that must be rendered to the Father of Eternal Mercy by the worthy administration of the Sacrament of Penance. Let him be resolved to place no obstacle in the path of the rich graces which God wishes to impart to those who come to confession.

2. While in the confessional, the priest must elevate his mind and heart to God and follow the suggestions enumerated herewith to maintain the spirit of his saintly work.

When the first penitent enters the confessional, the confessor must think of the incomparable love of God the Father who gave His Only-begotten Son for this very person, and thus give himself to God to work with the same love for the salvation of the soul before him. As the second comes, he must consider the great love of God the Son for the penitent and unite himself to this divine love. As the third approaches, he must recall the infinite love of the Holy Ghost for this soul and cooperate with Him for the same purpose. When the fourth penitent kneels down, the priest must envision the ineffable love of the Son of God who became incarnate for the salvation of this very soul. The confessor then continues to recall the divine love manifested in the other mysteries of Holy Faith, imploring Almighty God to apply the fruits of each to the soul of each penitent.

Let the priest also dwell upon the incomparable charity of the maternal heart of Mary, begging her blessing and assistance upon the work in hand. He might also invoke the saints as well as the martyrs, confessors, patriarchs and apostles.

This method will help the confessor to maintain the spirit of recollection and to cultivate a great love of prayer. Likewise, it will render the task of hearing confessions less burdensome and fatiguing, for love and fervor will fill his heart.

It is well for the priest to keep a crucifix in the confessional to be a constant reminder of the ardent love of the Sacred Heart of Jesus for souls. So, too, in difficulties it will urge the confessor to seek light and strength from the Divine Saviour, especially when dealing with sins against the Sixth Commandment.

3. After confession, the priest should kneel humbly before the altar to beseech Christ's mercy on behalf of his penitents, and to ask forgiveness for any errors of judgment he may have unknowingly committed while engaged in his sacerdotal labor in the confessional. He should thank Our Lord Jesus Christ for the graces bestowed on the confessor and the penitents, and ask Him to compensate for any deficiency in himself or in the persons who have come to confession. He should beg the Blessed Virgin Mary, the angels and the saints to offer to the Son of God every one whom Divine Providence has directed to his ministry, with the earnest prayer that none of these souls may perish.

CHAPTER VII

FIDELITY TO THE SECRECY OF CONFESSION

ONE OF the most important qualifications of the good confessor is fidelity to the secrecy of confession. This obligation is established on a foundation of divine law, natural law and ecclesiastical law. Consequently, a breach of this weighty trust can never be considered light or unimportant.

It is, therefore, always a grievous sin to reveal anything heard in confession. A priest may not refer, either directly or indirectly, during the lifetime or even after the death of the penitent, to matters revealed to him in the sacred tribunal. He may not mention anything that has been discussed with the penitent before confession with a view to receiving the Sacrament of Penance. Nor may he speak outside the confessional, even in conversation with the penitent himself, of anything revealed there unless express or tacit permission is given. Neither may the confessor mention the sin of an accomplice to his partner in crime, even as a means of urging him to confess his share of the guilt; nor may the priest speak of hearing the confession of one who has come to him secretly and has stated or implied that he wishes the fact to remain unknown. He may not discuss sins which are widely publicized, but are known sacramentally to the priest. The confessor is also forbidden to discuss with a fellow-priest the sins of a penitent who has been heard by both, nor may he refer in general terms to the sins confessed by people living in a small place or by the members of a religious community.

Penances must not be revealed, especially when they are such as are customarily associated with mortal sins. Peculiarities of penitents should not be discussed when they are known only through confession. Likewise, when a priest has heard only a few penitents in a certain locality, he should refrain from praising the virtues of any particular one or from saying that his sins were only venial, because this might result in making known indirectly the faults of the others and in insinuating that they confessed mortal sins.

The confessor is not permitted to employ the knowledge obtained in the confessional to guide his actions, whether in doing or omitting anything, without the penitent's permission, if by so doing he runs the risk of revealing indirectly the sin confessed.

If a difficult case of conscience should arise, the confessor may consult another priest so long as he can do this without revealing in any way the identity of the penitent.

It is dangerous to mention any matter which the confessor has heard discussed outside the confessional as well as within its walls. It would be wiser not to mention the subject.

If a person should say to the priest, "I am telling you such and such a thing as if I were in the confessional," he is obliged by the natural law to respect the truth, but is not held by the secrecy of the confessional, even though the priest should believe so, because the seal of confession applies only to sacramental confession.

There are other persons held by the same secrecy as the confessor, namely the superior who has granted permission to absolve from a reserved sin, if the priest has inadvertently or imprudently revealed the person for whom the absolution is asked. Likewise the priest who is taken into consultation, when the identity of the penitent has been revealed involuntarily or with the consent of the person concerned. Those who through malicious curiosity or accident have overheard the confession of another person are bound strictly to the secrecy of confession. Interpreters used to translate confessions in foreign languages are also bound by the same obligation.

When giving a mission in a parish, a preacher should be careful not to speak, even in general terms, of sins that prevail in that parish, lest he be guilty of breaking the seal of confession.

Finally, every confessor should be most faithful to avoid the slightest mention of what he has heard in confession because such an indiscretion gives scandal to the laity, makes the Sacrament of Penance odious, robs people of their liberty to confess their sins, and is the cause of many sacrileges with the consequent loss of souls. God will demand a strict account of confessors who are too free in speaking about things that should be wrapped in perpetual silence, and, so far as possible, banished from their thoughts.

CHAPTER VIII

SEVEN POINTS TO BE OBSERVED BY CONFESSORS

It does not surprise me that the Holy Ghost, formulating the Apostles' Creed, has placed among the great dogmas of faith the mystery expressed in the words, "I believe in the remission of sins." This indeed is the purpose and end of all the other mysteries. "This is all the fruit, that the sin thereof should be taken away" (Isa. 27, 9). This is a wonder surpassing all visible miracles performed by Christ on the bodies of men, excelling in the same degree as the soul excells the body and as truth is above the shadow. The miracles performed by the Master on men's bodies were but shadows of those He effects upon their souls in confession. There the blind are made to see, the lepers are cleansed, and the dead are brought back to life.

O God, what admirable changes are wrought in men's souls through the Sacrament of Penance! In a moment the soul passes from the depths of evil to the heights of grace, from death to life, from hell to paradise. He who was a slave of the devil becomes a child of God; he who belonged to the Prince of Darkness becomes the possession of the Prince of Light. He who was the abode of the demons passes from an abyss of misery into an ocean of beatitude. O loving Saviour, what graces Thou didst bestow upon us in instituting this Sacrament! How thankful we should be to Thee!

So great is this grace that even if venial sin alone were effaced by the reception of the Sacrament of Penance, that in itself would be more precious than deliverance from all human ills.

What renders this great favor of God so much more bountiful is that He does not content Himself with forgiving sin, but also gives to man this same power. Weak as we are, encompassed with frailty, we share the prerogative of God made Man. O admirable power of God, shared with His creatures! O power divine! *Quis potest dimittere peccata nisi solus Deus?* (Mark 2, 7).

But the greater the grace, the more rigorous will be the accounting demanded and the more culpable those who make improper use of the Sacrament of Penance. Not one single detail must ever be omitted that might help to exercise the holy ministry worthily. Seven recommendations are appended here.

1. *Preparation*

If zeal for souls has brought you to the confessional, you will leave nothing undone for the accomplishment of this work. You must see that the penitent begins his confession properly and say yourself the words: *Dominus sit in corde tuo, et in labiis tuis, ut rite confitearis omnia peccata tua, in nomine Patris et Filii et Spiritus Sancti. Amen.* Open your heart and show the fulness of your desire to help him. Urge him to make three acts: a) an act of renunciation; b) an act of oblation; c) an act of devotion to the Blessed Virgin Mary, to the angels and to the saints. These acts will serve to drive away the evil spirit and open the floodgates of grace.

2. *Instruction*

All theologians agree that a knowledge of the principal mysteries of religion is necessary to eternal salvation. "This is eternal life that they may know thee, the only true God and Jesus Christ, whom thou hast sent" (John 17, 3). Without this knowledge no one can properly receive the sacrament.

A confessor cannot, without incriminating himself before God, administer the Sacrament of Penance to a person who is ignorant of the fundamental mysteries of our holy faith. The priest must be satisfied therefore that his penitent has a sufficient knowledge of the Blessed Trinity, the Incarnation, Redemption and Judgment. He is also obliged by necessity of precept to know and accept the Our Father, the Creed and the Commandments of God and of the Church and whatever is essential to the proper reception of Penance and Holy Eucharist.

3. Interrogation or Examination

The confessor must not be satisfied merely to hear confessions. He must take the trouble to question his penitents, following the experience of so many priests who realize the necessity of such questioning. What excuse could a confessor make if, through his carelessness, certain souls did not fully accuse themselves of their transgressions?

Does not the judge in civil life question the culprit? Why should not the spiritual judge do likewise? Give careful attention to this subject, questioning those whom you believe to be insufficiently prepared.

4. Contrition and Attrition

Perfect contrition, or imperfect, which is attrition, is as essential to the Sacrament of Penance as confession. Consequently, the priest who wishes to apply the fruit of this Sacrament to souls is no less obliged to help them to conceive sorrow for their sins than he is to hear their confession well.

For this purpose, it is necessary to point out to the penitent his principal sins, especially those to which he is most attached or which are most dangerous. Make him see the ugliness of sin. Teach him to know that while in mortal sin he is in the grip of Satan, dead to grace and destined to be damned. Make him realize that there are many in hell who have not fallen so low as he; that he has delivered to Satan his soul that cost so much to the Son of God. For the satisfaction and passing pleasure of a moment, he has doomed himself to suffer hell forever. He has exchanged the eternal for the transitory.

You should also impress upon the penitent that in spite of having received so many graces he has wasted them all, giving his body and soul to evil, using his faculties to serve Christ's enemies. Every time a sinner commits a mortal sin he crucifies anew the Son of God (Heb. 6, 6).

In recalling these things to the sinner, you must be careful not to discourage him, lest he turn completely from God. Let kindness lead him to a realization of his sins. Tell the penitent that he mentions the true state of his soul only in order that he may make an act of perfect contrition or at least attrition, either of which must come from God; for it is a divine gift, man being incapable of supernatural sorrow.

You should urge the sinner to make a firm purpose of amendment and to have a resolute intention of avoiding occasions which have hitherto led him into sin.

5. Remedies

The confessor is not only a teacher, a judge and a mediator; he is also the physician of souls. Consequently, he must not only banish sin from men's souls, but must also apply remedies to prevent its recurrence. He must bind up the wounds of their souls, assuage their spiritual ills and help sinners to recover completely. Likewise, he must suggest preventive methods to ensure their future safety from such hideous diseases of the soul. He must urge them to accept and use the remedies he suggests just as an ordinary doctor would insist that his medicine be taken; he must impress upon them that they are spiritually ill, and that they must use the remedies he is giving them. Otherwise, they will surely die for all eternity.

Six efficacious means are herewith suggested for spiritual patients.

1. Avoid evil companions and places which lead to sin.

2. Go to confession and Holy Communion frequently. Choose a good confessor. Cultivate the proper dispositions required to draw the fullest fruits from the Sacraments. Have a constant devotion to the Mass. Assist piously at Vespers and listen attentively to the preaching of the Word of God.

3. Before beginning your work in the morning kneel humbly at your bedside and adore God, renewing your good resolutions to avoid sin. At the close of the day, make an examination of conscience; recall your firm determination to overcome sin. Ask the assistance of the Blessed Virgin Mary and of all the saints.

4. Cultivate an ardent devotion to the Mother of God. Since this devotion is of such paramount importance, every confessor should endeavor to implant it firmly in the hearts of his penitents, recommending some particular acts in her honor daily, counselling them to take her as protectress and guide, saying the beads, wearing the scapular;

reciting the Litany of the Blessed Virgin Mary. He should also urge them to unite the devotion to St. Joseph to that of Our Lady.

5. Read good books of devotion and piety, such as *The Imitation of Christ* and the Lives of the Saints. Parents should be reminded of their duty in this respect and see that their children make use of good Catholic literature.

6. In addition to these five means suggested, another most fruitful and salutary practice may be added, the annual retreat. The making of a retreat in a monastery or convent among religious is an excellent aid to piety and a consoling help to persons who are really in earnest about their eternal salvation. The confessor should, therefore, urge his penitents to take advantage of the many closed retreats offered the faithful.

These general remedies being helpful to all are strongly recommended. Almsgiving should also be urged and works of mercy, both spiritual and corporal.

Since these things are all so necessary for conversion, it is obvious that a person who would object to carrying out the confessor's recommendations would lack the proper dispositions for a betterment of life and for the reception of the grace of absolution.

6. *Penance and Absolution*

The confessor should be mindful of three things in connection with penance and absolution.

First, the penance he gives should be made up of various prayers or acts, for example, five Our Fathers, the beads, a prayer or a psalm, alms deeds, fasting on a certain day or hearing Mass. He should not confuse the penitent by giving him a penance made up of a number of these prayers and acts mixed together. Let him rather choose one or other of them.

Secondly, the Council of Trent recommends a penance in conformity with the sins committed and the persons involved, lest confessors, by giving penances which do not suit the gravity of the offence, become participators by connivance in the penitents' sins. St. Charles reminds priests of this same fact when he counsels them to give a penance commensurate with the sin committed, following the custom and practice of Sacred Scripture, where we find the guilty obliged to do penance in proportion to their crimes.

Thirdly, the penitent should be exhorted to perform his penance as soon as possible. The priest should encourage him to do the acts or say the prayers with a deep spirit of piety and with a firm resolution not to fall into sin again, and to make voluntary acts of virtue in order to draw greater graces upon himself.

Finally, everything should be done to arouse in his soul a lively sense of sorrow. The confessor must help him to make a fervent act of contrition, assuring him that if he has confessed his sins as well as possible, and has the requisite contrition, his soul will be purified by the absolution he is about to receive, just as truly as if he were to stand in the presence of Jesus Christ Himself and hear from His lips the words of pardon he craves.

The words of absolution must be pronounced with attention and devotion. The priest must be mindful that at the very moment he speaks these precious words, the forgiveness of heaven is granted, the Blood of the Lamb is applied to the penitent, and the life of grace is restored to his soul.

7. After Absolution

First, the confessor must tell the sinner what a great favor he has just received in having his sins forgiven and in being snatched from the jaws of hell. The priest should remind the sinner that a moment ago he was a child of the devil, and now is a son of God, and that the deliverance which has just come to him surpasses even the deliverance of an afflicted man freed from the most grievous sufferings.

Secondly, the priest should exhort the penitent earnestly not to waste the grace of God, but to conserve it with fidelity. Then the confessor should make him understand that he should prefer to lose even his most cherished possession rather than separate himself from God again by sin.

Thirdly, the priest should urge him to go to the altar and, kneeling before Our Lord in the blessed Sacrament, he should thank God for His infinite mercy and goodness in having freed him from the fetters of sin. Then, the confessor should have the penitent say a prayer to the Blessed Virgin Mary to invoke her protection, to thank her for this grace, remembering that all blessings come to us through the hands of Mary.

Every confessor should pray daily for his penitents that they may receive the strength and help they need to live up to the instruction they have received.

The priest should send his penitents away with a wish and a blessing: "Go in peace," or "May God bless you."

CHAPTER IX

FURTHER ADVICE TO CONFESSORS

To THE SUGGESTIONS already made in the preceding chapters, we add the following advice because its practical application is of great importance to the confessor.

All confessors should be extremely careful not to contradict or condemn one another. They should be closely united in a spirit of charity, following the same rule of conduct and the same maxims of the Gospel, so that the Holy Ghost may guide, bless and sanctify their harmonious work. Thus their penitents will be impressed and encouraged to follow their injunctions. Let confessors, then, sedulously observe all that has been recommended in this book, as well as what is to follow.

The priest, representing the Son of God as judge of mankind, should always give the appearance of understanding his great responsibility. He should wear his cassock and surplice when hearing confessions, occupying the confessional or some suitable place in the church where he may be seen by all. His very bearing and manner should give edification.

The confessor must radiate the good odor of Christ everywhere, and by word and example further the work of Our Divine Lord in humility, patience and charity.

The penitent must be taught to kneel in all humility in the confessional, with hands joined and eyes cast down or looking at the Crucified Saviour. The confessor should not speak in a loud tone nor permit the penitent to do so, lest their voices reach those waiting outside.

If there arises a question of reconciliation or restitution, or of some proximate occasion of sin, the confessor should not wait until the end of the confession to dispose the penitent, but should do so at the moment of questioning, when he finds him guilty of one of these sins.

The confessor must not ask useless questions, but examine the penitent on necessary points. He must insist on important details, such as the number of times each mortal sin has been committed, and the length of time that has elapsed since his last confession.

If discord or enmity exists towards another, the priest should encourage the penitent to complete reconciliation, even offering to assist in this if necessary.

If one is engaged in court actions or litigation, the confessor must urge him to try to settle the dispute amicably, if it is possible.

If the penitent should accuse himself of having spoken against his neighbor's reputation, the priest should oblige him to repair the damage. If the statements are true but not generally known, he should be told to endeavor to undo the harm caused, by admitting that he was wrong in having spoken so, then to say whatever good things he can about the person he has sinned against. If the statement is false, he should strive to contradict it, in the presence of the persons who heard it, and in every place where it is possible any harm may have been done.

The confessor should advise the penitent to ask pardon of him who has suffered. Each private individual, being the master of his own reputation, may forgive in entirety the evil spoken against him, and consequently, the sinner is not held to any further reparation. I say "private individual" as distinct from a public man, who is not master of his own reputation which is necessary for the public good.

If the detraction be of long standing, and, perhaps, entirely forgotten by all, then it is better left unnoticed, lest in seeking to rectify the wrong done, greater trouble may be stirred up. In this case, it would be better to counsel the sinner to say everything he can in favor of the person involved and enhance his good standing in the community.

In dealing with a person held to restore another's goods, here is the course of action to be followed. The confessor should first find out whether the penitent is bound to make restitution. In cases where the person is about to discharge the obligation, and suggests that he would prefer to make restitution anonymously, the priest should assist him if it be deemed expedient.

Married couples living in dissension or actually separated should not be absolved if they cannot give a legitimate reason for their condition.

The confessor should make the penitent cognizant of the duties of his state. Parents, teachers, children and servants should be carefully instructed in their respective obligations.

If there is question of vows that the penitent cannot fulfil, the confessor may commute them for easier things, for example, instead of a pilgrimage or something similar that the penitent has promised to carry out, it would be well to oblige him to make several confessions and communions.

CHAPTER X

AN EFFECTIVE WAY TO CONVERT SINNERS

IN CONCLUSION I shall set down an instruction imparted by the Most Blessed Mother of God,[1] concerning the manner in which one should deal with sinners, in public and private, in order to effect their conversion.

When you preach, go into the pulpit bearing with you the cannon, the fire and the terrible weapons of the Word of God, to combat sin and destroy it in the souls of men. When you must address a sinner to bring him back to God, treat him with gentleness, patience, kindness and charity. Deal with him as if he were a sick man covered with wounds and ulcers. Do not show anger towards him, but act like the wise physician who, treating a very sick patient, would display no impatience and anger but rather understanding and pity.

The first thing to be done to effect the cure of the sick soul, that is, the sinner, is to arouse him to the point where he will discover the seriousness of his condition. Help him as much as possible, showing him kindness and compassion.

When the penitent realizes his true condition, you must bathe his injuries with warm wine, that is, you must shower him with every affection, speak to him with patience and charity, and at the same time make him understand that you seek only the glory of God in bringing him back to his Maker. Impress upon his mind the great love and mercy which Christ cherishes for those sinners who return to Him.

---

* In the French edition a number of chapters are devoted to a very detailed examination of conscience. Cf. *Oeuvres Complètes,* Vol. IV, p. 294 ff. These chapters have been omitted in the present English edition.

[1] This effective way of converting sinners was given to St. John Eudes by the Blessed Virgin Mary through Marie des Vallées, a saintly woman of Coutances. See footnote, p. 136.

Recall the conversion of St. Peter, St. Paul, St. Mary Magdalen, St. Augustine, the good thief and countless others.

Anoint his wounds with oil, that is, with the words of Sacred Scripture and the living examples of Christ, His Mother and the Saints. For example, if there be question of inducing one to forgive an enemy, show him the charity of Christ forgiving His enemies even at the hour of death.

Above all else, banish bitterness from your own life. Never bring the vinegar of bitterness to a sinner, but show patience and kindness at all times, even if the one you are trying to help should become angry with you.

If all these expedients should fail, exhort him to pray to God for strength and grace to triumph over self and to be converted. At least, have him allow you to pray in his name. As an effective prayer the "Hail Mary, Daughter of God the Father" is suggested.[2]

---

[2] The prayer that St. John Eudes mentions here is a beautiful salutation to the Blessed Virgin Mary. It is recited daily in the two religious orders founded by him, the Congregation of Jesus and Mary and the Order of Our Lady of Charity. Priests and religious will find this prayer very helpful, especially when dealing with hardened sinners.

Ave, Maria, Filia Dei Patris,	Hail Mary, Daughter of God the Father,
Ave, Maria, Mater Dei Filii,	Hail Mary, Mother of God the Son,
Ave, Maria, Sponsa Spiritus sancti,	Hail Mary, Spouse of the Holy Ghost,
Ave, Maria, templum totius Divinitatis,	Hail Mary, Temple of the Divinity,
Ave, Maria, candidum lilium fulgidae semperque tranquillae Trinitatis,	Hail Mary, Immaculate Lily of the resplendent and ever-peaceful Trinity,
Ave, Maria, rosa praefulgida caelicae amoenitatis,	Hail Mary, Radiant Rose of Heavenly Fragrance,
Ave, Maria, Virgo virginum, Virgo fidelis, de qua nasci, et de cujus lacte pasci Rex caelorum voluit,	Hail Mary, Virgin of Virgins of whom the King of Kings did will to be born,
Ave, Maria, Regina Martyrum, cujus animam doloris gladius pertransivit,	Hail Mary, Queen of Martyrs, whose soul was pierced with a sword of sorrow,
Ave, Maria, Domina mundi, cui data est omnis potestas in caelo et in terra,	Hail Mary, Queen of the Universe, to whom all power has been given in heaven and on earth,
Ave, Maria, Regina cordis mei, Mater vita, dulcedo, et spes mea carissima,	Hail Mary, Queen of my Heart, My Mother, My life, My consolation, and my dearest hope,
Ave, Maria, Mater amabilis,	Hail Mary, Mother Most Amiable,
Ave, Maria, Mater admirabilis,	Hail Mary, Mother Most Admirable,
Ave, Maria, Mater misercordiae,	Hail Mary, Mother of Mercy,

If in spite of your efforts the sinner still remains hardened in heart, then be sure that God will reward your efforts and will repay you just as truly as if you had succeeded.

Ave, Maria, gratia plena, Dominus tecum;	Hail Mary, full of grace, the Lord is with thee;
Benedicta tu in mulieribus;	Blessed art thou amongst women;
Et benedictus fructus ventris tui, Jesus;	And blessed is the fruit of thy womb, Jesus;
Et benedictus sponsus tuus Joseph;	And blessed be thy spouse, St. Joseph;
Et benedictus pater tuus Joachim;	And blessed by thy father, St. Joachim;
Et benedicta mater tua Anna;	And blessed by thy mother, St. Anne;
Et benedictus filius tuus Joannis;	And blessed be thy adopted son, St. John;
Et benedictus Angelus tuus Gabriel;	And blessed be thy angel, St. Gabriel;
Et benedictus Pater aeternus, qui te elegit;	And blessed be the Eternal Father who chose thee;
Et benedictus Filius, que te amavit;	And blessed be the Divine Son who loved thee;
Et benedictus Spiritus sanctus, qui te sponsavit;	And blessed be the Holy Ghost who espoused thee;
Et benedicti in aeternum omnes qui benedicunt tibi, et qui diligunt te. Amen.	And blessed be forever all those who bless and love thee. Amen.

Part IV

MEDITATIONS
ON
THE PRIESTLY OBLIGATIONS

Part IV

MEDITATIONS ON THE PRIESTLY OBLIGATIONS[1]

FIRST MEDITATION

General Obligations of the Priesthood

FIRST POINT

DIGNITY AND HOLINESS OF THE PRIESTHOOD

CONSIDER the dignity, the greatness and the holiness of the priestly state and what it means to be a priest.

To be a priest is to be an angel, for Sacred Scripture calls priests angels inasmuch as they perform on earth the duties of the angels in heaven. God wished to be surrounded and served by angels on earth as well as in heaven. These earthly angels are His priests who possess greater power than the angels, the cherubim or the seraphim in His heavenly kingdom. Priests therefore should be, if it were possible, purer than angels, more luminous than the cherubim, more consumed with divine love than the seraphim. They must be *lucernae ardentes et lucentes* (John 5, 35), so that they may enlighten and inflame souls with the fire of eternity.

---

[1] These meditations were originally "Part V" of *A Memorial of the Ecclesiastical Life.* They make up a very complete review of the obligations of the priesthood. The fact that some of them are lengthy should not deter the reader from using them. In this respect it might be well to recall the saint's advice in a short foreword to *A Memorial of the Ecclesiastical Life:* "If you find the meditations too long or too wide in scope, you may confine yourself to a single point or two, according to your requirements."

To be a priest is to be a visible god on earth. All Christians are called gods in Sacred Scripture: "I said you are gods" (John 10, 34), but priests enjoy this prerogative in a much more eminent degree than the rest of the faithful.

Priests are gods in power and dignity, since they are clothed with the infinite power of God. If it were not through this divine power, how could they bring God down upon the altar at the Holy Sacrifice of the Mass? How could they form Him in the hearts of the faithful and give the Holy Ghost to their souls? How could they forgive sin and communicate sanctifying grace?

God gives His divine power to priests in such an exalted degree that they may effectuate many marvels that He alone accomplishes.

He created this world and can create others. To his priests He gave the power to produce Christ in the Blessed Eucharist, which is indeed greater than to create an infinite number of physical worlds.

The supreme effect of the Father's power is to beget His Only Son from all eternity and to give Him to us by the Incarnation.

The greatest act that Christ ever performed on earth was to immolate Himself on the cross for us, and to give Himself in continual sacrifice for the glory of His Father.

The most sublime work of the Holy Ghost was to form the Sacred Body of Christ in the womb of the Virgin Mother, to form the Mystical Body of Christ, His Church, and to apply to men's souls the fruits of the Passion.

Yet, did not God entrust all these powers to His priests? Is it not their ordinary function to form the physical and Mystical Body of the Son of God, and to distribute to the faithful His Sacred Body and His Precious Blood, His Holy Spirit, His mysteries and His graces? Is it not their daily privilege to sacrifice Christ to the Eternal Father, and apply the fruits of His Passion and Death to souls?

O admirable power of God's priests! Certainly each one may say with Christ, the Sovereign Priest, "All power is given to me in heaven and in earth" (Matt. 28, 18). In heaven, for the priest opens and closes its gates; in earth, for he has power over the personal and Mystical Body of Christ, who is so subjected to His minister that it may be truly said: "And he was subject to them" (Luke 2, 51).

Thus, priests are gods in power, authority and dignity. O power and dignity of the priesthood which surpasses all the powers and dignities of heaven and earth, second only to the ineffable dignity of the Mother of God!

Thank God for having elevated you to so lofty a state. Remember that even as priests are clothed with the power and authority of God, so too they should be filled with His holiness, love, charity and other divine perfections. To you especially are addressed the words of Sacred Scripture: "Put ye on therefore, as the elect of God, holy, and beloved, the bowels of mercy, benignity, humility, modesty, patience" (Col. 3, 12).

SECOND POINT

THE PRIEST'S LIFE OUGHT TO BE A REFLECTION OF THE LIFE OF CHRIST

Consider how the priest is truly another Christ living and walking on earth: *Nolite tangere christos meos* (Ps. 104, 15). He takes Christ's place, represents His person, acts in His name and exercises His authority. Speaking to all priests in the person of His apostles, our Blessed Lord said: "As the Father hath sent me, I also send you" (John 20, 21). By these words He meant that He sends His priests to dispel the darkness of hell which overspreads the face of the earth, and in its place to illumine the world with heavenly light. He sends them to work for the destruction of the tyranny of sin and the establishment of the kingdom of His Heavenly Father in this world. He sends them to perpetuate on earth the life He led and the virtues He practised. He sends them to continue His own office of mediator, judge and saviour.

The three last-mentioned functions are the principal qualities with which Christ has endowed His priests.

First of all, priests are mediators between God and men, making known His divine will. Theirs is the duty of drawing men to God and of reconciling them with the Creator; theirs is the obligation of rendering to Him the homage, adoration, praise and satisfaction due to Him.

They, too, must deal with those important relations between God and man which have to do with His glory, the salvation of the world, and the application of the fruits of Christ's Passion to men's souls.

Secondly, priests are, with the Son of God, judges of the world, not in temporal things, which are merely transitory, but in things heavenly and eternal. They are judges not only of bodies but also of souls, rendering decisions which are not of passing moment, but which will live in eternity. To them must come the judges of this world. Kings and emperors must bend their knees and bow their heads in submission to priestly power and judgment.

Thirdly, with Christ priests are saviours of the world, favored with that very name in Sacred Scripture, "Saviours shall come up into Mount Sion" (Abdias 21). The Son of God shares with His priests the heavenly prerogative of Saviour, desiring that they should be associated with Himself in the salvation of souls. "We are God's coadjutors" (1 Cor. 3, 9). He desired that they should discharge the office of saviours and be employed in the continuation on earth of the greatest and most divine of all His works, the redemption of the world. "As the Father hath sent me, I also send you" (John 20, 21). Towards this one end, every duty and office of the priestly life is primarily directed.

In the work of saving souls Christ expended Himself completely, employing therein every moment of His time, His thoughts, words and actions, His works, sweat, tears, blood and His very life. Thus, too, priests must give to this work their heart, their thoughts and affections, their strength and their all, that truly they may say with St. Paul, "I most gladly will spend and be spent myself for your souls" (2 Cor. 12, 15). It follows, then, that, if souls are lost through the priest's negligence, the wounds of Christ, His sufferings and His blood will cry vengeance against him at the hour of death. "I will require his blood at thy hand" (Ezech. 3, 18).

Truly the priest is another Christ living and walking on earth. Consequently, his life should be a perfect image of that of the Saviour, or rather a continuation of Our Lord's life. The priest is obliged, then, to study what the Master said while He was on earth, what He did, the virtues He practised, His horror for sin and His perfect detachment from the things of the world. The priest must imitate Christ's purity, sobriety, humility, modesty and all His other virtues that his own life may reflect them in practice.

O my Saviour, I give myself entirely to Thee since Thou wast so kind as to make me a participant in Thy divine prerogatives. Fill me with Thy Divine Spirit, clothe me with Thy virtues that I may work for the salvation of souls and may say at the end of my life what Thou didst say at the end of Thine, "I have finished the work which thou gavest me to do" (John 17, 4).

THIRD POINT

DUTIES OF THE PRIEST TOWARDS GOD, TOWARDS MEN AND TOWARDS HIMSELF

Christ associates you with Him in His eternal priesthood and in His divine prerogatives by which you are clothed with His powers and are bound to continue His life on earth. Consider then what Christ is and what He does. Consider Him first, with regard to His Father; secondly, with regard to men; and thirdly, with regard to Himself.

Our Blessed Lord, the Sovereign Priest, is all in all to His heavenly Father who in turn is all in all to His Divine Son. Christ loves only His Father and the Father loves only His beloved Son. Christ's only desire is to make His Father known and loved, and the sole thought of the Eternal Father is to manifest the glory of His Son and have Him adored and loved by men. The Son is the glory and treasure of the Father, and in turn the Son's supreme happiness is to glorify His Father and do His will. Towards this end, Christ directed every gesture and act of His priestly life, fulfilling them with divine dispositions and intentions.

The priest is also the Father's inheritance as His very title implies, and God is his portion as he freely promised when he received tonsure, *Dominus pars hereditatis meae* (Ps. 15, 5). He must therefore be all in all to God and God must be his all. He must look upon God as his only inheritance and treasure, eschewing the world's fortunes and pleasures. He must have no other possessions on earth than God, to whom he should give his whole heart and affections. Consequently, he must be always on his guard to discharge with the greatest care and holiness his priestly duties, such as the celebration of Mass, the recitation of the Divine Office, the administration of the sacraments and the preaching of the Word of God.

Since these offices are of such a divine and saintly character, they should be carried out *digne Deo* (Col. 1, 10), that is, both exteriorly and interiorly in a way befitting the majesty of God, worthy of the excellence of our ministry, of the holiness of the Sovereign Priest with whom we are co-ministers, and worthy of the price of His Precious Blood, in the shedding of which we were elevated to the dignity of the priesthood.

If you would know what Christ is and what He does with regard to mankind and especially with regard to His Church, you have but to look with the eyes of faith at His accomplishments while He was on earth, especially His intense sufferings. These deeds are so many tongues that cry aloud: "Thus God loved the world; thus Jesus loved His Church; thus Christ loved souls." With the same breath these voices will say to you: "Thus, too, you must love the Church; thus you must work for the salvation of souls; thus, you must do all things, suffer all things, sacrifice even life itself if thereby you may be instrumental in contributing to the salvation of one soul." *Omnium divinorum divinissimum est cooperari Deo in salutem animarum.*[2]

When you consider Christ in regard to Himself, you learn that being the Sovereign Priest He wished also to assume the character of a host, that thus regarding Himself as a host destined to death and sacrifice for the glory of His Father, "He humbled himself, becoming obedient unto death" (Phil. 2, 8). His whole life on earth was but a continual death so far as the things of this world were concerned. "I came down from heaven, not to do my own will but the will of him who sent me" (John 6, 38). His very life was truly an unending sacrifice of all that was in Him for the honor of His Father.

He who is called to participate in the priesthood should be one with Christ in the character of host. He should regard himself as a victim

---

[2] St. Dionysius, *De Caelesti Hierarchia,* cap. 3.

to be perpetually immolated with the Saviour for the glory of God; he should be detached and separated from the things of the world. Dying to all he should live alone for the Master. He should humble himself constantly, and burn with divine love. His whole life should be a perpetual sacrifice of his inclinations, his interests, his happiness, his comforts, his strength, his health and his life for the glory of God and the salvation of souls.

O Jesus, Sovereign Priest and Pastor of souls, I adore Thee with all my heart and soul as my Captain, my Exemplar and my Guide. I ask Thy pardon for having neglected to follow Thy divine rule and for having committed so many transgressions in my sacerdotal life. I give myself to Thee that henceforth with the help of Thy grace I may follow Thee more perfectly in all that regards Thy heavenly Father, Thy holy Church and Thy divine Self. I am resolved to imitate those saintly dispositions with which Thou didst discharge the duties of the Priesthood while Thou wast on earth. Destroy within me whatsoever may stand in the way of accomplishing my desire. Possess me entirely and establish forever within me Thy life and reign for the glory of Thy holy Name.

Ejaculatory Prayer: "God so loved the world."
Sic Deus dilexit mundum (John 3, 16).

SECOND MEDITATION

Obligation of the Priest to Seek Perfection

FIRST POINT

THE PRIEST'S RELATIONS WITH GOD DEMAND EMINENT PERFECTION

Three principal reasons show that no one is more obligated to practise perfection and holiness than the priest. The first reason comes from what he represents with regard to God; the second from his state and condition; the third from his relations with the life of the faithful.

No one has received greater graces from God than has the priest; consequently, no one can have such great obligations. No man on earth approaches more closely to God or communes more familiarly with Him than does the priest. To no other does God come more closely. The Eternal Father shares His divine paternity with him; the Son shares His Priesthood with him; the Holy Ghost makes him His associate in erasing sin, infusing grace, illuminating men's minds and warming their hearts with charity in the reconciliation of sinners and the application of the fruits of the Passion.

Thus, the priest is God on earth, taking His place, representing His person, acting in His name and clothed with His authority. Necessarily then he must be filled with His holiness according to the recommendation of Sacred Scripture: "Be holy because I am holy" (Lev. 11, 44). The priest must honor and love God with the highest degree of fidelity and perfection possible, inasmuch as he is the recipient of God's greatest favors. Pray constantly to know and practise these truths.

SECOND POINT

THE PRIESTHOOD IS THE HOLIEST OF ALL STATES

No other profession equals or excels the priestly state. Priests are the first officers of the Great King, the principal ministers in His realm, the treasurers and dispensers of His mysteries. Into their keeping Christ has entrusted the fruits of His life and death, His mysteries and His graces. St. Paul calls priests "dispensers of the mysteries of God" (1 Cor. 4, 1). Truly, they are charged with the keeping of His glory, His very Self, His Body and Blood, His Mystical Body and His most precious treasures. Naturally, therefore, theirs must be a holiness far exceeding that of ordinary Christians.

Priests occupy the most exalted position in the Mystical Body of Christ, which is the Church. They are, as it were, the heart and the head of that Body, for they are one with the Sovereign Priest who is the Head and the Heart of the Church. It follows, then, that they must discharge their duties more nobly and more perfectly than the other members of the Church.

Who could be pledged to a higher degree of holiness that he who is consecrated to God in body and soul by the august sacrament of Holy Orders, who spends his days in the sanctuary engaged in the sacred ministry, who frequently dispenses the sacraments to the faithful, who daily offers the Holy Sacrifice of the Mass and receives within his soul the adorable Flesh and the Precious Blood of the Son of God?

Ponder well these truths and beg God to engrave them on your mind and heart that you may derive from them the grace He wishes to give you.

THIRD POINT

THE RELATIONS BETWEEN THE PRIEST AND THE FAITHFUL DEMAND THE HIGHEST DEGREE OF PERFECTION

The priest is called in Sacred Scripture, "The angel of the Lord" (Mal. 2, 7), "the light of the world" (Matt. 5, 14), "an example of the faithful" (1 Tim. 4, 12), for he must purify, illumine and perfect the other Christians. Hence, he must be a font of blessings, whose salutary waters flow abundantly in the house of the Lord. He must be adorned with a supereminence of Christian virtues that his life may be truly a rule and guide for all the faithful.

Be assured, then, that there is no one on earth more obliged to seek perfection than the priest. It is not sufficient for him to lead the life of an ordinary Christian, but he must live as a priest. In other words, he must live so holily that he may sanctify others. This is not merely a counsel but a commandment. The Christian must tend towards perfection because of his baptism, the religious because of his vows, and the priest because of the very holiness of his state.

Humble yourself, seeing yourself so far removed from this holiness. Ask God's pardon for your negligence and infidelity. Make the resolution henceforth to lead a truly priestly life. Adopt at once the means best suited to this end, namely, the renunciation of sin, the world and self; the imitation of Jesus, the Great High Priest, and the performance of all the clerical and priestly functions in His spirit and with His dispositions. Give yourself to Him for this purpose; beg the assistance of Mary, the Mother of priests, and invoke the help of all the saintly priests and levites.

Ejaculatory Prayer: "I will serve Thee, O Lord, I will serve Thee in holiness and justice before Thee, all the days of my life." *Serviam tibi, Domine, serviam tibi in sanctitate et justitia coram Te, omnibus diebus vitae meae.*

THIRD MEDITATION

Hatred for Sin

GRAVITY OF SIN IN ITSELF

Adore God in His infinite hatred of sin. Give yourself to Him that the Light Divine which knows the hideousness of sin, and His Spirit which hates the detestable monster, may make you also know and hate it.

Realize that sin is the cause of endless miseries, the source of all spiritual and temporal evils on earth, in purgatory and in hell. It has caused the damnation of countless souls. Sin is so great an evil that it would be better for a thousand worlds to be destroyed than for one soul to be lost. The Doctors of the Church all agree on this point.

Sin is so great an evil that even the attaining of some benefit or good could never justify it. Would it not indeed be a marvelous thing to save all the souls on earth and snatch them from the jaws of hell? Yet, if to obtain such an end it were necessary to commit even the slightest sin, it would not be permitted. It would be far better to allow all souls to perish rather than save them by sinning.

Even too, if such an impossibility could be conceived, that the humanity of the Son of God were to be destroyed, and could be saved only by committing a sin, again it would not be permitted.

Know then that sin is an evil of infinite magnitude, horrible and detestable beyond description. It draws down upon men the anger of God and earns for them eternal damnation. Only God can hate it as it deserves, only He can know its hideousness, only the blood of the

Son of God can destroy its effects on men's souls. It can be destroyed only by the very destruction of a God-Man. You may judge for yourself, then, the extent of your guilt when you sin, and how you should detest even the slightest sin. Learn what confusion should cover you and what penance your heart should know at the realization of your guilt. Know, too, the depth and sincerity of the penance you should perform, and what trepidation you should experience at the very thought of ever falling again and what care you should exercise in avoiding the occasions of sin. Ask God to keep you from sinning in the future.

SECOND POINT

SPECIAL GRAVITY OF SINS COMMITTED BY PRIESTS

The sins of priests are greater than those of the faithful. Since the grace given priests is much greater than that given to the laity, it follows that their ingratitude renders them more criminal. Hence, St. John Chrysostom observes that in the Old Law the sacrifice ordered by God in retribution for the sin of a priest equalled that commanded to be offered for the sins of the entire chosen people.[1] It follows, therefore, that the sins of the priest in the Old Law were regarded as being equal in gravity to the crimes of the entire nation. Yet, the priests of the Old Testament were but shadows of the priests of the New, for to them God had given but a fragment of the graces He has bestowed upon the priests of the Christian Church. It is clear, then, that the sins of a priest of Christ are hideous in the eyes of God. The Council of Trent declares that sins which in others might be considered slight are grave when committed by priests. *Levia etiam delicta, quae in ipsis maxima essent, effugiant.*[2]

Ask God to open your eyes to the importance of these truths that you may excite true contrition in your soul and obtain the grace to

[1] *De Sacerd.,* lib. 6, c. 11.
[2] Conc. Trid. Sess. 22 *De Reform.,* c. 1.

avoid every sin and whatever is displeasing to Him who called you to the holiness of the priesthood.

HOLINESS REQUIRED IN THE PRIESTHOOD

St. Paul speaking of Jesus Christ, the Sovereign Priest, says: "It was fitting that we should have such a high priest, holy, innocent, undefiled, separated from sinners and made higher than the heavens" (Heb. 7, 26). It seems that the Apostle could hardly find adequate terms to describe the Master's separation from whatever was sinful, because He was a Priest. It would seem as though the word "holy" were sufficient to describe His Priesthood, for St. Dionysius says that holiness is spotless purity, unblemished by anything which would need expiation. Yet, St. Paul adds, "undefiled, innocent, separated from sinners," to make clear the incompatibility between sin and the priesthood. Christ's Priesthood was that very priesthood we share. Thus we, too, must be holy, innocent, undefiled and spiritually separated from sinners as He was.

Judge how removed is your life from that ideal set by the Master. Endeavor to repair any faults of which you have been guilty. Resolve that in the future with God's grace you will avoid all sins, especially those opposed to clerical holiness, such as impurity, avarice, laziness, intemperance, pride and vanity.

Ejaculatory Prayer: "Have mercy on me, O God, according to Thy great mercy." *Miserere mei, Deus, secundum magnam misericordiam tuam* (Ps. 50, 1).

FOURTH MEDITATION

Renouncing the World

CHRIST'S SENTIMENTS REGARDING THE WORLD

Adore Christ, the Sovereign Priest, and consider the sentiments He felt and will ever feel towards the world. They number four.

First, there was His feeling of contempt, knowing as He did that the world is but futility and nothingness: "Vanity of vanities and all is vanity" (Eccles. 1, 2).

The second was a feeling of aversion, hate and indignation, springing from the knowledge that the world is the enemy of His Father and the object of the divine anger, as the Apostle explained, "If any man love the world, the charity of the Father is not in him" (1 John 2, 15).

The third was a spirit of patience towards the world, for though He has always had the desire to destroy it as He will do on the last day, yet with infinite patience He has suffered and will suffer it until the end of time.

The fourth was His disposition to make use of the things of the world while He lived here below, for the glory of His Heavenly Father. Guided by the Holy Spirit, He sought earthly goods only in so far as they were necessary. With a perfect detachment, He never desired any pleasure from the transitory things of this world.

Ask God to give you similar sentiments and dispositions.

SECOND POINT

Sentiments of the Blessed Virgin Mary and the Saints Regarding the World

Christ engraved His own sentiments upon the hearts of His Blessed Mother and of the saints, especially His sainted priests. The Apostles were the first priests, and on the eve of his death He cried to His Heavenly Father, "They are not of the world, as I also am not of the world" (John 17, 16), and St. Paul adds, "For whom I have suffered the loss of all things, and count them but as dung" (Phil. 3, 8). Whence it follows that the apostles, as well as all holy priests and saints have lived in a spirit of aversion towards the things of this world, regarding them as the enemy of God and with St. Ambrose as the body of Satan. They well realized that the things men esteem are but vanity and folly, or as the Inspired Writer says, "the bewitching of vanity" (Wis. 4, 12).

Offer your heart to the Mother of God and to all the saints that you may know and live their sentiments towards the things of the world. Beg them to destroy within your own soul by the power God has given them, any attachment you may have for the world and its pleasures.

THIRD POINT

Reasons for Hating the World

Two qualities render the world hateful. The first is its malice, the second its folly.

"The whole world is seated in wickedness," writes St. John (1 John 5, 19), and the Holy Spirit assures us that it is filled with folly, "for the wisdom of this world is foolishness with God" (1 Cor. 3, 19). Its malice is apparent in its vices which pose in the guise of virtues. Its folly is apparent in many things, but particularly in its changing fashions and styles. This changeableness is a true mark of worldly folly: "A fool is changed as the moon" (Ecclus. 27, 12).

Detest the world's malice and despise its folly, and to make doubly sure that you will not become contaminated, avoid worldlings and the places they frequent. Avoid worldly habits in your speech, your dress and your environment. Remember that Christ said: "You are the salt of the earth" (Matt. 5, 13), that is, you are to be the wisdom and the wise men of the earth. It would be ridiculous to watch a city's chief magistrate following a fool and going about clothed like him. It would likewise be ludicrous to witness the sad spectacle of a priest following the false maxims and customs of the world he is supposed to guide in divine wisdom. His action would be a direct denial of that beautiful quality Christ bestowed upon him in the words, "You are the salt of the earth." He would become a "salt which has lost its savour" which is fit only to be thrown out and trampled under foot.

If in the past you have followed the ways of the world, beg God to lead you aright in the future that your daily conduct may justify His words, "They are not of the world, as I also am not of the world" (John, 17, 16).

Ejaculatory Prayer: "Deliver me, O Lord, from the present wicked world." *Eripe me, Domine, de presenti saeculo nequam.*

FIFTH MEDITATION

Self-denial

SELF-DENIAL OF OUR DIVINE SAVIOUR

Adore our Blessed Lord when He says, "If any man will come after me, let him deny himself" (Luke 9, 23). Adore the thought, the love and the design that He had in your regard when He said these words. Ask His pardon for placing any obstacle in the way of its fulfilment. Give yourself to Him that you may effectuate what He meant by these words, and realize that He Himself first did what He asks of you, having given you the perfect example of self-abnegation. While He was on earth, He never acted according to His own desires, but rather He did the will of His Father. He never sought His own satisfaction nor His own interests, but those of His Father. "For Christ did not please himself" (Rom. 15, 3). He lived not for Himself, but for God. "I live by the Father" (John 6, 58). He shed His blood even to the last drop, gave His very life, "emptied Himself" (Phil. 2, 7), and concealed His very sacred humanity and divinity in the Blessed Sacrament to the end of time.

Thank Our Blessed Lord for all the glory He has ever given or will ever give to His Father, as well as for the manifold graces He has merited for us. Give yourself anew to Him that you may share His sentiments. "Let this mind be in you, which was also in Christ Jesus: Who being in the form of God, thought it not robbery to be equal with God; but emptied himself, taking the form of a servant" (Phil. 2, 5-7).

ALL CHRISTIANS SHOULD DENY THEMSELVES

Jesus not only requires you as a Christian to renounce the world, Satan and sin, but He also binds you to renounce yourself. "If any man will come after Me let him deny himself" (Luke 9, 23). St. Paul says that you must strip yourself of "the old man" (Col. 3, 9) because "you are dead" (*Ibid*. 3, 3). Elsewhere He says, "He that shall lose his life for me, shall find it" (Matt. 10, 39). "If any man . . . hate not . . . his own life . . . , he cannot be my disciple" (Luke 14, 26).

This self-denial should be practised for the following reasons:

First, we do not belong to ourselves. "Know you not that you are . . . not your own" (1 Cor. 6, 19). We belong to God by an infinity of titles. We have no right to dispose of our life, no right even to exist, to live, to speak or act, nor even think for ourselves, but only for Him to Whom we belong. Hence, we must renounce ourselves entirely that we may be wholly God's.

Secondly, we must follow Christ if we would be united to Him. We cannot do that if we do not renounce ourselves, for we are but darkness and sin and death. Yet, darkness cannot imitate light, nor sin grace, nor death life.

Thirdly, nothing in this world is more opposed to our eternal salvation than we ourselves. We bear within ourselves four demons more dangerous than the devils who roam this world. The first demon is our own mind, filled with darkness and poisoned with the venoms of sin, whence spring error and heresy. The second is our own will, which St. Bernard calls "an untamed beast, a ravening wolf, a cruel lion and the sole foundation of hell." The third is self-love, which is the source of untold disorders. The fourth is ambition, pride and arrogance, with which we are born and which cease only with death. From these latter spring a multitude of vices.

In addition, sin has perverted all that is in us, filled us with darkness and malice, unleashed all our dormant passions. It has corrupted our senses, weakened our will and made slaves of body and soul. Hence,

St. Paul calls the body "sinful flesh" (Rom. 8, 3), and refers to it as sin (Rom. 6, 6), and as death (Rom. 7, 24). Sin has poisoned the blood in our veins and the very marrow of our bones, and caused us to be "by nature children of wrath" (Eph. 2, 3). Self-renunciation, therefore, is not merely a counsel of perfection, but a commandment. If we would share in the redemption of Christ, in the grace and salvation of the new man, we must renounce the remnants of Adam, that is, the old man and self.

When we ponder these truths, we realize that we have no enemy more cruel than our own ego, that there is none we should fear more than our very selves. It is more necessary to renounce ourselves even than to renounce the demons who seek to destroy us. God's greatest chastisement would be to leave us to our own deserts. Let us pray constantly that He will protect us against ourselves, more even than against all the infernal powers.

THIRD POINT

Priests Are Under a Special Obligation to Renounce Themselves

All Christians are obliged to practise self-abnegation. As St. Luke points out, Christ said to all: "If any man will come after me, let him deny himself" (Luke 9, 23). We priests are held to this duty in an especial manner for three important reasons: first, because being the first and noblest members of the Mystical Body of Christ on earth, we must follow Christ more perfectly, which means, of course, complete self-denial; secondly, since we are consecrated to God and His Church by ordination, we no longer belong to ourselves; thirdly, since we must encourage others to denial of self, we should practise it ourselves.

Learn the necessity of self-abnegation and develop a great desire to practise it at all times. Cultivate the spirit, the love and desire which annihilated Christ, that you, too, may be annihilated for Him. Study St. Paul's words: "Mortify your members" (Col. 3, 5), and truly strive to mortify your eyes, your taste, your tongue, your passions, your mind, your self-love and your will. Be careful to renounce self when you begin any important action, and to surrender yourself to Jesus Christ, asking Him to purify your intentions so that you may do them with His spirit and virtue.

Ejaculatory Prayer: "Deliver me, O Lord, from the evil man: rescue me from the unjust man." *Eripe me, Domine, ab homine malo: a viro iniquo eripe me* (Ps. 139, 2).

SIXTH MEDITATION

The Love of God

REASONS WHY WE MUST LOVE GOD

We are in this world to love God. For that end we were created, and that alone is our center, our happiness and our sovereign good. God is worthy of our love because of His infinite goodness, His incomparable beauty and His incomprehensible perfections. Our obligations of loving Him are, therefore, infinite in scope because He is all heart and all love for us. From Him we have received an infinity of gifts and graces, both general and particular, as Christians and as priests. Yet, how often we have shown Him ingratitude instead of love, injuries and outrages instead of devotion, in our actions, our words and the improper use of our body and soul.

Be confounded with sorrow, weep tears of blood at the memory of your conduct. Yet, if you were to weep torrents you could never atone sufficiently for your ingratitude. Ask His pardon, crying, "Have mercy on me, O God, according to thy great mercy" (Ps. 50, 1).

Renounce your love for the world and its pomps. Renounce your own self and all creatures. Protest to God that you wish henceforth to follow His commandment: "Thou shalt love the Lord thy God with all thy whole heart and with thy whole soul, and with all thy strength, and with all thy mind" (Luke 10, 27). Offer to Him in consecration your heart, begging Him to destroy in it whatsoever is opposed to His sacred love. Beseech Him to take full possession of you that you may be consumed with the sacred fire of His love divine.

The First Way to Love God is to Avoid Sin

The first thing you must do if you would love God is to hate whatever is opposed to Him, that is, every kind of sin. You must, therefore, purify your soul by perfect penance. Separate yourself forever from any occasion which may lead you astray. Work valiantly to destroy in your life any bad habits, thus eradicating the roots of sin, particularly inordinate self-love and pride.

Ask God's guidance to know the state of your own soul. Examine your conscience rigorously. After discovering your weaknesses, pray that God's divine mercy may give you true contrition and the grace to make amends. Ask also for the grace to remain aloof from dangerous occasions and temptations. Take the means necessary to attain these ends. Make the resolution to put them into practice daily. But, be on your guard against relying upon your own resources, seeking rather your strength in the grace and mercy of God, whom you must invoke unceasingly.

The Second Way to Love God is to Keep His Commandments

In order to love God truly you must establish in your heart a firm resolution of keeping God's commandments and those of His Church, as well as following the rules and obligations of your calling. You must discharge every duty well, especially those directly concerned with your priestly functions and the practice of the virtue of religion. Seek in all things to please and serve the Master.

If you examine yourself carefully on these points, you will find much to humiliate you. Be not discouraged. Form a real desire to fulfil all your obligations out of love for Him. Invoke the help of heaven and the intercession of Mary and the angels and saints, particularly those whose lives were filled with divine love.

Ejaculatory Prayer: "I love Thee, O my God; I love Thee, O infinite Goodness; and I wish to love Thee more and more." *Amo Te, Deus meus, amo te, bonitas infinita, amo te, et magis atque magis amare volo.*

SEVENTH MEDITATION

Obligations and Duties Towards Christ

REASONS WHY WE MUST HONOR AND SERVE CHRIST

There are three principal reasons why as Christians we must honor, serve and love Christ.

First, we must honor all that belongs to Him, His divinity and His humanity, His body and soul, His thoughts, words, actions and sufferings because they are infinitely holy, divine, admirable and adorable and merit infinite love and praise.

Secondly, we should honor and love all that honors and loves God. Yet everything in Christ renders to God the Father homage and love worthy of His supreme grandeur. In fact, God receives no honor and glory but through His Son Jesus, as the words of Mother Church so clearly state: "Through Him and with Him and in Him is given Thee, O Father Omnipotent, in union with the Holy Ghost, all honor and glory." It is certain that not a single good act is done except through Jesus Christ. "Without me you can do nothing" (John 15, 5). It is He who thinks, speaks and suffers in the members of His Mystical Body all things which are pleasing to the Creator. It is through Him and with Him and in Him that the angels and saints glorify God: "Through Whom the angels praise and the dominations adore Thy Majesty."

Thirdly, we are bound to love and serve Christ because of the privations, humiliations and sufferings He endured as well as the gifts He bestowed upon us. What has He not done for us? What has

He not given up? What has He not suffered because of us? He gave all, suffered all, endured all.

O Jesus, what should I not endure and do for Thy sake? Even if Thou hadst done nought for me, I should do all for Thee because Thou didst render such great glory to the Eternal Father, and because Thou art so lovable and adorable! O Good Jesus, may I be all Thine, my body and my soul, my life, all that I have and all that I am!

SECOND POINT

SPECIAL REASONS WHY PRIESTS SHOULD HONOR AND SERVE CHRIST

Besides our obligations towards Christ as Christians, we as priests have a multitude of additional obligations. We are clothed with a dignity possessing the quality of the infinite. Through our priesthood we are associated with Him in His noblest prerogatives, in His role as Mediator between God and man, Sacrificer of the Eternal, Saviour of the world.

Likewise, we are made cooperators with Him in the salvation of souls, receiving from Him the right to continue His most lofty tasks on earth, such as illuminating men's minds, reconciling them with their Maker, washing away their sins and bringing sanctifying grace to their souls. We have received the power of offering the Holy Sacrifice of the Mass and of giving His Body and Blood to the faithful as well as to ourselves.

Within our keeping are placed His treasures, mysteries, merits and grace; He entrusts to us His Body and Blood, His Church and every precious gift which is His. We take His own place in the world, with full powers to continue the work of redemption, discharging His own priestly functions. We receive graces in keeping with the high state to which He has called us, for it is true that He always bestows graces in conformity with the office to which He calls a chosen soul. When He bestowed the priesthood upon us, its wealth of graces came to us, unless we put some hindrance in their way.

Thinking over these things, what mind could conceive or what tongue express the depth and breadth of the priest's obligation to be all in all to Jesus? How could he but employ all his time, his life, his mind, his heart and his will and all that he has or knows or is in His service and for love of Him? If he acts differently, what a dreadful death he must expect! What a judgment! What a hell!

THIRD POINT

MEANS TO SERVE CHRIST

We must seek the means best suited for serving Christ. We may do so by thoughts, words, actions, mortifications, vocal and mental prayer, by acts of adoration and love. The best method is to work unceasingly to imprint upon our hearts a living image of His life and His virtues. We must fulfil our priestly duties with His spirit and His dispositions. We must seek always to act in a way worthy of Him in Whose honor and for Whose glory the sacerdotal office is discharged.

This desire shall be our aim. We must give ourselves to Christ that we may thus act, begging Him who set us in His place, to engrave within our being His image, so that loving Him with all our hearts we may become partakers of His saintly virtues and divine dispositions.

Ejaculatory Prayer: "I live, now not I: but Christ liveth in me." *Vivo autem, jam non ego: vivit vero in me Christus* (Gal. 2, 20).

EIGHTH MEDITATION

Devotion to the Blessed Virgin Mary

EVERY CHRISTIAN SHOULD HONOR THE BLESSED VIRGIN MARY

Adore God in His infinite love for the Blessed Virgin Mary, in the great designs He had upon her from all eternity and in all the effects of grace and glory which He has worked and will work through her in heaven and on earth. Rejoice with her in all the favors conferred upon her by Almighty God. Thank the Blessed Trinity and associate yourself with the Father, the Son, and the Holy Ghost in their love for her, and in their zeal for her honor that you may thereby honor and love her becomingly.

Know that true devotion to the Mother of God is but a continuation of the love, respect and submission with which Christ honored her on earth. Adore these sentiments in the Divine Heart of Jesus and give yourself to Him that His sentiments may be yours. Since He associated you with Him in His relationship of Son of Mary, He desires you to partake of His own sentiments and dispositions towards her. Pray that He may engrave them upon your heart, that you may honor and venerate her as your mother.

Consider the multitude of reasons obligating you to honor Mary, because of the perfection and excellence with which He endowed her, because of the service and honor she rendered and renders continually to the majesty of God, and because of the immense and incomprehensible blessings you have received through her intercession. "All good things came to me together with her" (Wis. 7, 11). "We are filled with all good things through (her)" (Tobias 12, 3).

O great and holy Mary, how admirable thou art! All worthy of praise and honor art thou! What obligations are mine to revere, serve and love thee and to be only thine! This I desire with all my heart; therefore, I offer thee and give thee my body and my soul, my heart, my mind, my life, my being with all its capabilities, my time and my eternity. To thee I protest that I wish that in all these things I may render thee homage now and hereafter. It is my earnest wish that I may lead others to praise, glorify and serve thee. Use on my behalf, I beg thee, the powers God hath given thee over men; possess me entirely so that thy Divine Son may establish the reign of his grace and love in my soul.

SECOND POINT

Special Union of Mary and Priests

There is a particular alliance between the Blessed Mother and priests. As the Eternal Father made her a partaker in His divine paternity, giving her the power of forming Christ within her womb, so, too, He communicates this same fatherhood to his priests in permitting them to form Christ in the Blessed Eucharist and in the hearts of the faithful. Christ made Mary a cooperator in the work of redemption; He also makes his priests coadjutors in the salvation of souls. The Holy Ghost associated Mary with Himself in the most divine of all His operations and in the mystery of the Incarnation; He associates priests with Him to continue this mystery in each Christian soul where Christ is reincarnated by Baptism and in the Blessed Eucharist. Since all graces coming from God pass through Mary's hands, so, too, they are given to you by the ministry of His priests. Mary is the treasury of the Blessed Trinity; priests also share this prerogative. Finally, as through Mary, Jesus was offered to His Eternal Father at the very first, as well as at the very last, moment of His life, so He is immolated and offered to God daily by His priests at Mass.

Because of this close alliance with Mary, priests owe her particular obligations of love, honor and service. They should be clothed with her virtues and dispositions. Humiliate yourself for neglecting your obligations to her. Form a great desire to fulfil them worthily. Offer yourself completely to Mary Immaculate and beg her to help you.

THIRD POINT

MEANS OF HONORING THE BLESSED VIRGIN MARY

If you have a true devotion to the Blessed Virgin Mary, seek the means of honoring and serving her. You may honor her by thought, applying yourself to the consideration of her mysteries, her virtues, her actions and her sufferings, as well as by interior acts of veneration and praise for her perfect cooperation with the grace of God. You may also honor her by words, in inciting others to love her, and by vocal prayer, principally the rosary. Lastly, you may serve by action, offering to her every deed you do, particularly almsgiving, fasts and mortification.

You may quite commendably enter any sodality or religious association established in her honor. Your devotion will also be strengthened by having her picture ever near you, and by observing her feasts with special affection.

Yet, the most efficacious of all means is the imitation of her virtues, especially her humility and submission to the divine will, her purity and hatred for sin, her love for God, her charity towards men, her patience, meekness and zeal for the salvation of souls.

With sorrow realize how far removed you are from this ideal; yet, you are amongst her chosen children. Pray to your heavenly Mother that she may obtain for you true repentance for your past transgressions, and the grace of God to be more faithful in the future.

Ejaculatory Prayer: "O Mother most amiable, show thyself a mother to me." *Mater amabilis, monstra te esse Matrem.*

NINTH MEDITATION

Obligations Towards the Church

FIRST POINT

WHAT THE CHURCH IS WITH REGARD TO THE THREE DIVINE PERSONS AND TO PRIESTS

Adore the Three Divine Persons of the Blessed Trinity in all that They mean to the Church, Their incomprehensible love and lofty designs upon it from all eternity. Adore and bless all that They have effectuated through the Church or will ever accomplish. Study the love and zeal of the Father, the Son and the Holy Ghost that you may learn to love and serve the Church as the beloved daughter of the Eternal Father, who gave her His Son to be her Spouse, and His Holy Spirit to be her Soul and Heart.

The Church is the sister, the mother and the spouse of Christ, as well as His Body and His fulness, as St. Paul remarks: "Which is his body and the fulness of him who is filled all in all" (Eph. 1, 23). The Church is likewise Christ's accomplishment and His perfection, His inheritance, His kingdom, His house, His treasure and crown, His glory and delight.

Moreover, the Church is the mother who engendered you for God by baptism, bears you within her womb, is the nurse who nourishes you with the divine word, as well as with the Body and Blood of her Spouse. The Church is your queen, your governess and directress, guiding you on the road to eternity. She is your teacher who instructs you in the eternal truths of heaven. She has given you the Sacrament of

Holy Orders, whereby you have been made a partaker of the priestly office with its privileges, graces and blessings.

How much then should you love and respect the Church! With what zeal you should serve her! How you should venerate her sacraments, ceremonies and customs! What sorrow you should know when she is made to suffer! What a duty is yours to thank God for having established her on earth! How you should pray that He may guide her always, sanctify and solidify her and give her priests according to His Heart!

SECOND POINT

CHRIST'S LOVE FOR HIS CHURCH

Adore Christ in all that He means to His Church, and remember that He is her Redeemer, Saviour, Founder, Brother, Spouse, Head, Doctor, Judge and Pastor; He is her Physician, Advocate and Mediator. Yet, at the same time He is her Servant for He said: "The Son of man is not come to be ministered unto, but to minister" (Matt. 20, 28). He is the Church's food, her life, her heart, her treasure, her reason for existence, her happiness and her God. He calls her His dove and well-beloved, His spouse and His sister and His heart, "My heart hath forsaken me" (Ps. 39, 13). He speaks of her as His dear soul, "I have given my dear soul into the hand of her enemies" (Jer. 12, 7).

Behold in the Sacred Heart of Jesus, His sentiments of zeal, care, vigilance and love for His Church. His love is apparent in three principal ways: first, in all the marvelous things He did on her behalf; secondly, in all that He suffered for her; thirdly, in the infinitely precious gifts He bestowed upon her.

Thank Him for all these favors; unite your heart with all the honor and love which has ever been or ever will be rendered Him by His Church. Embrace the sentiments expressed in the words of the Apostle, "For let this mind be in you, which was also in Christ Jesus" (Phil. 2, 5). Beg Him to inflame your heart with those dispositions, that you may truly say, "The zeal of thy house hath eaten me up" (Ps. 68, 10).

THIRD POINT

Our Duties Towards the Church

When the Son of God called you to the priesthood, He made you a partaker with Him in those all important qualities and offices He exercised in the Church, namely saviour, chief, doctor, father, pastor, physician, mediator, servant and judge.

Weigh well the obligations attached to these lofty prerogatives. Seek to ascertain how you have discharged them, and you will be astonished to find that there is much for which to reproach yourself and implore His pardon. Make the resolution to be more assiduous and faithful in the future.

In order that you may truly appreciate and love these high qualities which you share, picture the burning love which animated the apostles and all holy priests in their devotion to the Church. Study their zeal, vigilance and affection in spreading the Gospel and sanctifying the Church. Learn how meticulous they were about the cleanliness and the appointments of God's temples; how carefully they carried out the liturgy; how faithfully they obeyed all Church laws and with what holiness they administered the sacraments. See how devoted they were to the preaching of the word of God, and how anxious they were at all times to insure the salvation of the faithful.

Consider the sacrifices and sufferings of the apostles and all holy priests on the Church's behalf; see how they lived, not for themselves but for the Church, using their thoughts, words, actions, their strength, minds, their all, for that one object alone, so that truly they could say, "I most gladly will spend and be spent myself for your souls" (2 Cor. 12, 15).

Let shame engulf your soul as you realize how far you have wandered from the noble example set you by the saints. Beg them to help you know their zeal. Resolve to try to imitate the ideal they have set. Beseech Mary, the Mother of Christ, to help you by her prayers.

Ejaculatory Prayer: "Holy Mary and all Holy Priests and Levites, intercede for me." *Sancta Maria et omnes Sacerdotes et Levitae, intercedite pro nobis.*

TENTH MEDITATION

The Cassock, the Surplice and the Biretta

Meaning of the Cassock and Surplice

The black cassock signifies that the priest who wears it should at all times be in mourning for Christ, his Crucified Saviour. It means, too, that he should be dead to sin, to the world and to himself, doing penance for his own sins and for the sins of the world. It signifies finally that the priest's body should be at all times mortified in such manner that in him Christ's life is made evident to the faithful.

The surplice represents the "new man," our Lord Jesus Christ, as emphasized by the words used at ordination: "May the Lord clothe thee with the new man created in justice and holiness according to God." It follows that the priest must be like Christ, clothed with His perfection, humility, charity, modesty, purity and His other virtues.

The ordaining prelate when bestowing the surplice calls it the "habit of holy religion." Likewise, he prays that Almighty God may free the candidate from all the slavery of secular dress whose ignominy is put off. Since the Holy Ghost speaks through the Bishop, these words show us the purpose of the surplice in the mind of God.

How many careless or worldly priests there are who by their lives make a mockery of these words and ceremonies! The Church demands that the clerics who wear the surplice, lead a life in conformity with Christ's. Yet there are priests who live as worldlings, and look upon their clerical dress as a bar and a hindrance to pleasures which they renounced at ordination. The Church, through the person of the

Bishop, asks Almighty God to forgive the ordinands' sins, and to free them from the slavery of secular dress. Yet these same clerics cultivate an inordinate love for it, rather branding their own clerical attire as something of which to be ashamed.

O frightful blindness! O damnable profanation of sacred and holy things! Ask God to help you always to respect the attire of your calling, and to lead a life in conformity with the holiness of your clerical dress.

SECOND POINT

THE MEANING OF THE BIRETTA

The biretta is simply a cross which clerics wear on their head to show that the cross of Christ is their crown and their glory, whereby they re-echo St. Paul's words, "God forbid that I should glory, save in the cross of our Lord Jesus Christ; by whom the world is crucified to me, and I to the world" (Gal. 6, 14).

Engrave these truths upon your heart. Thank God for having given you the privilege of wearing the robe of religion. Ask His pardon for any profanation you may have made of it. Begin to practise with renewed zeal all that it requires and demands of you. Take seriously the meaning of the cassock, the surplice and the biretta. Treat them with fitting reverence. Pray God to give you the strength to persevere in your good resolution.

Ejaculatory Prayer: "Let thy priests, O Lord God, put on salvation." *Sacerdotes tui, Domine Deus, induantur salutem* (2 Par. 6, 41).

Part V

MEDITATIONS ON
TONSURE AND HOLY ORDERS

Part V

MEDITATIONS ON TONSURE AND HOLY ORDERS[1]

FIRST MEDITATION

Tonsure

FIRST POINT

TONSURE BINDS US TO STRIP OURSELVES OF THE SPIRIT, WAYS AND MAXIMS OF THE WORLD

TONSURE is the door into the clerical state. If we would understand the dispositions necessary for its reception and the obligations it imposes, we must consider the ceremonies attached to its bestowal. These ceremonies are, as it were, oracles of the Holy Ghost explaining what it means to be a cleric and what is expected of such a one in his daily life.

When the candidate for tonsure has laid aside his secular dress, which the Pontifical calls *ignominiam saecularis habitus,* he presents himself before the ordaining bishop. He is clothed in a cassock, *habitus sacrae religionis,* and bears a lighted candle in his right hand. These externals are to remind the young man that henceforth he must be stripped of the spirit of the world, its ways and maxims, and be vested

---

[1] *Meditations on Tonsure and Holy Orders,* like the preceding series on the priestly obligations, are taken from "Part V" of the original edition of *A Memorial of the Ecclesiastical Life.* They will furnish excellent material for meditation in preparation for the anniversary of one's ordination. Seminarians can find no better meditations for the ordination retreats.

with the spirit of religion and holiness. His only aim in embracing the clerical life must be to seek the honor and glory of the Saviour, and so to spend his days before God and man that he will be truly "a burning and shining light" (John 5, 35).

Humble yourself before God because of your unworthiness. Realize that you cannot enter this holy state without the grace of God. Beg Him to grant you this grace. Pray to the Blessed Virgin Mary and to all the holy priests and levites to obtain it for you.

SECOND POINT

Tonsure Obligates Us to Detach Ourselves from the Pleasures and Honors of the World

The Bishop cuts, in the form of a cross, the hair of the candidate receiving tonsure. The hair is waste matter which grows from the flesh, often growing from flesh that is dead rather than alive. It signifies the pleasures, honors and vanities of the world. These things in turn are the products of a world which is itself dead and decaying. St. Paul says, *Omnia arbitror ut stercora* (Phil. 3, 8). Thus the true cleric must be detached entirely from worldly things, despising them *ut stercora*. He must crown himself with the cross of Christ, finding his treasure in poverty, his glory in ignominy, his delight in labor and mortification, his life in death to sin, to himself and to the world.

Realizing how remote we are from these holy dispositions, let us give ourselves wholeheartedly to the Son of God that we may acquire them. Let us work unceasingly that whatever within us is contrary to them may be destroyed. Let us beg the Blessed Virgin Mary, the angels and the saints to assist us.

TONSURE OBLIGATES US TO SERVE CHRIST AND BE CLOTHED
WITH HIS VIRTUES

Publicly and distinctly the aspirant for tonsure says, *Dominus pars haereditatis meae et calicis mei, tu es qui restitues haereditatem meam mihi* (Ps. 15, 5). By these words he makes a solemn protestation that he chooses God for his portion, his inheritance and his treasure, despising all else. So, too, he makes evident his desire to belong entirely to God and to be in His absolute power and possession.

The ordaining prelate then clothes the young man with the surplice, saying: *Induat te Dominus novum hominem, qui secundum Deum creatus est, in justitia et sanctitate veritatis* (Eph. 4, 24). By these words the candidate is reminded that the surplice represents Christ, that he should be clothed with Him much more than an ordinary Christian. Thus, St. Paul writes, "For as many of you as have been baptized in Christ, have put on Christ" (Gal. 3, 27), meaning that Christians must be adorned with the Master's innocence, holiness and virtues.

These briefly are the dispositions necessary for entrance into the clerical state; these are the obligations and duties of him who has been tonsured.

If this great honor has already come to you, thank God for the favor He has conferred upon you, asking His pardon if your dispositions were unworthy, or your manner of discharging your obligations unsatisfactory. Pray to Our Lord, to His Blessed Mother and to the saints to supply what is wanting in you. Beseech them to obtain for you the grace to be more faithful in the future.

If you are preparing to receive the tonsure, resolve to live henceforth in conformity with its requirements, invoking heaven's assistance the while. Always put on your supplice with profound respect and devotion, saying, *Induat me Dominus novum hominem, qui secundum Deum creatus est in justitia et sanctitate veritatis.*

Ejaculatory Prayer: "The Lord is the portion of my inheritance and of my cup: it is thou that will restore my inheritance to me." *Dominus pars haereditatis meae et calicis mei, tu es qui restitues hereditatem meam mihi* (Ps. 15, 5).

SECOND MEDITATION

The Four Minor Orders in General

DUTIES TO JESUS CHRIST FOR HAVING ESTABLISHED THE FOUR MINOR ORDERS

Adore our Divine Saviour as the Author and Founder of the four Minor Orders, porter, lector, exorcist and acolyte. Honor Him as the font and source of grace contained in these sacraments.[1] With subdeaconship and the deaconship they represent degrees and participations in the priesthood, while together they constitute one perfect sacrament. Yet, this sacrament produces different graces flowing from its seven parts, just as a fountain with seven outlets diffuses its waters in seven separate channels. Revere the Divine Master in the holy plans He formulated for His Church, and the designs He had upon you in particular when He established Minor Orders.

Thank Him for all the effects of sanctifying grace produced in the Church by these orders. Offer Him all the glory they have ever effected or ever will effect in heaven and on earth, through their use by those upon whom they have been or are to be conferred. If you have already received them, renew your dispositions that you may make fruitful use of these orders. If you are about to receive them, give

[1] It is an article of faith that Holy Orders is a sacrament. Whether or not each of the various divisions of Holy Orders constitutes a distinct sacrament is open to question. The Episcopate, the Priesthood and deaconship present no controversy, but the subdeaconship and minor orders are in a different category. St. John Eudes regards them as sacraments and many theologians agree with him. Other learned divines, however, hold the opposite opinion, basing their arguments on sound reasoning.

yourself wholeheartedly to Him that you may know how He would have you receive them. Beg Him to destroy within you whatever is contrary to their fruition.

SECOND POINT

DUTIES TO OUR LORD FOR HAVING EXERCISED THE
FUNCTIONS OF THESE ORDERS ON EARTH

Consider the infinite love of Jesus for His Heavenly Father and His unbounded charity towards you, His chosen ministers, which impelled Him not only to establish these four Orders, but also to exercise their functions Himself while He was on earth.

He discharged the office of porter when He drove the money-changers from the Temple. And He still exercises the functions of this Office when He closes the doors of men's hearts, living temples of God, against the evil spirit and sin. So, too, He opens them to the Holy Spirit and to divine grace.

He discharged the office of lector when, as St. Luke says, being in the city of Nazareth, He entered the synagogue and arose to read, *"surrexit legere"* (Luke 4, 16). In His hands were placed the prophecies of Isaias and from them He read to the assembled people.

He discharged the office of exorcist when He expelled demons from men's bodies and vice from their hearts.

He discharged the office of acolyte for He assures us He is the "light of the world" (John 8, 12).

Thank Him, then, for the great honor He rendered to His Eternal Father in all these offices, and offer to the Father this same honor in reparation for the many transgressions of which you are guilty, either in unworthily preparing for the reception of these Orders, or in the manner in which you have carried out the functions they impose. Thank Jesus, too, for the graces and merits you have acquired through the faithful discharge of the Minor Orders, and in future when you make use of them, offer yourself wholeheartedly to Him that He may infuse into your heart the dispositions and intentions with which He exercised them.

DUTIES TO OUR LORD FOR HAVING CALLED YOU TO MINOR ORDERS

Consider the incomprehensible goodness with which Christ chose you to receive Minor Orders, through which you have been or will be clothed with several offices in the kingdom of the Great King. These offices are so noble and lofty that they surpass all the dignities and powers of the world, in the same measure that the spiritual is above the temporal, heaven above the earth, grace above nature and eternity above time.

Reflect that through these orders the Son of God has made you or will make you a participant in His noblest and highest qualities. For the Order of Porter entitles the recipient to share in that quality of the Saviour described in the Apocalypse: "These things saith the Holy One and the true one, he that hath the key of David, he that openeth, and no man shutteth; shutteth and no man openeth" (Apoc. 3, 7). The Order of Lector bestows upon you the quality of doctor and teacher; the Order of Exorcist shares with you the divine quality of power over demons; the Order of Acolyte gives you the quality described in the words of Sacred Scripture: "I am the light of the world" (John 8, 12).

Thank Christ for all these favors, and beg that they may arouse within you a great love for Him and a keen desire to serve and honor Him with all fidelity.

If you have already received the four Minor Orders, ask His pardon for any negligence you may have displayed in their exercise. Make the resolution to be more faithful in the future. If you have not yet received them, promise that when they are conferred upon you, you will endeavor to discharge worthily the obligations they will impose, and to make your life conformable to those high qualities of soul they demand. Ask the assistance and prayers of the Blessed Virgin Mary and of all holy priests and levites of the Church.

Ejaculatory Prayer: "Holy Priests and Levites, intercede for us." *Sancti Sacerdotes et Levitae, intercedite pro nobis.*

THIRD MEDITATION

The Order of Porter

EXCELLENCE OF THE ORDER OF PORTER

The first of the four Minor Orders is that which establishes porters in God's house. Yet it is so noble and so exalted a position that it raises those invested with it to a dignity and greatness far excelling even the highest earth can bestow. The porter thus occupies a position more exalted than any judge or president or governor or prince or king or emperor. This is true, too, of the Orders of lector, exorcist and acolyte.

Four reasons prove this statement.

First, the highest dignity of the world does not demand a sacrament. Yet, one cannot become a porter, lector, exorcist or acolyte without the bestowal of a sacrament.[1]

Secondly, all these Orders imprint on the soul of the recipient a divine mark or character, which no earthly honor can effect.

Thirdly, these Orders bestow sanctifying grace, provided no obstacle impede its infusion. No earthly dignity can produce such an effect.

Fourthly, not even a king nor an emperor has the right to open or close the doors of the church. A ruler may banish a subject from his kingdom, but he may not eject him from the Temple of God, nor may he drive devils from the bodies of the possessed.

Know then that there is nothing small in the Church. Even what appears to be trivial or inconsequential is in fact great, noble and important and must be treated with the utmost respect and reverence.

[1] See footnote on p. 213.

This is very evident, since it was necessary for Christ to institute a Sacrament in order to give to His chosen ones the power to open and close the doors of the church, ring the bells, read Sacred Scripture, exorcise the possessed, light the candles, present the wine and water for Mass, and finally to infuse into souls the grace to discharge their duties.

Be mindful, then, of your profound obligations to the Sovereign Monarch of the universe. Be grateful for the grace He has given you or will give you in appointing you porter in His House. Thank Him with all your heart and beg of Him light to understand the full extent of the obligations of your office and a plentiude of grace to discharge them worthily.

SECOND POINT

EXTERIOR FUNCTIONS OF THE ORDER OF PORTER

The Order of Porter has two distinct types of function, exterior and interior.

The *exterior* functions are those named in the Roman Pontifical of Clement VIII and the Pontifical of the Apostolic Library. They consist in ringing the church bells, opening and closing the doors of the Temple of God to the faithful, of barring them to the unfaithful, of admitting those worthy of entering the sacred edifice, of expelling those who would profane it by impiety or sacrilege. Likewise, the porter is charged with the care of the Sanctuary. He opens the book for the preacher, watches over the appurtenances of the church, is careful always that nothing is defiled or lost through his negligence. He must keep the church clean and maintain good order there at all times.

Ponder well your conduct regarding these matters. If you have been guilty of any negligence or failure of duty, ask God's pardon. Make the resolution that henceforth you will be assiduous in the discharge of your holy functions, above all to see that the church and particularly the sanctuary is scrupulously neat and clean, that God may not be dishonored in His own house by neglect and disorder.

Give yourself entirely to the Son of God that you may experience the fire of His zeal for the Temple of God, as enunciated by the Psalmist: "For the zeal of thy house hath eaten me up" (Ps. 68, 10).

INTERIOR FUNCTIONS OF THE ORDER OF PORTER

The *interior* or spiritual functions of this office are, according to the Pontifical, "to close against the devil and open to God by word and example the invisible House of the Lord, that is, the hearts of the faithful." The porter is so to live that his conduct and behaviour will be as so many bells calling, inviting and impelling men to know God and serve Him with love. This idea is suggested by the Inspired Writer in Exodus, when speaking of the robe of the High Priest: "And beneath at the feet of the same tunick round about, thou shalt make as it were pomegranates, of violet, and purple, and scarlet twice dyed, with little bells set between" (Exod. 28, 33).

Be humbled at the realization of how far you fall short of this ideal. Examine yourself carefully that you may discover what exists in you that is contrary to it. Pray God that you may have the grace necessary to rectify whatever is wanting in you.

Ejaculatory Prayer: "May the Lord open your heart in his law." *Adaperiat cor vestrum in lege sua* (2 March. 1, 4).

FOURTH MEDITATION

The Orders of Lector, Exorcist and Acolyte

FUNCTIONS OF LECTOR

There are two types of functions, exterior and interior, attached to the office of those ordained as lectors in the house of God.

The *exterior* functions are to dispense the word of God to the faithful by reading to them those holy doctrines befitting the Temple of the Lord. The lector should read clearly and distinctly with the intention of edifying and instructing. This part of the office of lector is so important that the Holy Ghost, speaking through the words of the *Pontifical* says that "those who discharge this function well will be associated with the apostles who from the beginning of Christianity, so worthily dispensed the word of God."

The lector also sings the lessons of the Church offices, and in addition blesses the bread and new fruits of the earth.

The *interior* functions are, according to the *Pontifical,* "to believe with his heart, and to effect in practice that which he reads, that he may teach the faithful by word and example." Thus, the ordaining prelate says to the young aspirant to the office of lector: "When you read in the church, you are assigned to an elevated position where you may be seen and heard by all. This signifies that you should possess all the virtues in an eminent degree that you may indeed be a guide and a model of the spiritual life to those who see and hear you."

Ask God's pardon for any faults you may have committed in the exericse of the office of lector. Make the resolution of being more faithful in the future and beg the assistance of His grace.

FUNCTIONS OF EXORCIST

The *exterior* functions of the office of exorcist are to expel demons from the bodies of those possessed, to notify the faithful when it is time to receive Holy Communion, and to pour water on the hands of the priest at Mass.

The *interior* functions are to banish from the body and soul of the exorcist whatever is sinful and unbecoming lest he himself become the prey of those very devils he seeks to rout. Hence, the Holy Spirit speaking through the *Pontifical* calls exorcists "spiritual rulers for casting out devils, with all their multiform wickedness, from the bodies of the possessed," and "approved physicians of Thy Church, confirmed by the gift of healing and by heavenly virtue."

Thank God who has given you, or who is about to give you the privilege of sharing in these excellent prerogatives. Humbly ask His pardon for having abused them. Be resolved in the future to use them to the best possible advantage that they may produce their desired fruits in your own soul for the glory of His Holy Name.

FUNCTIONS OF ACOLYTE

The *exterior* duties of acolyte are to carry candles on certain occasions during ecclesiastical functions, to light the candles and present the wine and water for Mass.

The *interior* duties are outlined by the Holy Ghost speaking through the Bishop. "Strive worthily," he says, "to fulfil the office once you have received it. For you shall not be able to please God, if, carrying in your hands a light before Him, you serve the works of darkness, and thereby set an example of faithlessness to others. But as Truth says: 'Let your light shine before men that they may see your good works and glorify your Father Who is in Heaven' (Matt. 5, 16). And as the Apostle Paul says: 'In the midst of a crooked and perverse generation shine as lights in the world, holding forth the word of life' (Phil. 2, 15). 'Therefore let your loins be girt and lamps burning in your hands, that you may be children of the light' (Luke 12, 35). 'Cast off the works of darkness and put on the armor of light' (Rom. 13, 12). 'For you were heretofore darkness, but now light in the Lord. Walk then as children of the light' (Eph. 5, 8). What that light is upon which the Apostle so much insists, he himself points out adding: 'For the light is in all goodness, and justice, and truth' (Eph. 5, 9). Be, therefore, solicitous, in all justice and goodness and truth, to enlighten yourselves and others and the Church of God. For then will you worthily supply wine and water in the Divine Sacrifice, when, by a chaste life and good works, you shall have offered yourselves as a sacrifice to God."

Weigh well these words and give yourself to Christ that you may possess the fruit He would have you enjoy. Offer Him thanksgiving for having been called to the office of acolyte, humiliation and contrition for past infidelities, and determination to be faithful in the future and a fervent prayer for heavenly grace.

Ejaculatory Prayer: O most blessed Light divine,
                       Shine within these hearts of Thine,
                       And our inmost beings fill.

                       O lux beatissima
                       Reple cordis intima
                       Tuorum fidelium.

FIFTH MEDITATION

The Order of Subdeaconship

DUTIES TO OUR LORD FOR HAVING INSTITUTED AND PERFORMED THE DUTIES OF SUBDEACONSHIP

Adore Christ as the author and Founder of subdeaconship. Honor Him in the designs upon His Church as well as upon you when He established it. Adore Him as the source of the graces contained in this Sacrament, graces earned at the price of His Precious Blood. Adore Him too as He carried out the functions of this Order. The office of Subdeaconship is to serve, that is, to serve God and the Church in the sacrifice of the altar and to assist the Deacon. For this purpose Christ came on earth. "The Son of man is not come to be ministered unto, but to minister," says Sacred Scripture (Matt. 20, 28). Thus, our Saviour spent His life serving God and men. "Behold my servant," said the Eternal Father referring to Him (Isa. 42, 1). And St. Paul says He took the form of a servant, *formam servi accipiens* (Phil. 2, 7). He brought His life to a close by the menial task of washing His apostles' feet.

Thank Him for the honor rendered His Father by the institution and exercise of this Order, as well as for the graces He merited for mankind through its operation. Offer to Him the glory rendered by those who have worthily discharged the functions of the subdeacon, offering yourself likewise to Him that you, too, may know the dispositions becoming to a servant of God and His Church.

SECOND POINT

The Goodness of Our Lord in Calling You to Subdeaconship

Consider the goodness of Christ whereby He chose you from among thousands and honored you with the privilege of subdeaconship. Realize, too, that He thereby associated you with Himself in His mission of Servant of God and the Church.

Thus, before ordaining those who are to become subdeacons, the bishop reminds them to consider attentively and seriously the burden they are about to assume and the obligations they are contracting. He reminds them that they are still free to withdraw and engage in worldly pursuits, *ad saecularia vota transire,* but after having received subdeaconship they will belong to the Church as perpetual servants: *In ecclesiae ministerio semper mancipatos.* To serve her with purity and holiness, they will henceforth be obliged to live in perfect chastity and continence.

Consequently, when you have received or when you will receive this order, know that you will have given, consecrated and delivered yourself wholly to the Church and to God to live chastely in a degree of perfection not asked of others. Be mindful also that "to serve God is to reign," *servire Deo regnare est,* and that the service of Christ is more honorable than any man could envision. The chaste ecclesiastic is an angel of God on earth.

Thank God for the precious favors you have experienced through your admission to subdeaconship. Ask His pardon for any unfaithfulness of which you have been guilty. Renew your profession of service and chastity, begging Him for the grace to discharge worthily the functions of your Order.

THIRD POINT

FUNCTIONS OF SUBDEACON

The *external* functions of subdeacon are as follows:

1. To prepare the water for the altar and for baptism.

2. To assist the deacon in the ministry of the altar.

3. To carry the sacred vessels to the altar for the Sacrifice of the Body and Blood of Christ.

4. To wash the corporals and purificators in a vessel especially reserved for the purpose, and afterwards disposing of the water so used, by emptying it into the baptistery. Likewise, he is to wash the other altar linens, always discharging his duties *studiose, nitide et diligentissime.*

The *interior* functions are to employ the water of divine doctrine to wash and purify the spiritual corporals and cloths of the true altar of the Church. That altar is Christ Himself and the corporals and cloths are the members of Christ, that is, God's faithful. The subdeacon must so regulate his own life and morals that they may render him able to discharge worthily the duties of an office which demands holiness and probity.

Thus, when the bishop consecrates a subdeacon, the Church speaking through the mouth of the ordaining prelate begs God to bless, sanctify and consecrate the ordinand. Holy Church implores Him to constitute the subdeacon a tireless and watchful sentinel of the heavenly army. She begs God to send down upon the ordinand the Spirit of wisdom and understanding, counsel and fortitude, knowledge and piety, and the Spirit of the fear of the Lord.

Then the bishop places the amice on the young man's head, saying: "Receive this amice by which is signified the curbing of the tongue." As he places the maniple on the aspirant's left arm, he says, "Receive the maniple by which is signified the fruit of good works." Then he clothes him with the tunic, saying, "May the Lord clothe thee with the tunic of sweetness and the garment of joy."

These things show clearly that the subdeacon should be filled with the gifts of the Holy Ghost; that he should know how to control his tongue, practise good works and have as his only joy the serving and honoring of God.

Consider these truths and give yourself completely to the Spirit of God that you may acquire gratitude, love and penance and a firm resolution to give yourself wholeheartedly to Jesus, invoking His grace and the assistance of His Mother, and of the holy priests and levites in heaven.

Ejaculatory Prayer: "O Lord, for I am thy servant: I am thy servant, and the servant of thy church." *O Domine, quia ego servus tuus: ego servus tuus et servus Ecclesiae tuae.*

SIXTH MEDITATION

The Order of Deaconship

FIRST POINT

DUTIES TO CHRIST FOR HAVING INSTITUTED DEACONSHIP

Adore our Saviour as the Author and Founder of the Order of Deaconship, and the source of all the graces contained in this sacrament. Adore Him, too, in the designs He conceived for His Church and for you in particular when He instituted deaconship. Thank Him for the honor given His Father through its medium and for the manifold graces it has brought to mankind. Ask His pardon for not having discharged its obligations properly, giving yourself unreservedly to Him with the firm intention of working only for His honor and glory.

SECOND POINT

THE CHIEF DUTY OF THE DEACON IS TO PREACH THE GOSPEL

One of the most beautiful and saintly qualities with which the Eternal Father endowed His Son is enunciated in these words of Sacred Scripture: "I am appointed King by him over Sion his holy mountain preaching his commandment" (Ps. 2, 6). Christ was the sovereign Preacher of the divine word. The principal office He discharged while on earth was to preach and He Himself stated that He had been sent from heaven for that purpose, "I must preach the Kingdom of God: for therefore am I sent" (Luke 4, 43).

The Master has associated you or will associate you with Himself in this noble and sublime office, for one of the principal duties of the deacon is to preach the word of God. "The deacon must minister at the altar, baptize and preach," says the bishop to the ordinand.

Thank God, then, for this favor He confers upon you. Realize your unworthiness, and give yourself to the Saviour that you may excite within your heart the proper dispositions to discharge your duties worthily. Seek to know the dispositions with which the Lord exercised these functions. Endeavor to put into practice the injunction already given or about to be given you by the bishop: "Take care that you may illustrate the gospel, by your living works, to those to whom you announce it with your lips, so that it may be said of you, *Blessed are the feet of those who preach the gospel of peace, who bring glad tidings of good things.*" These words mean simply that you should so live that your every action may be as it were a tongue or a voice, *vox clamantis* (Matt. 3, 3), exhorting the faithful to serve and love God.

THIRD POINT

ADDITIONAL DUTIES OF THE DEACON

The remaining duties of the deacon are:

1. To serve the priest at the altar. Deacons are therefore the levites of the Gospel, carrying out in the New Law those duties devolving upon the levites of the Old Testament, who served the priests in the tabernacle.

2. To confer the Sacrament of Baptism.

3. To administer Holy Communion. Hence, the *Pontifical* calls them "co-ministers of the Body and Blood of Christ," inasmuch as they cooperate with the priest in the administration of the Body and Blood of Our Lord.

Christ fulfilled all these duties while He was on earth. He was the servant of His Father: *Ecce servus meus* (Is. 42, 1). He baptized the apostles: *Hic est qui baptizat in Spiritu Sancto* (John 1, 33). With His own hands He administered to them His Body and Blood.

Thus, in elevating you to the dignity of the deaconship He has shared His own prerogatives with you. What admirable goodness! What heartfelt praise you should offer Him! What confusion should fill you at the realization of your failure to live up to His generosity and for the indignities and ingratitude you have offered Him! How saintly should be the life of a deacon! No wonder St. Paul says that a deacon must be proved before being received; they must be "chaste, not double-tongued, not given to much wine, not greedy of filthy lucre: holding the mystery of faith in a pure conscience" (1 Tim. 3, 8-9).

Finally, take well to heart the words of the bishop, "Be ye pure and chaste as becoming ministers of Christ and dispensers of the mysteries of God." Ask our Blessed Lord for these requisites.

Ejaculatory Prayer: "Grant, O Lord Jesus, that among Thy dispensers I may be found faithful." *Da mihi, Domine Jesu, ut inter dispensatores tuos fidelis inveniar.*

SEVENTH MEDITATION

The Priesthood

DUTIES TO OUR LORD IN RETURN FOR THE INSTITUTION OF THE PRIESTHOOD

Adore Christ as the sovereign Priest, Author of the Order of the Priesthood and Source of all graces contained in this august sacrament. Adore Him in all His holy designs upon His Church and upon you when He founded it. Adore Him in His divine exercise of the functions of the priesthood while He was on earth, thanking Him for the glory He rendered His Father, and for the grace He bestowed upon the whole Church and upon you in particular. Ask His pardon for having impeded the operation of this grace within your own soul, and beg Him to help you to be more faithful in the future.

SECOND POINT

EXCELLENCE OF THE SACERDOTAL FUNCTIONS

Ponder what the bishop says to the young man presented as a candidate for the priesthood.

He reminds him that the ancients, whom God commanded Moses to appoint to govern the Chosen People, were but figures and shadows of the priests of the New Law; and that the priests of today are the successors of the seventy-two disciples selected by the Master. They are *doctores fidei, comites Apostolorum, cooperatores ordinis episcopalis.*

The bishop then instructs the ordinand that the sacerdotal office comprises the following functions:

1. To change the bread and wine into the Body and Blood of Christ, to offer Him sacrifice and give Him the people.
2. To preach the word of God.
3. To baptize.
4. *Praeesse,* that is, to rule and guide souls towards eternity.
5. To forgive sins or withhold absolution.
6. To bless. Hence when the bishop anoints the hands of the ordinand with holy oil, he says: "Deign to consecrate and sanctify, we beseech Thee, O Lord, these hands by this holy anointing and our blessing; that whatsoever they may bless may be blessed; and that whatsoever they may consecrate may be consecrated and sanctified in the name of the Lord Jesus Christ. Amen."

Remember that all these qualities and functions belong only to the divine and infinite power of God. Consequently, when He admitted you to the priesthood, He elevated you to a divine and infinite dignity. Consequently, you incur obligations which are infinite in character and obligate you to thank God constantly, to love Him and to surrender yourself completely to Him that you may worthily discharge your duties. Let this be your resolution.

THIRD POINT

MEANS OF CONSERVING THE GRACE OF ORDINATION

Weigh well the words spoken by the Holy Ghost through St. Paul: "Neglect not the grace that is in thee, which was given thee by prophecy, with the imposition of the hands of the priesthood" (1 Tim. 4, 14).

"I admonish thee that thou stir up the grace of God which is in thee, by imposition of my hands" (2 Tim. 1, 6).

If Timothy, to whom these words were addressed, himself a saint and martyr, needed this salutary admonition, how much more is it necessary for you!

To preserve and revivify the grace of ordination, or to dispose yourself to receive it, three things are necessary:

1. Destroy within you by penance whatsoever is opposed to it.

2. Cultivate a high esteem of the priesthood and its duties. Entertain an intense desire to discharge its obligations in holiness. Put into practice the beautiful words spoken by the bishop to the ordinand:

"As you, therefore, beloved children, have been chosen by the voice of our brethren to be consecrated as our coadjutors, preserve the purity of your lives in unspotted holiness. Reflect seriously on what you do. Let your conduct be in conformity with the action you perform, so that celebrating the mystery of the Lord's death, you take heed to mortify your members from all vices and lusts. Let your doctrine be spiritual medicine for the people of God; let the odor of your life be the delight of the Church of Christ; so that you may build up the house, that is the family of God . . ."

3. Be ever mindful of your need of God's grace for the fulfilment of your priestly duties. Beg of Him that He may assist you. Pray to the Blessed Virgin and all the holy priests and levites in heaven.

Ejaculatory Prayer: "O sweet Jesus, grant that the odor of our life may be the delight of thy Church." *O bone Jesu, fac ut bonus odor vitae nostrae sit delectamentum Ecclesiae tuae.*

EIGHTH MEDITATION

The Feast of the Priesthood [1]

JESUS CHRIST IS THE SOVEREIGN PRIEST

Let us consider and adore our Lord Jesus Christ as the supreme High Priest, exercising with infinite sanctity the sacerdotal functions by which He procured unlimited glory for His Heavenly Father, destroyed sin, merited for us all the appropriate graces necessary to our salvation and placed before our eyes the living example and the perfect rule that we must follow if we would exercise worthily these same great functions.

Let us give profound thanks to Him for all these miracles, beseeching the angels, and the saints, especially all the holy priests and levites, and the Blessed Virgin Mary to help us to bless and thank our Sovereign Priest for His incomparable gifts.

SECOND POINT

INSTITUTION OF THE CATHOLIC PRIESTHOOD BY OUR LORD

Let us consider our good Saviour as the Founder, the Head and Superior of the Holy Order of the priesthood, as the Principle and the

[1] The Feast of the Priesthood was formerly celebrated by the Eudist Fathers, the Sulpicians and other religious congregations on November 13.

Fountain of the boundless wealth of graces and blessings contained in Holy Orders and as the Sanctifier of all holy priests and levites.

Let us thank Our Lord and summon all the angels and saints in heaven to thank Him with us, for the infinite favor conferred upon the Church in establishing the priesthood, and in raising up her Priests on whom He has bestowed such admirable powers, for the benefit of the faithful, enabling each chosen priest to offer the wonderful sacrifice of the altar, to administer on their behalf His Sacred Body and His Precious Blood, to wipe out the sins of the faithful and to reconcile them with God, in short, to close hell against them and to open heaven for them.

We shall also bless Our Lord, the High Priest, for the countless graces He has conferred on earth on all His holy priests and levites, and for all the glory and happiness which He communicates to them in heaven. We shall likewise thank the glorious company of priests for all the services they have rendered to the divine Majesty of God, and to His true Church. We shall offer to God all the honor that they accorded Him while on earth and will give Him forever in heaven. We shall ask them to unite us with their unceasing praise of God and to make us sharers in the virtues they practised here on earth as members of the priesthood.

THIRD POINT

INCOMPARABLE FAVOR WHICH OUR LORD HAS GRANTED US IN CALLING US TO THE PRIESTHOOD

Let us consider the incomparable favor which Our Lord has bestowed in having called each of us to a state so noble, so holy, so worthy of admiration as the priesthood. We must give Him deepest thanks for this inestimable privilege, and beg all the saints of heaven to bless and glorify Him for it on our behalf.

Then we shall make a careful examination of our innumerable sins, offences and negligences, in our sacerdotal functions, that we may humble ourselves most deeply at the feet of our Redeemer, asking His pardon with great contrition, and offering Him in satisfaction all the honor rendered to His majesty by all the holy priests and levites, in the performance of these same functions. We must implore our Divine Master to repair our defects Himself, while we promise henceforth to begin with His help to live as veritable priests, and to discharge with fitting fervor and sanctity the functions of His divine Priesthood, beseeching Him to grant us all the graces we need for this end. We must also ask the Blessed Virgin Mary and all holy priests to aid us to obtain these graces from the infinite mercy of the omnipotent High Priest.

Ejaculatory Prayer: "Thou art a priest for ever."
Tu es sacerdos in aeternum (Ps. 109, 4).

Part VI

MEDITATIONS
FOR
THE ANNUAL RETREAT

Part VI

MEDITATIONS FOR THE ANNUAL RETREAT[1]

FIRST MEDITATION

The Holy Sacrifice of the Mass

FIRST POINT

THE DIGNITY AND HOLINESS OF THE MASS

REFLECT on the greatness, the holiness and infinite dignity of this august mystery.

It is the most marvelous action ever performed in heaven or on earth; it is a divine sacrifice with Christ as its victim, offered to God by God for intentions and ends which in themselves are infinite. It is the supreme sacrifice of Calvary by which Our Lord confers three ineffable favors upon you: He comes to you, He sacrifices Himself for you, and He gives Himself to you.

Cultivate a great love and appreciation of the Holy Sacrifice of the Mass, at which myriads of angels gather in holy awe. Thank the Son of God for having established it in His Church, and for having given you the privilege of offering it and of receiving His Sacred Body and Blood in Holy Communion.

[1] These short and practical meditations are taken from the original edition of *A Memorial of the Ecclesiastical Life*. See *Oeuvres Complètes*, Vol. III, p. 124 ff. They may be used for morning meditation or for daily examination during the annual retreat.

SECOND POINT

FAULTS COMMITTED IN THE CELEBRATION OF MASS

Examine yourself carefully on the faults you have committed in offering the Holy Sacrifice. Examine both your interior and exterior deportment. Have you prepared worthily for Holy Mass? Have you made a proper thanksgiving afterwards?

What fruit have you reaped from the scores of Masses that you have offered and from the many Communions you have received? What advancement in virtue or what amendment of life have you gained?

Have you been assiduous in preventing profanations and irreverence in the churches where Mass is offered? Has your behaviour been in keeping with what is expected in reverence and devotion to the Mass?

Ask God's pardon for any faults of which you may have been guilty. Pray Our Lord to help you repair the evil your negligence or culpability may have caused. Make the resolution of being more careful in the future. Beg God's help to persevere.

Ejaculatory Prayer: "Bear in mind what you do. Let your conduct be in conformity with the action you perform." *Agnoscite quod agitis: imitamini quod tractatis.*

SECOND MEDITATION

The Sacrament of Penance

CHRIST'S GOODNESS IN HAVING INSTITUTED THIS SACRAMENT

Let us consider the goodness and mercy of Christ in having established in His Church this great sacrament by which He confers three special favors upon us.

First, Our Blessed Lord pardons our sins through sacramental penance, wipes away all our transgressions, no matter how enormous or numerous. Consequently, our indebtedness to Him is equal to His infinite kindness. Sin being infinite in malice, the Divine Son bestows an infinite good upon us when He pardons us. Even in the remission of one venial sin, He confers upon us a spiritual favor greater in value than He would give us if He were to cure the greatest physical sufferings we could conceive. It is obvious that even the smallest sin surpasses the greatest material ill.

Let us think, then, of our obligations to God because of the manifold sins He has forgiven us. Let us thank Him constantly.

Secondly, through the Sacrament of Penance, He applies His Precious Blood to our souls to cleanse and purify them from sin. The Sacrament of Penance is, as it were, a spiritual blood-bath wherein Christ washes us whenever we will. O unspeakable love! He could have wiped away our sins in a thousand other ways, but He chose this sacrament to show us His infinite love.

Thirdly, not only does Penance destroy our sins, but it fills our souls with sanctifying grace, increasing the grace that is already within us, or reestablishing it if we have lost it through mortal sin. Instantly, our souls are adorned with His virtues, with the gifts of the Holy Ghost, with the beatitudes, and we become children of God, temples of the Divine Spirit, heirs of the Eternal Father, co-heirs with the Son. Let us thank Him unfailingly for His mercy.

DISPOSITIONS NECESSARY FOR THE WORTHY RECEPTION OF THE SACRAMENT OF PENANCE

In receiving the Sacrament of Penance, it is necessary to have the proper dispositions for its worthy reception. Otherwise, what was meant to be a remedy becomes a poison, what was intended to be a grace becomes a sin. Thus, salvation is endangered and a sacrament is received sacrilegiously. Moreover, the oftener we go to confession, so much the more should we be on our guard against carelessness, routine and the lack of true repentance.

The dispositions with which we should approach this great sacrament are as follows: 1. We should realize that of ourselves we cannot have true contrition; hence, we should constantly invoke God's assistance and the help of the Blessed Mother and of the saints; 2. We should examine our conscience very carefully; 3. We should have true sorrow for our sins and a firm purpose of amendment; 4. We should make our confession clearly and sincerely, concealing or minimizing nothing of a serious nature; 5. We should be very docile to the admonitions of the confessor; 6. We should faithfully execute the penance as soon as it can conveniently be done; 7. We should range ourselves on God's side against ourselves, putting on His zeal that we may destroy within us the enemy of our souls, sin itself. In a word, we should make each confession as though it were our last, and as though we were about to face the Omnipotent Judge from whom nothing will be hidden.

Let us examine ourselves on the manner of making our confessions in the past, invoking God's pardon for any negligence of which we may have been guilty. Let us make the resolution to repair our past faults by a genuine confession in which we shall have a fulness of His grace. Let us beg His help for the future.

Ejaculatory Prayer: "Have mercy on me, O God, according to thy great mercy." *Miserere mei, Deus, secundum magnam misericordiam tuam* (Ps. 50, 3).

THIRD MEDITATION

Mental and Vocal Prayer

EXCELLENCE OF PRAYER

Prayer, either mental or vocal, is a conversation with God. Therein you render Him homage, make known your wants and beg light and grace from Him.

It is, indeed, a high privilege that you, a miserable sinner, a mere nothing, should be able to commune with the Creator. Surely, He bestows upon you a tremendous favor in permitting you even to approach His august presence or to lift up your eyes to Him. "And dost thou think it meet to open thy eyes upon such an one, and to bring him into judgment with thee?" (Job, 14, 3).

Christ was not more insistent upon any point than that of prayer. Why? First of all, because He loves you so much that His chief happiness consists in conversing with you, unworthy though you are. Hence, Sacred Scripture says, "My delights were to be with the children of men" (Prov. 8, 31). Secondly, He realizes that you of yourself are nothing, and can do nothing. Thirdly, He wishes to enrich you with His gifts. You must ask Him continually for what you need, thus making manifest your utter dependence upon Him and your realization that He alone can help you since He is the source of all good.

SECOND POINT

DISPOSITIONS NECESSARY FOR PRAYER

Reflect on the interior and exterior dispositions with which the creature should approach his Creator. Man is indeed a humble subject in the presence of his Sovereign, a sinner before the Saint of saints, a criminal before the Supreme Judge.

Recall how Christ prayed to His Father during His years on earth. Think, too, how Mary and the saints prayed.

Examine yourself carefully for any faults you may have committed in vocal or in mental prayer.

Have you prepared yourself sufficiently? "Before prayer prepare thy soul," says Sacred Scripture (Ecclus. 18, 23). Have you neglected any obligatory prayers? Have you chosen unsuitable times or inappropriate places? Have you permitted yourself to become the prey of distractions? Have you been reverent and recollected? Have your prayers been fruitful for advancement in the ways of God? Have you taken advantage of the graces and gifts attached to the prayers you have said? Have you distracted others at prayer? Remember you must respect others who are communing with the Master and do nothing to hinder their devotions.

Ask God's pardon for any faults of which you may have been guilty. Beg His grace to be more faithful in the future. Seek the means best suited to help your prayers become meritorious. Avoid the occasions of distraction.

Ejaculatory Prayer: "We ought always to pray and not to faint." *Oportet semper orare, et non deficere* (Luke 18, 1).

FOURTH MEDITATION

Submission to the Will of God

IMPORTANCE OF SUBMISSION TO THE DIVINE WILL

The divine will is the principle, the end and center of all things. It is infinitely powerful, wise and good. It ordains and disposes of whatever happens in this world and in eternity. In all its decrees it is infinitely adorable for it takes its origin in the most perfect justice, goodness and charity towards us. It does all things for the best in the most admirable manner conceivable.

The divine will is manifested in various happenings, by the Commandments, by the precepts of the Church, by our duty, our obligations and our state in life.

The Son of God did not choose His own will but the will of His Heavenly Father. He was entirely subjected to His Father's mandates, no matter how difficult they were.

The Blessed Virgin and the saints followed a similar path of conformity to the divine will.

Our salvation, our perfection, our happiness, our peace, our well-being, and even our liberty, depend on our constant cooperation with the will of God, following the example of Jesus, Mary and the saints.

SECOND POINT

How Have You Practised Submission to God's Will?

Examine yourself on your failures to submit to God's will shown in various events of your life, as well as in your observance of the commandments and in the precepts of the Church. Above all else, ask yourself how you have cooperated with that divine will insofar as it affects your state in life. Ask the Master's pardon and be resolved in the future to correct whatever is wanting in you.

Ejaculatory Prayer: "Behold I come that I should do thy will, O my God." *Ecce venio ut faciam voluntatem tuam, Deus.*

FIFTH MEDITATION

Obedience

NECESSITY AND IMPORTANCE OF OBEDIENCE

The virtue of obedience is so necessary to eternal salvation that Our Lord came on earth to teach it to us by word and example. He practised it unceasingly during His life, doing nothing except by obedience. Not only did He obey His Heavenly Father, but likewise He was subject to Mary and Joseph. So, too, He bowed to Herod and Pilate and His executioners who represented the powers of darkness "This is your hour, and the power of darkness" (Luke 22, 53) He was obedient even unto death and unto the death of the cross.

The saints have always loved this holy virtue, preaching it incessantly and practising it scrupulously.

The Scripture, the Fathers and Doctors of the Church all agree that where there is not obedience there cannot be true virtue.

Thank Our Lord for the inspiring example He has given us.

SECOND POINT

How Have You Practised Obedience?

Examine yourself on the many faults of which you are guilty in regard to the submission of mind and will to those who for you take God's place. Ask His pardon for your transgressions.

Ejaculatory Prayer: "Obey your prelates." *Obedite praepositis vestris* (Heb. 13, 17).

SIXTH MEDITATION

Charity

EXCELLENCE OF CHARITY

Charity is the queen and mother of all the other virtues, their end, their soul, their very life. Consequently, where charity does not exist, there is no true virtue possible.

Charity brought Christ forth from the bosom of His Father that He might descend into the womb of the Virgin Mother. It prompted Him to come on earth and lead a life of suffering and misery for thirty-four years, finally dying on the cross. It impelled Him to give Himself to us continually in the Blessed Sacrament.

Charity is the dominant theme of the New Testament, the sole commandment Christ gave before His death. Weigh well His words: "This is my commandment, that you love one another, as I have loved you" (John 15, 12). Consider, too, the words of the Apostle Paul: "Charity is patient, is kind; charity envieth not, dealeth not perversely, is not puffed up; is not ambitious, seeketh not her own, is not provoked to anger, thinketh no evil; rejoiceth not in iniquity, but rejoiceth with the truth; beareth all things, believeth all things, hopeth all things, endureth all things" (1 Cor. 13, 4·7).

The flower and perfection of charity is the meekness which our Saviour recommended in His words, "Learn of me, because I am meek, and humble of heart" (Matt. 11, 29).

The greatest work of charity is to labor for the salvation of souls.

This, indeed, surpasses all else that a Christian might ever accomplish on earth, or as St. Dionysius says, "It is the most divine of all divine things."

SECOND POINT

How Have You Practised Charity?

Examine yourself on the faults you have committed against charity in thoughts, words, actions or omissions against this virtue, in relation to those with whom you live.

Also consider what transgressions you have been guilty of in the matter of your zeal for the salvation of souls.

Ask God's pardon and make a firm purpose of amendment.

Ejaculatory Prayer: "This is my commandment, that you love one another." *Hoc est praeceptum meum, ut diligatis invicem* (John 15, 12).

SEVENTH MEDITATION

Humility

NECESSITY OF HUMILITY

Humility consists in maintaining a very low degree of self-esteem, in despising, hating and avoiding honor and glory as well as the praises of men. It seeks abjection, ignominy and scorn.

Without humility it is impossible to please God or save one's soul, according to the words of our Saviour: "Amen I say to you, unless you be converted, and become as little children, you shall not enter into the kingdom of heaven" (Matt. 18, 3).

Humility is the measure of perfection and holiness of souls on earth and of their glory in eternity, for the Son of God said when He was here on earth: "Whosoever therefore shall humble himself as this little child, he is the greater in the kingdom of heaven" (Matt. 18, 4).

Since there is no virtue more necessary than humility, it follows that no vice is more to be avoided than vanity, especially by those who profess to be devout.

Think of the multitudes of angels damned by one defiant thought of pride; think of the number of souls who enjoyed a high degree of holiness, but were hurled into hell because of arrogance and pride.

Reflect upon the sublime examples of humility given by the Son of God, as well as by His Mother and the saints.

Consider in particular these matters regarding which you should practise humility.

SECOND POINT

How Have You Practised Humility?

Make a serious and thorough examination of the faults you have committed against humility by thought, word and deed.

Ascertain your true sentiments towards yourself. Do you take pleasure in the esteem and praises of men? Do you seek to avoid whatever may be disparaging to you? Are you boastful? Do you receive with humility deserved corrections or warnings? Do you cling stubbornly to your own opinion in your discussions with others? Do you submit willingly to your superiors? Do you act and speak so as to draw to yourself the praises of those about you? Do you not really esteem yourself before all else? Do you covet dignity and advancement? Do you take a secret pride in your knowledge, experience, industry, ability or whatever talent you may have which you deem important?

Ask Christ to forgive the many sins you may have committed against humility. Beg Him to help you to repair the evil you have caused and take the good resolution to dispel by every means in your power whatever is opposed to this beautiful virtue, that you may acquire and practise humility in the future. That your success may be assured, have this intention at your Masses, Communion and in your prayers. Study your soul, that you may truly know yourself and learn well these three truths: 1. you are nothing, you have nothing, of yourself you can do nothing; 2. you are of yourself sinful, having within yourself the source of every evil; 3. you have richly merited God's anger and eternal punishment if you have committed a serious sin.

Never willingly accept the praises of creatures, but offer them to God to whom they belong rightly: "To the king of ages, immortal, invisible, the only God, be honor and glory" (1 Tim. 1, 17).

Humble yourself at the beginning and the end of every action, ever mindful of your unworthiness and following the injunction of Sacred Scripture, "The greater thou art, the more humble thyself in all things; and thou shalt find grace before God" (Ecclus. 3, 20).

Reject at once any thoughts or sensations of vanity which may come to you. Turn them into occasions of abasing yourself in the light of your own nothingness.

Close your eyes from faults of others, and see only your own. When you witness or learn of your neighbor's weaknesses, be humbled yourself, realizing that there is no crime which you yourself might not commit if it were not for God's grace.

When others blame you, accept it that you may learn self-condemnation. Seek not to be regarded as a master, or a learned man or an outstanding personality.

Love and embrace the abjectness which comes from your faults. Willingly accept all humiliations, confusion, contradictions and afflictions which God sends you, not merely as trials to sanctify you, but as just deserts for your sins and as means by which to humble your pride.

Ejaculatory Prayer: "Humble thyself in all things: and thou shalt find grace before God." *Humilia te in omnibus et coram Deo invenies gratiam* (Ecclus. 3, 20).

EIGHTH MEDITATION

Modesty, Simplicity and Truth

EXCELLENCE OF MODESTY, SIMPLICITY AND TRUTH

Consider the words of St. Paul, "I . . . beseech you, by the mildness and modesty of Christ" (2 Cor. 10, 1), "put ye on therefore, as the elect of God, holy and beloved, the bowels of mercy, benignity, humility, modesty, patience" (Col. 3, 12). "Let your modesty be known to all men. The Lord is nigh" (Phil. 4, 5).

Study the admirable modesty of Christ and His Blessed Mother who are the models and exemplars we as Christians must follow.

Ponder the words of the Son of God, "Be ye therefore wise as serpents and simple as doves" (Matt. 10, 16), and be reminded that simplicity is a virtue dear to the heart of God. It is the direct opposite of duplicity, worldly wisdom and prudence, as well as of useless thoughts, desires, words and actions.

Remember that Christians must cherish a great love of truth: 1. because Christ is the Eternal Truth and is called in Sacred Scripture "faithful and true" (Apoc. 19, 11); 2. because Christians are called in the Scripture "the faithful"; 3. because Christ Himself called liars and deceivers children of Satan, who in turn is the father of lies and the author of deceit.

How Have You Practised Modesty, Simplicity and Truth?

Make an examination of conscience regarding the faults you have committed against these virtues, paying particular attention to the modesty you should display when in church, in your own room, walking in public or talking with your neighbor. Are you guilty of duplicity or artifice?

Do you go to extremes in dress, in eating or in the furnishings of your home or room? Are you guided by the maxims of the world? Are you curious about secular events, given to following foolish fashions or inclined to listen to or read useless things?

Are you disposed to be singular or odd, thus causing a rift in that spirit of union which should exist between you and those with whom you live? Are you faithful to your word and your promise? Is your manner of speaking simple, sincere and candid? Do you exaggerate?

Ejaculatory Prayer: "Let your modesty be known to all men." *Modestia vestra nota sit omnibus hominibus* (Phil. 4, 5).

NINTH MEDITATION

The Manner of Performing Our Actions

IMPORTANCE OF DOING ALL THINGS WELL

It is of the utmost importance that we perform all our actions, even the smallest, in the best possible manner. Several reasons demand this. First of all, we are children of God, created to His image and likeness. Consequently, we must imitate Him, according to the words of the Apostle, "Be ye therefore followers of God, as most dear children" (Eph. 5, 1). God performs His every work divinely, and so we too must endeavor to discharge every obligation and perform every action with a perfection becoming sons of God and in obedience to the Saviour's commandment, "Be you therefore perfect, as also your heavenly Father is perfect" (Matt. 5, 48).

Secondly, Christ, who is our exemplar and to whom we must conform our lives, rendered infinite glory to His Father, even in the smallest things, for He did all for love of Him.

Thirdly, God bestows even the smallest things upon us, such as every morsel of bread we eat or every drop of water we drink, with the same love that pours upon us His greatest blessings. Thus, He is as much concerned with those things which may appear trivial as He is with the significant, as we are reminded when Scripture tells us that even the hairs of our head are numbered. Consequently, we must show the same interest in our smallest actions as in the important ones.

Fourthly, when we act negligently and without proper dispositions, we rob God of the glory due Him in time and eternity, purchased for us by the shedding of Christ's blood. In addition, we lose the treasures of grace that otherwise would be laid up for us in heaven, had our motives been holy. Finally, it is much easier to do our duty with fervor and devotion than it is to act coldly and carelessly.

SECOND POINT

How Have You Performed Your Actions up to Now?

The proper manner of acting is outlined by St. Paul when he says, "Whether you eat or drink, or whatsoever else you do, do all to the glory of God" (1 Cor. 10, 31). These words mean simply that you should act with His dispositions as He Himself would do in our place, as far as you possibly can with the help of His grace.

Weigh carefully the faults you have committed in this respect: 1. in those actions directly concerned with God, as in those things connected with the virtue of religion and with our priestly duties; 2. in those affecting your neighbor; 3. in those that have a bearing upon your state in life, your profession or the office which is yours.

Ask God's pardon for any offenses of which you are guilty. Offer Him in reparation the honor His Son rendered Him by His holy life, and resolve henceforth to do well all that is required of you.

For this purpose:

1. Avoid laziness, coldness, lukewarmness and negligence.

2. Always have a right and pure intention, protesting to God that you wish to do nothing to please the world, nor to gain the esteem of men, nor to pander to your own satisfaction, nor your own temporal or spiritual interests, nor for merit or reward. On the contrary, make open avowal that you do everything for His glory and the fulfilment of His will as well as in thanksgiving for all Christ did while He was on earth.

3. Perform every action according to its appointed time and place. "Let all things be done decently and according to order" (1 Cor. 14, 40).

4. Let your smallest action include within it all possible perfection, remembering that whatever is done for God is great.

5. Perform all your actions with the dispositions becoming to them: for example, those of humility with a spirit of self-abasement; those of obedience, promptly and willingly; those of penance with mortification and hatred of self and of sin; those of charity towards your neighbor with an open heart filled with divine love; those of piety and religion with devotion.

6. Make an act of renouncement of self before each action, at least before the principal ones, thus giving yourself to Christ to enter into His spirit.

7. Upon the completion of the action, preserve these dispositions, uniting yourself to those which filled the Saviour as He performed similar ones, for He is and "worketh all in all" (1 Cor. 12, 6).

8. Do and suffer all for God. "Do his will with a great heart, and a willing mind" (2 Mach. 1, 3), that is, with the love and wish to please Him, thus putting into every action your sole desire of making His divine will your pleasure, your joy, your happiness and your paradise.

9. When you have performed the action, shut your heart against any self-satisfaction or vanity, remembering that even as you are nothing but sinfulness, so nothing could emanate from you of yourself but evil, God being the only source of good. Thus, too, you should remember that since you never really succeed in doing your best, your actions are usually full of faults which should be looked upon as useless in themselves and unworthy of merit.

Ejaculatory Prayer: "He hath done all things well."
Bene omnia fecit (Mark 7, 37).

TENTH MEDITATION

The Use We Should Make of the Faculties of Our Soul and Body

ALL THAT IS IN US BELONGS TO GOD

All that is in us belongs to God by three general titles which comprise an infinity of others: the title of creation, the title of conservation, and the title of redemption.

By creation and conservation all that is in our soul and body belongs to His Divine Majesty as many times as there are moments in our life on earth, because, after putting us in this world, God preserves us continually in being.

By redemption we belong to Him by as many titles as His Divine Son had thoughts, words and actions, bore sufferings and shed drops of His Blood. He employed these means, of which each is infinite in value, to snatch us from the captivity of sin and Satan. Thus, we have an infinity of obligations constraining us to use every faculty of our body and soul in His service and for the honor and glory of Him to whom we belong in entirety. "For you are bought with a great price. Glorify and bear God in your body" (1 Cor. 6, 20).

By Baptism we are made members of Christ. "Know you not that your bodies are the members of Christ?" (1 Cor. 6, 15) Hence, we are obliged to live His life, be animated by His spirit, make the same use of the powers of our soul and our senses that He did of His. Rather, we should say it is He who should use our faculties for the diffusion of His spirit.

By Baptism, too, as well as by Confirmation, our body and soul were made temples of the Holy Ghost, consecrated to God more solemnly than are chalices, ciboria or altars. Now, as in a holy temple there is nothing which may be used for profane purposes, so there must be nothing in us but what is used for the service and honor of Him to whom they have been consecrated, not only by Baptism and Confirmation, but also through the Holy Eucharist.

Thank God for all these favors.

SECOND POINT

How Have You Used the Faculties of Your Soul and the Members of Your Body?

What use have you made of the various faculties of your soul and body?

Humble yourself and be mindful that instead of having employed all your faculties in the service of Him who gave them to you, and to whom they belong, you have employed them to serve His enemies.

Ask His pardon with great sorrow in your heart. Offer Him in satisfaction all the honor His Son rendered Him, through the saintly use of His own all holy faculties.

Search your understanding, your memory and your will to see if there is anything there which displeases Him. Scrutinize the passions of your lower appetite, love, hatred, joy, sadness, fear, hope; examine all actions done with your eyes, your hearing, your taste, your tongue, your feet and your hands. Make a determined resolution to mortify and destroy whatever you discover to be at variance with His divine will, obeying the injunction of the Holy Ghost, "Mortify therefore your members which are upon the earth" (Col. 3, 5).

Make a new oblation and consecration of your body and soul to God, supplicating Him to employ His all powerful goodness in taking full and absolute possession of you, that He may thus destroy within you whatsoever is contrary to Him, and establish within you His kingdom and His adorable will.

Be resolved to imitate and follow Christ in the holy use to which He subjected His every faculty. Give yourself completely to Him, that He may fill you with His spirit and possess and govern you in all things.

Ejaculatory Prayer: "You are not your own. For you are bought with a great price." *Non estis vestri: empti enim estis pretio magno* (1 Cor. 6, 19-20).

Part VII

MASS AND OFFICE
FOR
THE FEAST OF THE PRIESTHOOD

INTRODUCTION

ST. JOHN EUDES labored for many years to revive the priestly spirit in the French clergy of the Seventeenth Century. He realized in the course of time that a solemn feast in honor of the priesthood of Jesus Christ and of all holy priests and levites would greatly help to develop the apostolic life in the members of his Institute and instil it into the seminarians of whom he had charge; and at an early date he decided to establish it. In 1649, he submitted to the approval of Doctors Basire and Le Moussu an Office of the Priesthood written by himself, and this he published in 1652 in the first edition of the *Proper* of his Congregation. On December 29th of the same year, His Lordship Claude Auvry, Bishop of Coutances, authorized all the faithful of his diocese, and especially the priests and clerics of his seminary, to make use of the Saint's Offices. At this time, the Feast of the Priesthood was allocated to November 15, and accordingly it is morally certain that it was celebrated in the seminary of Coutances on November 15, 1653.

Subsequently, the Saint continued to perfect his Office, as is shown by the editions of the *Proper* published by him in 1668 and in 1672. In these the hymns are more rhythmic, an octave is added to the Office, and in order to make it possible to celebrate the Feast and its octave before the Feast of the Presentation of the Blessed Virgin, the solemnity is advanced two days and so is kept on November 13. St. John Eudes wanted the renewal of the promises of the clergy in his Society to take place on the Feast of the Presentation, and thus the Feast of the Priesthood served as a preparation for that great act which, in those circumstances, could not fail to be carried out with the greatest possible fervor.

The Saint's Office in honor of the Priesthood of Jesus Christ and of all holy priests and levites is one of great beauty. It is at the same time a magnificent glorification of the heroes of the priesthood whose virtues and success it enthusiastically relates, a striking exposition of the dignity and the duties of a priest, and a fervent prayer that God should grant that His ministers should participate in the spirit and the virtues of their predecessors. In it the Saint was happy in his choice and arrangement of texts from Scripture and the Fathers; and those parts of the Mass and Office that are entirely his own, such as the hymns and the prose, are remarkable for their vigor and their loftiness of thought. He succeeded in introducing the whole of his beautiful teaching on the relations between the priests and the Blessed Virgin Mary, his personal duties and his mission with regard to the laity. When chanted in a major seminary, it could not fail to make a profound impression on the clerics, and the same may be said of the Office as a whole.

This Feast of the Priesthood was also adopted by the Priests of St. Sulpice and by Benedictines of the Blessed Sacrament. At St. Sulpice, it was first fixed for October 30, but later, with the consent of the Ordinary, it was celebrated on July 17, or on another day towards the end of the scholastic year. We cannot say at what precise date the Feast was introduced at St. Sulpice, but apparently it was not established there by Father Olier, but by his disciples some years after his death, which occurred in 1657. According to Father Faillon, the Feast began to be kept there about 1660, and he attributes to Father de Bretonvilliers the compositions of the Office and Mass used in its celebration. We believe, on the contrary, that the Fathers of St. Sulpice, being in touch with St. John Eudes, adopted his Office and Mass, retouching, perhaps, certain parts of it, especially the hymns.

Similarly, the Benedictines of the Blessed Sacrament also adopted the Feast of the Priesthood, which admirably suited their devotion towards the Holy Eucharist. For there is a close connection between the priesthood and the Eucharist, and in some respects the Feast of the Priesthood seemed to be a happy complement of the Feast of the Blessed Sacrament. That is why, when the Benedictines adopted it, they fixed its celebration for the Thursday after the Octave of Corpus Christi. On May 30, 1668, Cardinal de Vendome, the Legate *a latere* of Pope Clement IX, authorized them to celebrate this Feast, using the Office written by St. John Eudes and accommodated to the Benedictine rite. This Feast did not remain restricted to the three Institutes that we have mentioned; it was adopted in several dioceses, amongst others in that of Rouen, in which it is said to have been kept until the middle of the Nineteenth Century.

The Eudists were very attached to the Feast of the Priesthood, and St. John Eudes' immediate successor, Father Blouet de Camilly, "had it inserted in the letters of institution of several houses of the Congregation;" while the General Assembly of 1742 recommended that it be faithfully celebrated in all houses of the Institute. Nor did it cease to be celebrated till towards the middle of the Nineteenth Century, when its abandonment was doubtless due to the return to the Roman Liturgy. The Priests of St. Sulpice preserved it until the liturgy was reformed by Pope Pius X, when they had to give it up; but neither the Eudists nor the Sulpicians have relinquished hope of reviving some day a Feast that so happily harmonizes with their spirit and their works.

MASS OF THE FEAST OF THE PRIESTHOOD OF JESUS CHRIST

Introitus

Dominus dixit ad me: Filius meus es tu, ego hodie genui te: Tu es Sacerdos in aeternum, secundum Melchisedech. Ps. Benedicite, Sacerdotes Domini, Domino: benedicite, sancti et humiles corde, Domino.

V. Gloria Patri . . . Dominus dixit.

Oratio

Deus, tuorum gloria Sacerdotum, qui Unigenitum tuum nobis summum Sacerdotem, et animarum nostrarum Pastorem vigilantissimum dedisti; quique ei, ad sacrificandum tibi hostiam mundam, et ad promovendam humanis generis salutem, sanctos Sacerdotes et Levitas consortes tribuisti: quaesumus, beata Maria semper Virgine et iisdem sanctis Sacerdotibus intercedentibus, ut Spiritum gratiae cui servierunt, in Ecclesia tua excitare digneris, quatenus nos eodem repleti, studeamus amare quod amaverunt, et opere exercere quod verbo et exemplo docuerunt. Per eumdem Dominum.

Introit

The Lord hath said to me: Thou art my son; this day have I begotten thee: Thou art a priest for ever according to the order of Melchisedech. Ps. O ye priests of the Lord, bless the Lord: bless the Lord, O ye holy and humble of heart.

V. Glory be to the Father . . . The Lord hath said.

Collect

O God, the glory of Thy Priests, who didst give us Thy Only-Begotten Son to be our High Priest and the most watchful Pastor of Souls, and didst make all holy priests and levites His associates in offering to Thee a spotless victim and in promoting the salvation of the human race: grant, we beseech Thee, through the intercession of Blessed Mary ever Virgin, and of all the Holy Priests and Levites, that the spirit of grace be stirred up in Thy Church, so that filled with this same grace, we may love what they have loved, and accomplish in deed what they have taught by word and example. Through the same Lord.

Lectio Epistolae Beati Pauli Apostoli ad Hebraeos. (Cap. 7)

Fratres, alii sine jurejurando Sacerdotes facti sunt; hic autem cum jurejurando, per eum qui dicit ad illum: Juravit Dominus et non paenitebit eum: tu es Sacerdos in aeternum. In tantum melioris testamenti sponsor factus est Jesus. Et alii quidem plures facti sunt Sacerdotes, idcirco quod morte prohiberentur permanere: hic autem, eo quod maneat in aeternum, sempiternum habet Sacerdotium. Unde et salvare in perpetuum potest accedentes per semetipsum ad Deum: semper vivens ad interpellandum pro nobis. Talis enim decebat ut nobis esset Pontifex, sanctus, innocens, impollutus, segregatus a peccatoribus, et excelsior caelis factus: qui non habet necessitatem quotidie, prius pro suis delictis hostias offerre, deinde pro populi. Hoc enim fecit semel, seipsum offerendo, Jesus Christus, Dominus noster.

Graduale. Sacerdotes ejus induam Salutari, et Sancti ejus exsultatione exsultabunt. V. Isti sunt qui in omnibus praebuerunt semetipsos exemplum bonorum operum, in humilitate, in modestia, in charitate.

Alleluia, alleluia. V. Hi sunt servi boni et fideles, qui miniterium suum honoraverunt: ideo constituit eos Dominus super omnia bona sua.

Lesson from the Epistle of St. Paul the Apostle to the Hebrews. Chapter 7.

Brethren, others were made priests without an oath: but this with an oath, by him that said unto him: The *Lord hath sworn and he will not repent: Thou art a priest for ever.* By so much is Jesus made a surety of a better testament. And the others indeed were made many priests, because by reason of death they were not suffered to continue: but this, for that he continueth for ever, hath an everlasting priesthood: whereby he is able also to save for ever them that come to God by him; always living to make intercession for us. For it was fitting that we should have such a high priest, holy, innocent, undefiled, separated from sinners, and made higher than the heavens: who needeth not daily (as the other priests) to offer sacrifices, first for his own sins, and then for the people's: for this he did once, in offering himself, Jesus Christ, Our Lord.

Gradual. I will clothe his priests with salvation, and his saints shall rejoice with exceeding great joy. V. These are they that show themselves an example of good works, in humility, in modesty, in charity.

Alleluia, alleluia. V. These are good and faithful servants, who have honored their ministry: therefore the Lord made them masters over all his possessions.

Post Septuag, omissis Graduale, Alleluia, et Sequentia, dicitur:

Tractus—In omnibus exhibeamus nos ipsos sicut Dei ministros, in multa patientia, in humilitate, in suavitate, in charitate non ficta: nemini dantes ullam offensionem, ut non vituperetur ministerium nostrum. V. Inter vestibulum et altare plorabunt Sacerdotes, ministri Domini, et dicent: Parce, Domine, parce populo tuo, et ne des haereitatem tuam in opprobrium, ut dominentur eis nationes. V. Hi sunt boni milites Christi Jesu, qui bonum certamen certaverunt; ideo beatificavit eos in gloria, et dedit illis coronas perpetuas.

Tempore Paschali, loco Gradualis, dicitur:

Alleluia, alleluia. V. Talis decebat ut nobis esset Pontifex, sanctus, innocens, segregatus a peccatoribus, et excelsior coelis factus. Alleluia. V. Secundum eum qui vocavit vos Sanctum, et ipsi in omni conversatione sancti sitis. Scriptum est enim: Sancti eritis, quoniam ego sanctus sum. Alleluia.

Sequentia
Gaudeamus jubilantes,
Sacerdotum celebrantes
Sacrate solemnia.

Haec est dies laetabunda,
In qua Patrum veneranda
Laudamus magnalia.

After Septuagesima, the Gradual, Alleluia, and the Sequence are omitted and the following is said:

Tract—In all things let us exhibit ourselves as the ministers of God, in much patience, in humility, in sweetness, in charity unfeigned: giving no offense to any man, that our ministry be not blamed. V. Between the porch and the altar, the priests, the Lord's ministers, shall weep and shall say: Spare, O Lord, spare thy people; and give not thy inheritance to reproach, that the heathen should rule over them. V. These are good soldiers of Christ Jesus, who have fought the good fight; and therefore he made them blessed in glory, and gave them everlasting crowns.

In Paschaltide, instead of the Gradual, the following is said:

Alleluia, alleluia. V. It was fitting that we should have such a high priest, holy, innocent, undefiled, separated from sinners, and made higher than the heavens. Alleluia. V. According to him that hath called you, who is holy, be you also in all manner of conversation holy: because it is written: You shall be holy, for I am holy. Alleluia.

Sequence
Come we jubilant, rejoicing,
Festive rites and solemn voicing
Of the Priesthood's sacred feast!

This the day of joy unbounded,
When we praise with awe well-founded
Lofty deeds performed by priest.

Sit vox laeta, sit canora,
Sit laus pura, sit decora
Puritate pectoris.

Laudet caelum, terra, pontus,
Laudet simul tota virtus
Spiritus et corporis.

Te laudamus unitatem,
Aeternamque Trinitatem,
Ortum, finem omnium.

Te laudamus Salvatorem,
Sacerdotum fundatorem,
Caput, Patrem, gaudium.

Horum Matrem te Mariam,
Et sororem et Reginam
Omnis laudet Spiritus.

Vos consortes Dei Patris,
Patres estis Dei fratris,
Quos unxit Paraclitus.

Prae Angelis sublimavit,
Apostolis sociavit
Vos Sacerdos maximus.

Vos a cunctis honorari,
Super omnes exaltari
Rex jubet Altissimus.

Vos legati Numinis,
Fratres almae Virginis,
Et patres fidelium.

Sacri linguae Flaminis,
Summi tubae Principis,
Et doctores gentium.

Hi caelorum docent leges,
Christi Jesu pascunt greges
Verbis, factis, precibus.

Let the voice of joy resounding
Lift its praise in pure tones sound-
ing,
Rising from the heart made pure.

Praise be sung by earth, sky, ocean;
Likewise let the heart's devotion
And the soul's give praise most sure.

One in Godhead we acclaim Thee,
Trinity eterne proclaim Thee,
Source of all things and the End.

God Our Saviour now we praise,
Hearts to Priesthood's founder raise,
To Our Head, Our Father, friend.

By all souls let praise be lifted
To thee, Mary, priesthood's gifted
Mother, Queen and Sister fair.

God the Father's own, no other,
Fathers, ye, of God your Brother,
Chrismed by the Spirit rare.

You the great High Priest hath
lifted
Higher than the angels gifted,
Joined you to the apostles' train.

You the Most High King com-
mandeth
Honour'd be by all, demandeth
You o'er all mankind to reign.

Envoys of the Godhead here,
Brethren of the Virgin Fair,
Fathers of the faithful true.

Tongues of sacred fire flaming,
Trumpets of the Prince acclaiming,
Teachers of mankind anew.

Thus they teach the laws of heav'n,
Feeding to Christ's flock the leav'n
By each word and prayer and deed.

Pravos mores dissipant,
Carnem, mundum superant,
Expellunt daemonia.

Foedas horrent voluptates,
Stultas spernunt vanitates,
Mundi calcant somnia.

Vanum ejus rident fastum,
Asperantur tanquam lutum
Cuncta temporalia.

Domus Dei vigiles,
Et columae stabiles,
Moestorum laetitia.

Justis augent gratiam,
Reis donant veniam,
Dant cunctis solatia.

Sub perenni tam piorum,
Tam potentum patronorum
Laetemur custodia.

Ut a Sanctis adjuvemur,
Corde magno subsequamur
Sanctorum vestigia.

Circa domos, intra templa,
Corda, voces et exempla
Christum Jesum praedicent.

Bone Jesu, bonitatem
Ostende supplicibus:
Da sanctorum sanctitatem
Sanctis sequi moribus.

Intus flagrant charitatis
Divinis ardoribus:
Foris lucent sanctitatis
Praeclaris operibus.

Baneful habits they expel,
Mastering the flesh as well,
World and devil they exceed.

Sinful lusts they hold in horror,
Foolish vanities in terror,
Stamping out the world's vain
dreams.

They laugh at earthly vanity,
They spurn with holy sanity,
Each thing that transitory seems.

Watchmen of the House of God,
Pillars sound, unmoved, unawed,
Joy to those by sorrow swayed,

Graces for the just they win,
Pardon give for guilt of sin,
Comfort unto all dismayed.

Let us then rejoice, protected
By the constant help effected
By such holy guardians strong.

May we generously follow,
Helped by saints, whose way we hal-
low,
In their holy steps along.

Round our homes, within our
temples,
Let our hearts, lives, and examples
Herald forth our Lord Christ Jesus.

Gentle Jesus, show Thy favor
To all creatures suppliant here;
Grant they may with pious savour
Go the way of saints, nor fear.

Charity within a-flaming
From the burning fires divine;
Sanctity without, acclaiming
By their lives and deeds they're
thine.

Hos sacravit castitas,	Them hath chastity renown'd
Decoravit pietas,	And sweet piety hath found,
Sacravit humilitas,	And humility made sound;
Coronavit charitas,	Charity their brows hath crown'd,
Spes, fides et gratia.	Hope and Faith and grace adorn'd.
O beata Trinitas,	O most Blessed Trinity
O vera felicitas	Rare bliss of Divinity
Et Sanctorum sanctitas,	And all saints' affinity!
Immensae clementiae	Boundless be the mercies dear,
Immensae sint gratiae,	Boundless be all graces here.
Aeterna sit gloria,	Everlasting glory be.
Amen dicant omnia:	Let all creatures join to say
Amen. Alleluia.	Amen. Alleluia.

Sequentia sancti Evangelii secundum Matthaeum. (Cap. 5)

Continuation of the holy Gospel according to St. Matthew. Chapter 5.

In illo tempore, dixit Jesus discipulis suis: Vos estis sal terrae. Quod si sal evanuerit, in quo salietur? Ad nihil valet ultra, nisi ut mittatur foras et conculcetur ab hominibus. Vos estis lux mundi. Non potest civitas abscondi supra montem posita. Neque accendunt lucernam, et ponunt eam sub modio, sed super candelabrum, ut luceat omnibus qui in domo sunt. Sic luceat lux vestra coram hominibus, ut videant opera vestra bona, et glorificent Patrem vestrum qui in caelis est. Nolite putare quoniam veni solvere legem aut Prophetas: Non veni solvere, sed adimplere. Amen quippe dico vobis, donec transeat caelum et terra, iota unum aut unus apex non praeteribit a lege, donec omnia fiant. Qui ergo solverit unum de mandatis istis minimis, et docuerit, sic homines, minimus vocabitur in regno caelorum: Qui autem fecerit et docuerit, hic magnus vocabitur in regno coe-

At that time, Jesus said to his disciples: You are the salt of the earth. But if the salt lose its savour, wherewith shall it be salted? It is good for nothing any more but to be cast out, and to be trodden on by men. You are the light of the world. A city seated on a mountain cannot be hid. Neither do men light a candle and put it under a bushel, but upon a candlestick, that it may shine to all that are in the house. So let your light shine before men, that they may see your good works and glorify your Father who is in heaven. Do not think that I am come to destroy the law or the prophets. I am not come to destroy, but to fulfil. For amen I say unto you, till heaven and earth pass, one jot, or one tittle shall not pass of the law, till all be fulfilled. He therefore that shall break one of these least commandments, and shall so teach men, shall be called the least in the kingdom of

lorum. Dico enim vobis, quia nisi abundaverit justitia vestra plus quam Scribarum et Pharisaeorum, non intrabitis in regnum caelorum.

heaven. But he that shall do and teach, he shall be called great in the kingdom of heaven. For I tell you, that unless your justice abound more than that of the scribes and Pharisees, you shall not enter into the kingdom of heaven.

Credo

Offertorium

Sacerdotes sancti ut palma florebunt, et sicut cedri Libani exaltabuntur. Judicabunt nationes et dominabuntur populis, et regnabit Dominus illorum in perpetuum. Alleluia.

Creed

Offertory

The holy priests shall flourish like the palm tree: they shall grow up like the cedars of Libanus. They shall judge nations, and rule over people: and their Lord shall reign for ever.

Secreta

Deus, qui Filium tuum Unigenitum pro nobis Sacerdotem et hostiam esse voluisti: praesta quaesumus, beata Maria semper Virgine intercedente, cum omnibus sanctis Sacerdotibus et Levitis, ut sicut nos, immensa clementiae tuae largitate, divini ejus Sacerdotii participes effecisti, ita et nosmetipsos cum eo, in hac sacrosancta oblatione, in qua omnis sanctitatis fontem constituisti, hostiam vivam et sanctam tibi in aeternum consecrare et immolare digneris. Per eumdem Dominum.

Secret

O God, who didst will that Thy Only-begotten Son shouldst be priest and victim for us, grant, we beseech Thee, that as through the intercession of the Blessed Mary ever Virgin and all Thy holy priests and levites, we have been made sharers in Thy Divine Priesthood, through the greatness of His bounty, Thou wouldst deign also to consecrate and immolate us to Thee as a living and holy victim in union with Him in Thy holy oblation, which Thou didst make the fount of all holiness. Through the same Lord.

Communio

Gratias agimus tibi, Domine Jesu, qui eras, qui es, et qui venturus es: quia fecisti nos Deo nostro regnum et sacerdotes. Alleluia.

Communion

We give Thee thanks, O Lord Jesus, who art and who wast and who art to come: because thou hast made us a kingship for our God, and priests. Alleluia.

Postcommunio

Domine Jesu Christe, Pastor bone, qui dixisti: Rogate Dominum messis,

Postcommunion

Lord Jesus Christ, Good Shepherd, who didst say: Pray the Lord

ut mittat operarios in messem suam: te supplices exoramus, intercedente beatissima Virgine Maria Matre tua, cum omnibus sanctis Sacerdotibus et Levitis, ut operarios fideles in vineam tuam mittas; omnes Sacerdotes et Levitas dignos sacris altaribus ministros efficias; et Ecclesiae tuae plures alios Sacerdotes et Pastores juxta Cor tuum concedas; ut tecum et cum ipsis aeterno Patri aeternae laudis hostiam offerre mereamur. Qui vivis et regnas cum eodem Deo Patre, in unitate Spiritus Sancti Deus. Per omnia saecula saeculorum.

of the harvest that He may send laborers into His harvest, we humbly beseech Thee, through the intercession of the Blessed Mary ever Virgin and all Thy holy priests and levites, that Thou mayst send faithful laborers into Thy vineyard; that Thou mayst make all priests and levites worthy ministers of Thy sacred altars; and that Thou mayst grant us many other priests and pastors according to Thy heart; in order that with Thee and them we may offer a victim of praise to Thy Eternal Father, who livest and reignest with the same God the Father in the unity of the Holy Spirit, forever and ever. Amen.

OFFICE OF THE FEAST OF HOLY PRIESTHOOD
OF
OUR LORD JESUS CHRIST

FIRST VESPERS

Ant. Dominus dixit ad me: Filius meus es tu, ego hodie genui te: tu es Sacerdos in aeternum, secundum ordinem Melchisedech.

Dixit Dominus et psalmi de die Dominica, ultimo loco *Laudate Dominum omnes gentes.*

Ant. Pax vobis, dicit Dominus Jesus Sacerdotibus suis: Sicut misit me Pater, et ego mitto vos, accipite Spiritum sanctum.

Ant. Vos estis sal terrae, vos estis lux mundi: sic luceat lux vestra coram hominibus, ut glorificent Patrem vestrum qui in caelis est.

Ant. Secundum eum qui vocavit vos sanctum, et ipsi in omni conversatione vestra sancti sitis: scriptum est enim: Sancti eritis, quoniam ego sanctus sum.

Ant. Hoc est praeceptum meum, ut diligatis invicem, sicut dilexi vos; et discatis a me quia mitis sum et humilis corde.

Ant. The Lord hath said to me: Thou art my son; this day have I begotten thee. Thou art a priest for ever according to the order of Melchisedech.

Psalms for Sunday. Last psalm, *Laudate Dominum omnes gentes.*

Ant. Peace be to you, says the Lord Jesus to His priests: As the Father hath sent me, I also send you. Receive ye the Holy Ghost.

Ant. You are the salt of the earth; you are the light of the world. So let your light shine before men that they may glorify your Father who is in heaven.

Ant. According to him that hath called you, who is holy, be you also in all manner of conversation holy: for it is written: You shall be holy, because I am holy.

Ant. This is my commandment, that you love one another, as I have loved you; and learn of me, because I am meek, and humble of heart.

Capitulum, Heb. 7, 24

Christus Jesus, eo quod maneat in aeternum, sempiternum habet Sacerdotium: unde et salvare in perpetuum potest accendentes per semetipsum ad Deum, semper vivens ad interpellandum pro nobis.

Hymnus
Jesu, Sacerdos maxime,
Apostolatus Ordinis
Rex et Pater sanctissime,
Nostris adesto canticis.

Aaron genus clarissimum,
Divinitati proximum,
Melchisedech regalia
Vox intonat magnalia.

Laudamus orbis Lampades,
Duces Dei certaminum,
Caelestis aulae Praesides,
Christi Columnas militum.

Vos Agnus agnos convocans,
Pugnam lupis denuntiat:
Res mira! per vos militans
Agnus lupos exterminat.

Ex ore vestro, Numinis
Romphaea sacra fulgurat:
Quae saevientis daemonis
Truces catervas dissipat.

Contra cohortes Tartari,
Agni sequamur praelia:
Ut donet agnos subsequi
Agni decoros gloria.

Little Chapter, Heb. 7, 24

Christ Jesus, for that he continueth for ever, hath an everlasting priesthood: whereby he is able also to save for ever them that come to God by him; always living to make intercession for us.

Hymn
Jesus, our great High Priest we sing.
Herald of Holy Ordination,
Father all-holy, holy king,
Accept our chant of exultation.

We praise the line of Aaron famed,
Nigh unto God, by Godhead named.
Our voices sing the holy things
Melchisedech in offering brings.

We laud these beacons of earth's ball,
God's champions in His cause divine,
The provosts of the heavenly hall,
The columns of Christ's fighting line.

The Lamb assembling you His flock,
Forthwith the wolf abandons flight.
A Miracle! the wolf to mock
God's Lamb doth conquer bestial might!

The sacred glaive of spirit fire
From out your unctuous lips doth flash
And put to flight the threatening dire
Of hostile cohorts' baneful clash.

Gehenna's hosts their stand oppose,
We see the Lamb disperse their ranks,
That He would grant us lambs like those
As worthy of His praise and thanks.

O candidati Principes,
Splendor decusque Virginum:
O purpurati Martyres,
Flos et corona Martyrum.

Carnis dolosae fascinum
Ex corde nostro pellite:
Fraudes et arma daemonum
Oratione frangite.

Praesta, beata Trinitas,
Origo, finis omnium,
Patrum tenere semitas
Nunc et per omne saeculum.
                              Amen.

V. Elegit eos Dominus Sacerdotes sibi.

R. Ad sacrificandum ei hostiam laudis.

Ad Magnif. Ant. Beata es, Maria, Regina et Mater Sacerdotum; quia Dominum Jesum portasti summum Sacerdotem: Tibi honor, tibi laus, tibi gloria in aeternum. Alleluia.

Oremus: Deus, tuorum gloria Sacerdotum, qui Unigentium tuum nobis summum Sacerdotem, et animarum nostrarum Pastorem vigilantissimum dedisti, quique ei ad sacrificandum tibi hostiam mundam, et ad promovendam humani generis salutem, sanctos Sacerdotes et Levitas consortes tribuisti: quaesumus, beata Maria semper Virgine iisdemque sanctis Sacerdotibus et Levitis intercedentibus, ut Spiritum gratiae cui servierunt in Ecclesia tua excitare digneris; quatenus nos eodem repleti,

O white-robed leaders, shining fair,
With glistening Virgins' beauty white!
As martyrs oft ye well do wear
The flower's crown, the martyrs' right.

Dispel afar the wiles of sin
Which lure the flesh, assail the heart.
Break Thou the Devil's powers within,
By might of word his cunning thwart.

Grant, Blessed Trinity Divine,
Beginning of all things and End,
That we may keep the Fathers' line,
Now and forever onward tend.
                              Amen.

V. The Lord hath chosen them to be his priests.

R. To offer him a sacrifice of praise.

At the Magnifiant. Ant. Blessed art thou, O Mary, Queen and Mother of priests, because thou didst bear Jesus the High Priest. To thee honor, praise and glory forever. Alleluia.

Let us pray. O God, the glory of Thy Priests, who didst give us Thy Only-Begotten Son to be our High Priest and the most watchful Pastor of Souls, and didst make all holy priests and levites His associates in offering to Thee a spotless victim and in promoting the salvation of the human race: grant, we beseech Thee, through the intercession of Blessed Mary, ever Virgin, and all the holy Priests and Levites, that the spirit of grace be stirred up in Thy Church, so that filled with this same

studeamus amare quod amaverunt, et opere exercere quod verbo et exemplo docuerunt. Per eumdem Dominum.

grace, we love what they loved, and accomplish in deed what they taught by word and example. Through the same Lord.

MATINS

Invit. Jesum, Mariae Filium, Regem Sacerdotum, *Venite adoremus.

Invit. Come, let us adore Jesus, Son of Mary, King of Priests.

Hymnus
Salvete, mundi Sydera,
Gentis sacrae pars inclyta,
Cleri decus sanctissimi,
Praeclara sors Altissimi.

Hymn
Hail, shining stars of lowly earth,
The sacred sons of spotless birth,
The glory of all holy clerks,
Whose lot it is to share God's works.

Pars vestra Jesus optima,
Pars ejus et vos intima:
Paracliti sacrarium,
Summi Parentis gaudium.

Jesus your highest part, and best,
And ye to Jesus dearest blest:
Of Holy Ghost the sacred shrine,
The joy of Highest Sire divine.

Imago Matris Virginis,
Lucerna Christi corporis,
Caput, sinus, cor, ubera:
Quis tanta laudet munera?

The Image of the Virgin Spouse,
The light of Christ's own body's house,
The heart, the head, the gen'rous breast:
How sing such lofty functions best?

Virtutis auro fulgidi,
Hostes acerbi criminum,
Aeternitatis arbitri,
Pax et salus fidelium.

Who shine as with all virtues' gold,
Fierce enemies to crime and sin:
The judges of th'eternal fold
Are ye; believers' peace within.

Per vos ubique gentium
Regnum Dei protenditur:
Per vos tyrannis daemonum
Languet, ruit, subvertitur.

By you God's kingdom reaches wide,
Comprising peoples far and near;
By you the devils' sway denied
Doth falter, fail, collapse from fear.

Vobis datur mysteria
Parvis loqui, non turgidis:
Divina per vos gratia
Sanctis datur, non perfidis.

To utter mysteries is yours
Unto the simple, not the proud:
Through you God's grace most freely pours
Not for the faithless but the vowed.

Vos horruistis noxia,
Et falsa mundi somnia:
Christus dedit clarissimum
Vitae perennis praemium.

Ye have forsworn all evil things,
The world, and dreams it falsely
    brings:
Christ hath the gift most shining
    giv'n,
To show the life of endless heav'n.

Terrae polique Lumina,
Obscura cuncta tollite:
Urbis sacrae Munimina,
Cives sacros defendite.

Ye shining lights of sky and earth
Destroy all darksome evil blight:
Ye sentinels of heaven's girth
Defend her citizens in light.

Praesta, beata Trinitas,
Origo, finis omnium,
Patrum tenere semitas,
Nunc et per omne saeculum.
                        Amen.

Grant, Blessed Trinity divine,
Beginning of all things and End,
That we may keep the Fathers' line,
Now and forever onward tend.
                        Amen.

FIRST NOCTURN

Ant. Talis decebat ut nobis esset Pontifex, sanctus, innocens, segregatus a peccatoribus, et excelsior caelis factus.

Ant. It was fitting that we should have such a high priest, holy, innocent, undefiled, separated from sinners, and made higher than the heavens.

Psalmi trium Noct. de Confessore Pontifici.

Ant. Ego elegi vos de mundo, ut eatis, et fructum afferatis, et fructus vester maneat.

Psalms for the three nocturns are those for a Confessor Pontiff.

Ant. I have chosen you out of the world, that you should go and should bring forth fruit, and your fruit should remain.

Ant. Vobis data est omnis potestas caelorum: Quaecumque enim ligaveritis in terra, erunt ligata et in caelo; et quaecumque solveritis super terram, erunt soluta et in caelo.

Ant. All power is given to you: whatsoever you shall bind upon earth, it shall be bound also in heaven: and whatsoever you shall loose upon earth, it shall be loosed also in heaven.

V. Sacerdotes tui induantur justitiam.
R. Et Sancti tui exultent.

V. Let thy priests be clothed with justice.
R. And let thy saints rejoice.

Lectio Prima
De Epistola B. Pauli Apostoli ad Hebraeos. Cap. 5, 1-7.

Omnis pontifex ex hominibus assumptus, pro hominibus constituitur, in iis quae sunt ad Deum, ut offerat dona et sacrificia pro peccatis: qui condolere possit iis qui ignorant et errant: quoniam et ipse circumdatus est infirmitate: et propterea debet, quemadmodum pro populo, ita etiam et pro semetipso offerre pro peccatis. Nec quisquam sumit sibi honorem, sed qui vocatur a Deo, tanquam Aaron. Sic et Christus non semetipsum clarificavit, ut Pontifex fieret; sed qui locutus est ad eum: Filius meus es tu, ego hodie genui te. Quemadmodum et in alio loco dicit: Tu es Sacerdos in aeternum secundum ordinem Melchisedech. Qui in diebus carnis suae, preces supplicationesque ad eum, qui possit illum salvum facere a morte, cum clamore valido et lacrymis offerens, exauditus est pro sua reverentia.

R. Benedictus Deus et Pater Domini nostri Jesu Christi: Qui Filium suum Unigenitum per Spiritum sanctum unxit in Regem et Sacerdotem in aeternum, ut immolet ei hostiam sanctam immaculatam. V. Sanctus, sanctus, sanctus Dominus Deus, Rex regum et Princeps sacerdotum. Qui Filium suum Unigenitum per Spiritum sanctum unxit.

First Lesson
Epistle to the Hebrews. Chap. 5, 1-7.

Every high priest taken from among men, is ordained for men in the things that appertain to God, that he may offer up gifts and sacrifices for sins: who can have compassion on them that are ignorant and that err: because he himself also is compassed with infirmity. And therefore he ought, as for the people, so also for himself, to offer for sins. Neither doth any man take the honour to himself, but he that is called by God, as Aaron was. So Christ also did not glorify himself, that he might be made a high priest: but he that said unto him: *Thou art my Son, this day have I begotten thee.* As he saith also in another place: *Thou art a priest for ever, according to the order of Melchisedech.* Who in the days of his flesh, with a strong cry and tears, offering up prayers and supplications to him that was able to save him from death, was heard for his reverence.

R. Blessed be God and the Father of Our Lord Jesus Christ, who anointed His Only-Begotten Son as King and Priest for ever, that He might offer Him a holy and spotless victim. V. Holy, holy, holy Lord God, King of Kings and Prince of Priests. Who anointed His only-begotten Son.

Lectio Secunda
De libro Ecclesiatici. Cap. 44, 1-15.

Laudemus viros gloriosos, et parentes nostros in generatione sua. Multam gloriam fecit Dominus magnificentia sua a saeculo. Dominantes in potestatibus suis, homines magni virtute et prudentia sua praediti, nuntiantes in Prophetis dignitatem Prophetarum, et imperantes in praesenti populo, et virtute prudentiae populis sanctissima verba. In peritia sua requirentes modos musicos, et narrantes carmina scripturarum. Homines divites in virtute, pulchritudinis studium habentes, pacificantes in domibus suis. Omnes isti in generationibus gentis suae gloriam adepti sunt, et in diebus suis habentur in laudibus. Qui de illis nati sunt, reliquerunt nomen narrandi laudes eorum. Sapientiam ipsorum narrent populi, et laudem eorum nuntiet Ecclesia.

R. Jesus ingrediens mundum dicit: Hostiam et oblationem noluisti, corpus autem aptasti mihi. In capite libri scriptum est de me ut faciam voluntatem tuam: *Deus meus volui, et legem tuam in medio cordis mei. V. Dominus divit ad me: Tu es Sacerdos in aeternum, secundum ordinem Melchisedech. *Deus meus
. . .

Lectio Tertia
Cap. 50, 1-15.

Hi sunt Sacerdotes sancti, qui in vita sua suffulserunt domum, et in

Second Lesson
Ecclesiasticus. Chapter 44, 1-15.

Let us now praise men of renown, and our fathers in their generation. The Lord hath wrought great glory through His magnificence from the beginning. Such as have borne rule in their dominions, men of great power and endued with their wisdom, shewing forth in the prophets the dignity of prophets, and ruling over the present people, and by the strength of wisdom *instructing* the people in most holy words. Such as by their skill sought out musical tunes, and published canticles of the scriptures. Rich men in virtue, studying beautifulness: living at peace in their houses. All these have gained glory in their generations and were praised in their days. They that were born of them have left a name behind them, that their praises might be related. Let the people show forth their wisdom: and the church declare their praise.

R. Jesus coming into the world said: sacrifice and oblation thou wouldst not: but a body thou hast fitted to me. In the head of the book it is written of me that I should do Thy will; I have willed it, O my God, and Thy law is in the midst of my heart. V. The Lord hath said to me: Thou art a priest for ever according to the order of Melchisedech. *O my God . . .

Third Lesson
Chapter 50, 1-15.

These are holy priests, who in their life propped up the house and

diebus suis corroboraverunt templum. In diebus ipsorum emanaverunt putei aquarum, et quasi mare adimpleti sunt supra modum. Qui curaverunt gentem suam, et liberaverunt eam a perditione. Qui praevaluerunt amplificare civitatem, qui adepti sunt gloriam in conversatione gentium, et ingressum domus et atrii amplicaverunt. Quasi stella matutina in medio nebulae, et quasi luna plena in diebus suis lucent. Et quasi sol refulgens, sic illi effulserunt in templo Dei. Quasi arcus refulgens inter nebulas gloriae, et quasi flos rosarum in diebus vernis, et quasi lilia quae sunt in transitu aquae et quasi thus redolens in diebus aestatis. Quasi ignis refulgens, et thus ardens in igne. Quasi vas auri solidum, ornatum omni lapide pretioso. Quasi oliva pullulans, et cypressus in altum se extollens, in accipiendo ipsos stolam gloriae, et vestiti eos in consummationem virtutis. In ascensu altaris sancti gloriam dederunt sanctitatis amictum. Et circa illos corona fratrum: quasi plantatio cedri in monte Libano, sic circa illos steterunt: quasi rami palmae: et omnes filii eorum in gloria sua.

R. Beata es Maria, Dei Genitrix Virgo, Regina et Mater Sacerdotum: *Quia Dominum Jesum portasti, Pastorem magnum animarum, et Principem sacerdotum. Tibi laus, tibi honor, tibi gloria in saecula saecu-

in their days fortified the temple. In their days the wells of water flowed out: and they were filled as the sea above measure. They took care of their nation and delivered it from destruction. They prevailed to enlarge the city and obtained glory in their conversation with the people and enlarged the entrance of the house and the court. They shone in his days as the morning star in the midst of a cloud, and as the moon at the full. And as the sun when it shineth, so did they shine in the temple of God. And as the rainbow giving light in the bright clouds, and as the flower of roses in the days of the spring, and as the lilies that are on the brink of the water, and as the sweet smelling frankincense in the time of summer. As a bright fire, and frankincense burning in the fire. As a massy vessel of gold adorned with every precious stone. As an olive tree budding forth, and a cypress tree rearing itself on high, when they put on the robe of glory and were clothed with the perfection of power. When they went up to the holy altar, they honoured the vesture of holiness. And about them was the ring of his brethren: and as the cedar planted in mount Libanus, and as the branches of palm trees, they stood round about them: and all their sons in their glory.

R. Blessed art thou, O Virgin Mother of God, Queen and Mother of priests: *Because thou didst bear the Lord Jesus, the great Pastor of souls, and the Prince of priests. To thee praise, to thee honor, to thee

lorum. V. Beatam te dicent omnes Pastores et Sacerdotes. *Quia . . . Gloria Patri . . . *Quia . . .

glory forever. V. All Pastors and Priests will call thee blessed. *Because . . . Glory be to the Father . . . *Because . . .

SECOND NOCTURN

Ant. Ego sum lux mundi, et vos lux mundi estis. Qui vos audit, me audit: et qui vos spernit, me spernit.

Ant. I am the light of the world, and you are the light of the world. He that heareth you, heareth me: and he that despiseth you, despiseth me.

Ant. Nolite tangere Christos meos: qui hos tangit, tangit pupillam oculi mei.

Ant. Touch ye not my anointed: he that toucheth you toucheth the apple of my eye.

Ant. Hi sunt lucernae ardentes et lucentes super candelabrum sanctum.

Ant. They are lights burning and shining upon a holy candelabrum.

V. Sacerdotes meos induam Salutari.
R. Et Sancti mei exultatione exultabunt.

V. I will clothe my priests with salvation.
R. And my saints shall rejoice with exceeding great joy.

Lectio IV: Sermo sancti Ephrem, Syri Diaconi De Sacerdotio.

O miraculum stupendum! O potestas ineffabilis! O tremendum Sacerdotii mysterium, spirituale ac sanctum, venerandum et irreprehensible, quod Christus in hunc mundum veniens etiam indignis impertitus est! Genu posito, lacrymis atque suspiriis oro ut hunc Sacerdotii thesaurum inspiciamus: thesaurum, inquam, his qui eum digne et sancte custodiunt. Scutum siquidem est refulgens et incomparabile, turris firma, murus indivisibilis, fundamentum solidum ac stabile, a terra ad axem usque coeli pertingens. Quid dico, fratres? Excelsos illos

Lesson IV: Sermon of St. Ephrem, Syrian Deacon On the Priesthood.

O wondrous miracle! O power unutterable! O tremendous mystery of the Priesthood, holy and spiritual mystery, worthy of reverence and blameless, which Christ hath by His advent into the world imparted even to those unworthy! On bended knees, with tears and sighs, I pray that we may look into this treasure of Priesthood; a treasure, I say, to those who guard it with fitting holiness. For it is indeed a matchless bright shield, a strong tower, a wall unbreakable, a firm and stable foundation, reaching from earth to highest heaven! What am I saying, breth-

axes contingit, imo in ipsos coelos coelorum sine impedimento atque labore ascendit, et in medio Angelorum simul cum Spiritibus incorporiis facile versatur. Quid dico, in medio supernarum Virtutum? Quin et cum ipso Angelorum Domino atque Creatore, datoreque luminum familiariter agit et quantum vult confestim quae postulat, facile et cum suo jure quodammodo impetrat.

R. Isti sunt Principes Sacerdotum, qui viventes in carne plantaverunt Ecclesiam sanguine suo: * Calicem Domini biberunt, et amici Dei facti sunt. V. In omnem terram exivit sonus eorum, et in fines orbis terrae verba eorum. Calicem . . .

Lectio V

Non desisto, Fratres, laudare et glorificare illius dignitatis profunditatem, quam nobis, nobis inquam, Adæ filiis, sancta elargita est Trinitas. Per hanc mundus salvatus est, et creatura illuminata. Per hanc et mortis potentia destructa est, et inferni vires deperditæ, ipsaque Adæ maledictio exterminata est atque soluta, et cœlestis thalamus apertus est et adornatus. Quid dicam? quid eloquar? aut quid laudibus efferam? Excedit quippe intellectum et orationem, omnemque cogitationem, donum altitudinis dignitatis sacerdotalis. Et, sicut arbitror, hoc est quod Paulus, quasi in stuporem mentis actus, innuit exclamans: O altitudo divitiarum sa-

ren? It even attaineth those supernal regions, ascending without let or labor from the depths to the very heavens, and there with incorporeal spirits, surrounded by angels, holdeth free and familiar intercourse. But why do I say surrounded by the Heavenly Powers except it be that it treateth—familiarly with the very Lord and Creator of angels Himself, the Giver of Light, asking forthwith whatsoever it will, making petition as it were with certain seemly ease and right?

R. These are Princes of Priests, who living in the flesh have planted the Church with their blood: they have drunk the chalice of the Lord, and were made the friends of God. V. Their sound hath gone forth into all the earth: and their words unto the ends of the world. The chalice . . .

Lesson V

Nor do I desist, brethren, from giving praise and glory to that profundity of dignity which the Holy Trinity hath liberally bestowed upon us, the sons of Adam. Thereby the world hath been saved and the creature enlightened. Thereby both the power of death hath been destroyed and the forces of hell spoiled; both the curse of Adam destroyed and broken, and the heavenly bridal chamber adorned and thrown open. What shall I say and declare? what in the way of praise? Forsooth, this gift of the lofty dignity of the Priesthood hath outrun mind and speech and all thought. And this I think is what St. Paul indicates when,

pientiæ et scientiæ Dei, quam incomprehensibilia sunt judicia ejus, et investigabiles divinæ viæ ejus! Altivolans e terra in cœlum, nostra postulata Deo celerrime defert, et Dominum pro servis suis deprecatur.

R. Hi sunt vere Sacerdotes et Martyres, qui pro Christi nomine sanguinem suum fuderunt: * Et tradiderunt corpora sua ad supplicia, hostiam viventem, sanctam, Deo placentem. V. Isti sunt qui venerunt ex magna tribulatione, et laverunt stolas suas in sanguine Agni. Et tradiderunt.

Lectio VI

O potestas ineffabilis, quæ in nobis dignata est habitare, per impositionem manuum sacrorum Sacerdotum! O quam magnam in se continet profunditatem formidabile et admirabile Sacerdotium! Felix ille, qui in hac ipsa dignitate administrat pure et irreprehensibiliter! Discamus igitur, Fratres, quoniam magna est et multa, immensa ac infinita ipsius Sacerdotii dignitas. Gloria Unigenito, gloria et soli bono, illud suis præbenti discipulis per sanctum novum Testamentum: ut et ipsi nobis, per impositionem manuum suarum super dignos, exemplum demonstrent. Cuncti ergo honoremus Sacerdotes; cuncti hac venerandi Sacerdotii sublimitate decoratos prædicemus beatos: certo scientes quod si quis amicum Regis

stricken with an amazement of mind, he exclaims: O the depth of the riches of the wisdom and the knowledge of God! how incomprehensible are His judgments, and how unsearchable his ways! Flying from earth to high heaven, it bears most swiftly to God above our requests, praying the Lord for His servants.

R. These are truly priests and martyrs, who shed their blood for the name of Christ: and they delivered up their bodies to torments, a living victim, holy, pleasing to God. V. These are they who are come out of great tribulation and have washed their robes in the blood of the Lamb. And they have delivered up . . .

Lesson VI

O power unutterable, which hath deigned to dwell in us through the laying on of hands of holy priests! What great depths lie within this awful and wonderful Priesthood! Happy the man who purely and blamelessly ministers in this dignity! So let us know, brethren, that great and manifold, vast and boundless is the dignity of the Priestly Office itself. Glory be to the Sole-Begotten, glory also to the Only Good, who offers this through the new and holy covenant to His disciples, that these in turn, by the laying of their hands upon worthy men, may furnish an example unto us. Therefore, let us all give honor to Priests and all pronounce those to be happy who have been adorned by this sublime **and**

amet, hunc ipsum multo amplius a Rege amari. Quocirca amemus Sacerdotes Dei, siquidem amici ipsius sunt boni, et pro nobis ac mundo deprecantur.

R. Vidi in circuitu sedis Seniores, sedentes super thronos, amictos stolis albis, et in capite eorum coronæ aureæ. Et audivi vocem de throno dicentem: * Isti ambulabunt mecum in albis, quia digni sunt, et florebunt sicut lilium in æternum. V. Hi sunt Sacerdotes sancti, qui Virgines permanserunt, et sequuntur Agnum quocumque ierit. Isti. Gloria Patri. Isti.

admirable office of Priesthood, knowing for sure that he will be loved much more by the King, who is a lover of the King's friend. Wherefore, let us love the Priests of God, seeing that they His friends are good and intercede for us and the world.

R. I saw round about the throne the ancients, sitting on thrones, clothed in white garments, and on their heads were crowns of gold. And I heard a voice from the throne, saying: These will walk with me in white garments, because they are worthy and have flowered like lilies forever. V. These are holy priests, who have remained Virgins, and follow the Lamb whithersoever he goeth.

THIRD NOCTURN

Ant. Ecce ego mitto vos sicut Agnos inter lupos: Estote ergo prudentes sicut serpentes, et simplices sicut columbae.

Ant. Gratias tibi, Domine Jesu, qui facis Sacerdotes tuos Angelos, et ministros altaris tui flammam ignis.

Ant. Isti sunt sancti Dei homines, de quibus os Domini locutum est dicens: Ego dixi, Dii estis vos, et filii Excelsi omnes.

V. Sanctificamini, omnes Ministri altaris.
R. Et sancti estote, quoniam ego sanctus sum.

Ant. Behold I send you as lambs among wolves. Be ye therefore wise as serpents and simple as doves.

Ant. I thank thee, Lord Jesus, who makest thy priests angels, and the ministers of thy altar a burning fire.

Ant. These are holy men of God, of whom the mouth of the Lord hath spoken saying: I said, You are gods, and all sons of the most High.

V. Sanctify yourselves, all ministers of the altar.
R. And be holy, as I am holy.

Lectio VII: Lectio sancti Evangelii secundum Matthaeum Cap. 5.

In illo tempore: Dixit Jesus discipulis suis: Vos estis sal terrae: quod si sal evanuerit, in quo salietur? Et reliqua.

Homilia sancti Joannis Chrysostomi Super Cap. 5. Matth.

Vos estis sal terrae: Non enim pro vestra, inquit, salute tantumodo, sed pro universo prossus orbe haec vobis doctrina committitur. Non ad duas quippe urbes, aut decem, aut viginti, neque ad unam vos mitto gentem, sicut mittebam Prophetas: sed ad omnem terram prorsus ac mare, totumque mundum, et hunc variis criminibus oppressum. Dicendo enim: Vos estis sal terræ, ostendit omnium hominum infatuatam esse naturam, et peccatorum vi corruptam: et idcirco illas ab eis maxime virtutes requirit, quæ cunctis necessariæ atque utiles sunt futuræ. Nam qui mansuetus est ac modestus, et misericors et justus, non intra se tantummodo hæc recte facta concludit, verum in aliorum quoque utilitatem præclaros hos faciet effluere fontes.

Lesson VII: The Reading of the Holy Gospel according to St. Matthew. Chap. 5.

At that time: Jesus said to his disciples: ye are the salt of the earth, but if the salt have lost its savour wherewith shall it be salted?

Homily of St. John Chrysostom on St. Matthew, Chapter 5.

Ye are the salt of the earth: this teaching is committed to you, not for your salvation alone, but indeed for that of the whole world. I send you not, forsooth, unto two cities, or ten, or twenty, nor unto one people do I send you, as I did the Prophets; but to the bounds of the whole earth and the seas, to the whole world, and a world oppressed by diverse crimes. For in saying: Ye are the salt of the earth, He shows that the nature of all mankind hath been subjected to foolishness and corrupted by the power of sin: and hence He requires of them those virtues in especial which will be necessary and profitable to all. For he who is gentle and modest, merciful and just, rightly concludes that these were wrought not within himself only, but he will proceed to put forth these fair fountains for the good of others as well.

R. Isti sunt Sancti, qui oves Domini paverunt verbo et exemplo, quia ipsum in tote corde suo dilexerunt. * Ipsi intercedant pro nobis ad Deum, ut mittat operarios in messem

R. These are the Saints who make the sheep of the Lord fear by word and example, because they love him with their whole heart. * May they intercede for us before the Lord, that

suam. V. Hi sunt fratrum amatores qui multum orant pro populo et universa sancta civitate. Ipsi.

Lectio VIII

Sed qui mundo corde est atque pacificus, et persecutionem pro veritate patitur, nihilominus in commune commodum vitam instituit. Ne igitur putetis, inquit, ad levia vos ducendos esse certamina, neque exiguarum rerum vobis ineundam esse rationem. Vos estis sal terræ. Quid igitur? Ipsine putrefacta medicati sunt? Nequaquam. Neque enim fieri potest ut ea quæ jam corrupta sunt, salis perfricatione reparentur. Non enim hoc fecerunt, sed ante renovata, sibique tradita, atque ab illa jam putredine liberata aspergebant sale, et in ea novitate conservabant quam a Domino susceperant. Liberare quippe a putredine peccatorum, Christi virtutis est. Ut autem ad illa iterum non revertantur, Apostolorum curæ est ac laboris.

R. Cum Agnus aperuisset librum, viginti quatuor seniores ceciderunt coram eo in facies suas dicentes: * Dignus es, Domine, accipere honorem, et gloriam, et benedictionem, quia fecisti nos Deo nostro Reges et Sacerdotes. V. Et adoraverunt viventem in sæcula sæculorum, et cantabant canticum novum dicentes. Dignus es. Gloria. Dignus es.

he may send laborers into his vineyard. V. These are lovers of their brethren, who pray greatly for their people and for all the holy city.

Lesson VIII

But he who is clean of heart and a peace-maker and suffers persecution for truth's sake, sets forth a life for the common benefit as well. Think not, therefore, he saith, that you shall be led forth to trivial contests or that you will be esteemed for mediocre deeds. Ye are the salt of the earth. What then? Hath that which was putrefied been healed? By no means! Nor is it possible that things already corrupt should be made whole by the application of salt. This they did not accomplish, but things previously renewed and committed to them and already divested of their rottenness these they purified by salt and preserved in that estate which they had received from the Lord. For it belongs to Christ's power to deliver from the rottenness of sin, but it is the concern and task of the Apostles that these should not again revert to that state.

R. When the Lamb had opened the book, the four and twenty ancients fell down before the Lord, saying: Thou art worthy, O Lord, to receive honor and glory and benediction, because thou hast made us to our God kings and priests. V. And they adored him that liveth for ever and ever, and sang a new hymn saying . . .

Lectio IX

Vides quemadmodum paulatim Prophetis hos meliores esse patefecerit. Non enim illos filios veteris Testamenti, neque mediocres ponit magistros, sed severos quosdam atque terribiles. Hoc est enim omnino mirabile, quia non adulantes, neque palpantes, sed e diverso salis instar urentes, fere omnibus se tam desiderabiles reddiderunt. Nolite ergo, inquit, mirari si, alios omittens, vos potissimum doceo, atque ad pericula tanta succingo. Considerate quippe quantis urbibus, quantisque populis vos sim missurus magistros. Propterea, non vos tantummodo volo esse sapientes, sed ut tales faciatis et caeteros. Hujusmodi autem Magistros, in quibus certe tantorum periclitatur salus, maxima debet pollere prudentia, tantasque illis virtutum adesse divitias, ut aliis quoque utilitatem aedificationis impertiant.

Te Deum.

AD LAUDES

Ant. Sacerdos in aeternum Christus Dominus, per Spiritum sanctum, pro nobis semetipsum obtulit hostiam Deo, in odorem suavitatis.

Psalmi de Dominica.

Ant. Ego elegi vos, ut sitis vasa munda, in honorem sanctificata, utilia Domino, et ad omne opus bonum parata.

Ant. Sacerdotes tui, Domine, induantur, sicut electi Dei, sancti et

Lesson IX

Now thou seest how He hath revealed these to be better, in a measure, than even the Prophets. For He regards those sons of the Old Covenant not as mild teachers but rather as stern and terrible. For this is altogether wonderful that not as flattering or coaxing, but rather as burning like salt they ingratiated themselves to such an extent with all men. Be not amazed therefore, He says, if passing over others I teach you in particular and gird you up for such dangers. Indeed, consider to what cities and peoples I am about to send you as teachers. Wherefore, I wish you to be not only wise, but to act even as they and others. But teachers such as these in whom the salvation of so many is certainly involved in peril, must shine with the greatest prudence, and they must possess such a wealth of virtues that they may impart also to others a useful edification.

Te Deum.

LAUDS

Ant. Christ the Lord, the Eternal Priest, hath delivered Himself for us, a sacrifice to God for an odor of sweetness.

Psalms for Sunday.

Ant. I have chosen you, that you may be clean vessels, sanctified in my honor, useful to the Lord, and ready to every good work.

Ant. Let thy priests be clothed, O Lord, as the elect of God, holy and

dilecti, viscera misericordiae, begnitatem, humilitatem, modestiam, charitatem.

Ant. Sacerdotes Dei, benedicite Dominum: Sancti et humiles corde, laudate Deum.

Ant. Sacerdotes Domini, laudate Deum, quia gloria et honore coronavi vos: et constituit vos Dominos domus suae, et Principes omnes possessionis suae.

Capitulum, Heb. 7.

Christus Jesus, eo quod maneat in aeternum, sempiternum habet Sacerdotium: unde et salvare in perpetuum potest accedentes per semetipsum ad Deum, semper vivens ad interpellandum pro nobis.

Hymnus
Hymnos Olympus intonet,
Psalmosque terra personet;
Totis medullis cordium
Christo canamus canticum.

Caeli colamus Principes
Regumque terrae Judices,
Jesu Sacristas inclytos,
Dei domus Arcarios.

Mundi bases fortissimas,
Ecclesiae custodias:
Regis superni nuntios,
Pacis perennis Angelos.

beloved, with the bowels of mercy, benignity, humility, modesty, charity.

Ant. O priests of God, bless the Lord: holy and humble of heart, praise God.

Ant. Priests of the Lord, praise God, because he crowned you with glory and honor: and made you masters of his house, and rulers of all his possessions.

Little Chapter, Heb. 7.

Christ Jesus, for that he continueth for ever, hath an everlasting priesthood: whereby he is able also to save for ever them that come to God by him; always living to make intercession for us.

Hymn
Heavens on high with hymns let ring.
To Christ let us exultant sing,
While earth its psalms of praise doth bring
To every heart a vibrant string.

With worship let us honor show
To Heaven's leaders praise bestow,
The judges of earth's kings, the Priests
Unstained of Christ, who spread His feasts.

The world's supporting pillars firm,
The Holy Church's guardians term,
The messengers of Heaven's King,
Bright angels lasting peace to bring.

Vos sacra caeli buccina
A Prole missa Virginis
Legatione caelica,
Arcana Jesu panditis.

Ye sacred trumpets of the sky
By Virgin's Son sent far and nigh,
Shed forth the mysteries secret
Of Jesus, His the envoys fleet.

Vos Spiritus Oracula,
Tormenta Christi bellica:
Per vos patent mysteria,
Per vos fugantur crimina.

Ye oracles of Spirit bright
Christ's fearsome threats do bring to
     light;
Through you the mysteries appear,
Through you all crimes are banished
     here.

Qua mente cernunt Angeli
Jesum, Mariae Filium,
Regem tremendum saeculi
Vobis in ara subditum!

In ways the Angels' flashing sight
Sees Mary's Son, Lord Jesus bright,
The King tremendous of the skies
To you on altar subject lies.

Agni stupent sanctissiman
Carnem, sacratis oribus,
Deo litari victimam
Escam dari mortalibus.

The flock beholds with awe, amazed,
The Flesh confected as they gazed,
By sacred words God's victim
     wrought,
And here as food to mortals brought.

Salutis orbis vindices,
Hostes salutis pellite:
Sacri polorum cardines,
Vitae fores recludite.

Who come to save the universe
Dispel ye far the foes adverse;
Be ye the axis of the poles
Whereon life's doors swing wide to
     souls.

Praesta, beata Trinitas,
Origo, finis omnium,
Patrum tenere semitas
Nunc et per omne saeculum.
                    Amen.

Grant, Blessed Trinity divine,
Beginning of all things and End,
That we may keep the Fathers' line,
Now and for ever onward tend.
                    Amen.

V. Sacerdotes Dei incensum et
panes offerunt. R. Ideo sancti erunt
Deo suo.

V. The priests of God offer incense and bread. R. And therefore
they shall be holy to their God.

A Bened. *Ant.* Vobis datum est
nosse mysteria Regni Dei, ad dan-
dam scientiam salutis plebi ejus, in
remissionem peccatorum eorum.

At the Benedictus. To you it is
given to know the mysteries of the
kingdom of heaven, to give knowledge of salvation to his people, unto
the remission of their sins.

Oremus

Deus tuorum gloria Sacerdotum, qui Unigenitum tuum nobis summum Sacerdotem et animarum nostrarum Pastorem vigilantissimum dedisti, quique ei ad sacrificandum tibi hostiam mundam, et ad promovendam humani generis salutem, sanctos Sacerdotes et Levitas consortes tribuisti: quæsumus, beata Maria semper Virgine, iisdemque sanctis Sacerdotibus et Levitis intercedentibus, ut spiritum gratiæ cui servierunt in Ecclesia tua excitare digneris; quatenus nos eodem repleti, studeamus amare quod amaverunt, et opere exercere quod verbo et exemplo docuerunt. Per eumdem Dominum.

Let us pray

O God, the glory of Thy priests, who didst give us Thy Only-Begotten Son to be our High Priest and the most watchful pastor of souls, and didst make all holy priests and levites His associates in offering to Thee a spotless victim and in promoting the salvation of the human race: grant, we beseech Thee, through the intercession of Blessed Mary, ever Virgin, and of all the holy Priests and Levites, that the spirit of grace be stirred up in Thy Church, so that filled with this same grace, we may love what they loved, and accomplish in deed what they taught in word and example. Through the same Lord . . .

AD PRIMAM

Ant. Sacerdos in aeternum.

R. Christe Fili . . . V. Qui natus es de Maria Virgine.

Lectio brevis: 1 Petr. 2. Vos autem genus electum, regale Sacerdotium, gens sancta, populus acquisitionis; ut virtutes annuntietis ejus, qui de tenebris vos vocavit in admirabile lumen tuum.

PRIME

Ant. The Eternal Priest.

R. O Christ, Son of the living God, have mercy on us . . . V. Who was born of the Virgin Mary.

Short Lesson: 1 Peter 2. But you a chosen generation, a kingly priesthood, a holy nation, a purchased people: that you may declare his virtues, who hath called you out of darkness into his marvellous light.

AD TERTIAM

Ant. Ego elegi vos.

Capit. Christus Jesus.

R. Sacerdotes tui * Induantur justitiam. Sacerdotes . . .

V. Et Sancti tui exsultent . . . Induantur justitiam. Gloria Patri . . . Sacerdotes.

TIERCE

Ant. I have chosen you.

Little Chapter. Christ Jesus.

R. Let thy priests be clothed with justice . . . Let thy priests . . .

V. And let thy saints rejoice . . . Be clothed with justice . . . Glory be to the Father . . . Let thy priests.

V. Sacerdotes meos induam Salutari.

R. Et Sancti mei exsultatione exsultabunt.

V. I will clothe my priests with salvation.

R. And my saints shall rejoice with exceeding great joy.

AD SEXTAM

Ant. Sacerdotes tui.

Capit. Abd. 1.

In monte Sion erit salvatio, et erit Sanctus. Et erit domus Jacob ignis, et domus Joseph flamma. Et ascendent Salvatores in monte Sion judicare domum Esau. Et erit Domino regnum.

R. Sacerdotes meos * Induam Salutari. Sacerdotes . . .

V. Et Sancti mei exsultatione exultabunt. Induam. Gloria Patri. Sacerdotes.

V. Sanctificamini, omnes Ministri altaris.

R. Et sancti estote, quoniam ego sanctus sum.

SEXT

Ant. Let thy priests.

Little Chapter. Abdias, 1.

And in Mount Sion shall be salvation, and it shall be holy: and the house of Jacob shall be a fire and the house of Joseph a flame. And saviours shall come up into Mount Sion to judge the house of Esau: and the kingdom shall be for the Lord.

R. I will clothe my priests with salvation . . .

V. And my saints shall rejoice with exceeding joy . . . I shall clothe . . . Glory be to the Father . . . I will clothe.

V. Be ye sanctified, all ministers of the altar.

R. And be holy, because I am holy.

AD NONAM

Ant. Sacerdotes Domini.

Capit. 1 Petr. 2.

Vos autem genus electum, régale Sacerdotium, gens sancta, populus acquisitionis; ut virtutes annuntietis ejus, qui de tenebris vos vocavit in admirabile lumen suum.

R. Sanctificamini * Omnes Ministri altaris. Sanctificamini . . .

V. Et sancti estote, quoniam ego

NONE

Ant. Priests of the Lord.

Little Chapter. 1 Peter 2.

But you are a chosen generation, a kingly priesthood, a holy nation, a purchased people: that you may declare his virtues, who hath called you out of darkness into his marvellous light.

R. Be ye sanctified, all ministers of the altar . . . Be ye sanctified . . .

V. And be holy, because I am

sanctus sum . . . Omnes . . . Gloria Patri . . . Sanctificamini . . .

V. Sacerdotes Dei incensum et panes offerunt.

R. Ideo sancti erunt Deo suo.

holy. All . . . Glory be to the Father . . . Be ye sanctified . . .

V. The priests of God offer incense and bread.

R. And therefore they shall be holy to their God.

AD SECUNDAS VESPERES

Ant. Vocavit nos Dominus vocatione sua sancta, ut nos divini sui Sacerdotii consortes faceret. Gratias Deo super inenerabili dono ejus.

SECOND VESPERS

Ant. The Lord hath called us by his holy calling, that we may be made partakers of his holy priesthood. Thanks be to God for his unspeakable gift.

Psalmi de Dominica, ultimo loco Memento Domine David.

Ant. Dei adjutores sumus, Dei et hominum mediatores, dispensatores mysteriorum Christi. Gratias Deo super inenarrabili dono ejus.

Psalms for Sunday. Last psalm, Memento Domine David.

Ant. We are God's coadjutors and the mediators of men, the dispensers of the mysteries of God. Thanks be to God for his unspeakable gift.

Ant. Isti sunt Sancti, qui fecerunt et docuerunt mandata Domini: ideo magni vocabuntur in Regno caelorum.

Ant. These are saints, who keep and teach the commandments of God: therefore they shall be called great in the Kingdom of heaven.

Ant. Hi sunt qui ad justitiam erudierunt multos; ideo fulgebunt quasi splendor firmamenti, et quasi stellae in perpetuas aeternitates.

Ant. These are they that instructed many in justice: therefore they shall shine as the brightness of the firmament, and as stars for all eternity.

Ant. Omnes sancti Sacerdotes, rogate Dominum messis, ut mittat operarios in messem suam.

Ant. All holy priests, pray ye the Lord of the harvest, that he send forth labourers into his harvest.

Capit. Hebr. 7. *Vide Laudes.*

Little Chapter. Hebr. 7. *See Lauds.*

Hymnus
Terræ Deos extollimus,
Patres Deorum psallimus;
Dei patres et filios,
Summo Parenti proximos;

Hymn
We praise those gods, the gods of earth,
We sing them bringing gods to birth;
The sons and sires of God be praised,
To highest Parent nearest raised.

Christos Dei sanctissimos,
Dignos Dei vicarios:
Nactos Dei consortium,
Sortemque cœli clavium.

God's holiest other Christs they be,
Vicars esteemed of Deity:
Born thus to share the life divine
And hold the keys to heaven's
    shrine.

Pupilla vos charissima,
Os, lingua, cor et viscera,
Manusque Regis gloriæ:
Sponsi, patres Ecclesiæ.

The eye most precious of the King
Of Glory, ye! His heart ye bring,
His mind, His hands, His lips and
    tongue,
As Church's Sponsors be ye sung!

O vos beatos Principes
Inter beatos Cœlites,
Jesu coruscos munere
Et Trinitatis fœdere!

O blessed Princes set on high
Amongst the blessed in the sky,
Shining with Jesus' splendid light
And Trinity's blest aura bright!

Per vos avernus clauditur,
Per vos Polus recluditur:
Divina per vos gratia
Novare curat omnia.

By you the jaws of hell are stopped,
By you the doors of Heaven oped:
By you doth work the grace divine
To renovate and to refine.

Videte quot miserrimas
Mentes draco nunc devorat,
Pœnas quibus teterrimas
Æternus ignis præparat!

Behold how many souls forlorn
The dragon now devours apace;
For whom most fearsome woes are
    sworn,
And who eternal fires must face.

Vos ergo Patris optimi
Rogate nunc clementiam:
Det hostis atrocissimi
Calcare nos ferociam.

Implore ye now the favor kind
Of God the Father gently just,
To grant us strength to leave be-
    hind
The fearsome foe, downtrod in dust.

Rogate Regem messium
Messes suas ut visitet:
Suum Redemptor Spiritum
In corde Cleri suscitet.

Beseech the King of harvests white
That He his fields would visit here;
That He Redeemer stir up bright
His spirit in the clergy dear.

Praesta, beata Trinitas,
Origo, finis omnium,
Patrum tenere semitas
Nunc et per omne saeculum.
         Amen.

Grant, Blessed Trinity divine,
Beginning of all things and End,
That we may keep the Fathers' line,
Now and forever onward tend.
         Amen.

V. Magna est gloria eorum in Salutari tuo.

R. Gloriam et magnum decorem impones super eos.

Ad. Magn. Beatam te dicent, O Maria, Dei Genitrix Virgo, omnes sancti sacerdotes et Levitae: quia ex te ortus est Christus Deus noster, Princeps Sacerdotum et magnus Pastor animarum. Alleluia.

Oremus. Deus, tuorum gloria sacerdotum, qui Unigentum tuum nobis summum Sacerdotem et animarum nostrarum Pastorem vigilantissimum dedisti, quique ei ad sacrificandum tibi hostiam mundam, et ad promovendam humani generis salutem, sanctos Sacerdotes et Levitas consortes tribuisti: quaesumus, beata Maria semper Virgine, iisdemque sanctis Sacerdotibus et Levitis intercedentibus, ut spiritum gratiae cui servierunt in Ecclesia tua excitare digneris; quatenus nos eodem repleti, studeamus amare quod amaverunt, et opere exercere quod verbo et exemplo docuerunt. Per eumdem Dominum.

V. Great is their glory in thy Salvation.

R. Thou hast laid upon them glory and great beauty.

At the Magnificat. All thy holy Priests and Levites shall call thee blessed, O Mary, because Christ Our God, the Prince of Priests and Great Shepherd of Souls was born of thee. Alleluia.

Let us pray. O God, the glory of Thy priests, who didst give us Thine Only-begotten Son to be our High Priest and the most watchful pastor of souls, and didst make all holy priests and levites His associates in offering to Thee a spotless victim and in promoting the salvation of the human race: grant, we beseech Thee, through the intercession of Blessed Mary, ever Virgin, and all the holy Priests and Levites, that the spirit of grace be stirred up in thy Church, so that filled with this same grace, we love what they loved, and accomplish in deed what they taught by word and example. Through the same Lord.

INDEX

Absolution, 164; withholding, 22
Acolyte, exterior and interior functions of, 225
Acts, before the divine office, 32; after the divine office, 33; before meditation, 29; after meditation, 30
Admonition, 161
Afflicted, consoling the, 57
Affliction, causes of, 50
Ambrose, St., 119, 189
Angel, the priest is a, 11
Attrition, 162
Augustine, St., 29, 47, 84, 117
Avarice, in the priest, 17
Ave, Maria, Filia Dei Patris, 171

Baptism, disposition for administration of, 45
Barradas, 84
Benedictum sit, 41
Bernard, St., 18, 76, 84; on study, 35
Biretta, the meaning of, 210
Blessed Sacrament, devotion to, 23
Blessed Virgin Mary, attitude toward world, 189; devotion to, 23
Body and Blood of Christ, the priest's power over, 5
Bonaventure, St., 141
Books, for sermon material, 84; for retreats, 68; frivolous and worldly, 85
Borromeo, St. Charles, 84
Brigid, St., 135

Cassock, meaning of, 208
Cathechism, the teaching of, 62, 121
Catherine of Siena, St., 136
Cemetery, care of, 22
Charity, excellence of, 254; practice of, 255; for sick, 20, 50; of confessor, 149

Chrysostom, St. John, 127, 131, 139, 141, 142, 186; on words of St. Paul, 136
Church, care of, 22; love for, 21; priest is the light of, 9
Clement, St., on powers of priest, 127
Confession, dispositions for hearing of, 45, 47; hearing of, 22; preparation of priest's, 38; thanksgiving after, 39; secrecy of, 157
Confessional, the priest in the, 45
Confessor, careless, 129; compared to preacher, 144; excellence of office of, 127; harm done by bad, 129; importance of duties of, 128; the good, 127; mercy of, 47; justice of, 47; seven points to be observed by, 160-166; piety of, 154; prudence of, 151; science of, 147
Conscience, examination of, 40
Contrition, in the penitent, 162; in the priest, 39
Cross, glory and treasure of, 58

Deacon, chief duties of, 231; additional duties of, 232
Deaconship, duties of, 231
Devotion, to the Blessed Sacrament, 23; to the Blessed Virgin Mary, 23
Differences, adjusting, 21
Dionysius, St., on priesthood, 8, 12, 21, 142, 180
Duties, of the dying, 54; of deaconship, 231; of subdeaconship, 227; of priestly state, 15, 234; of priest toward God, men and himself, 179; of priest toward the Church, 204
Dying, the priest and the, 53; duties of, 54; indulgences for the, 55

303